NEW WINESKINS

"People do not put new wine into old wineskins
. . . they put new wine into new wineskins."

Matthew 9:17

NEW WINESKINS

Re-imagining Religious Life Today

SANDRA M. SCHNEIDERS, I.H.M.

PAULIST PRESS
New York/Mahwah

Library of Congress Catalog Card Number: 85-62865

ISBN: 0-8091-2765-2

Published by Paulist Press
997 Macarthur Boulevard
Mahwah, N.J. 07430

Printed and bound in the United States of America

CONTENTS

III. REFLECTING ON SOME CONTEMPORARY CHALLENGES

To the Members
of
My Religious Congregation
The Sisters, Servants of the Immaculate Heart of Mary
and
To my two Religious Sisters
Anne, D.C. and Mary, O.P.
with deep affection and gratitude

INTRODUCTION

WOMEN RELIGIOUS AND THE THEOLOGY OF RELIGIOUS LIFE

Anyone who has followed closely the development of the literature on religious life since Vatican Council II is aware that all of the full-length systematic studies have been authored by men.[1] At first sight this seems strange since, as both men and women religious acknowledge, women religious have responded much more quickly and more radically to the Council's call for the renewal of religious life than have the men. Why, then, have women not written any of the contemporary theologies of religious life?

It seems to me that this apparent anomaly is highly indicative of the distinctive character of women's reflection on religious life. A systematic theology of religious life involves the elaboration of a theoretical framework within which all the elements of religious life can be explained and situated in relationship to each other and to the whole. By its very nature such an integrated theory is usually the creation of a single individual even though he or she may have drawn upon multiple resources in the formulation of the final synthesis. In other words, a systematic theology is characterized by the priority of theory according to which experience is organized and understood, and it is usually formulated by a single individual whose distinctive stamp it bears.

Observation leads me to the conclusion that the reflection of women religious on their life has been marked by diametrically opposite characteristics: by the priority of *experience* over theory and by the *collaborative* character of the reflection. My hypothesis is that women theologians have not written systematic theologies of religious life because that genre is not a suitable vehicle for the type of reflection in which women religious have been engaged.

The first major characteristic of women's reflection on re-

1

ligious life is its *rootedness in experience*. Women since Vatican II
have not tended to start with definitions, laws, or propositions
about religious life and to deduce from them what that life is or
should be. They have tended to examine their lived experience,
to reflect upon that experience, and to try to express its significance for themselves, the Church, and the world. Rather than
testing the validity of their experience by its conformity to the
theory, they have tested the validity of the theory by its adequacy
to their experience. The experience itself they have tested
against the Gospel criterion: By their fruits you shall know them
(Mt 7:20).

It is difficult to establish why or how women religious,
whose lives prior to Vatican II had been almost totally determined by canon law and the theology derived therefrom, liberated themselves so quickly from the technical and the legal
and embraced with such confidence their own experience which
they had been taught to distrust. Although the conscious articulation and thematization of the priority of experience emerged
slowly aided by the theology of liberation emanating from Latin
America, the functional priority of experience among women
religious was well established early in the process of renewal that
was launched by Vatican II. I am inclined to speculate that
women, long denied the serious theological formation of male
religious and clerics, had never completely internalized the theoretical and legalistic approach to religious experience that was
so pervasive in the post-Tridentine Church and that when in-
vited and challenged to renewal they turned spontaneously to
life rather than to law, to the Gospel rather than to speculative
theology. In any event, while men religious were more preoccupied with questions of what was theoretically possible within
the framework of canonical religious life, women were more
concerned with the revision of their concrete lives in accord with
the Gospel.

Women's tendency to assign priority to experience, to theo-
rize out of experience rather than to allow theory to prescribe
and limit experience, should not be regarded as a pedestrian incapacity for high level speculation.[2] On the contrary, it is a sure
instinct for the real nature of religious life which is not a static
essence to be described and analyzed but first and foremost a

life to be lived, an historical reality which is ever-changing and unpredictable. Experience enjoys a real priority over theory in relation to life, and women religious in particular have become convinced of this despite the fact that, for centuries, theory and law have exercised a practical supremacy.

The priority women religious have assigned to experience has given their reflection on religious life two interesting characteristics which are quite incompatible with the development, at least at the present time, of a systematic theology of religious life. Because it is rooted in experience, women's reflection has tended to be occasional and provisional.

The *occasional* character of women's reflection on religious life is evident from even a cursory perusal of what women have written. Events such as the publication of Leo Suenens' *The Nun in the World,* the appearance of the papal exhortation *Evangelica Testificatio,* the attempt of the Sacred Congregation for Religious and Secular Institutes to deal with the habit issue in the U.S. through the hierarchy rather than major superiors, the decline in the number of ordained ministers available for parish ministry, loss of congregational institutions for financial reasons, the emergence of the justice and liberation agenda at the Medellín Conference and the 1971 Synod of Bishops, and so on, have called sisters to reflect on issues and elements in their lives which vary widely in significance and which certainly have not been taken up in any kind of systematic or "logical" order. Response to events which directly affected their lives and the lives of those with and to whom they ministered has led women religious to reflect on such diverse questions as religious dress, lifestyle, community life, intercongregational living, daily Eucharist, the meaning of poverty, living alone, daily horaria, social activism, the possibility of permanent commitment, the necessity of local superiors, the role of ministry in religious life, among numerous others. The responses have varied in depth and intensity, frequently not in direct proportion to the theological importance of the issue but usually in proportion to its experiential impact on individuals and communities.

The *provisional* character of women's reflection on religious life is also directly related to the priority they have assigned to experience over theory. Unlike the propositions of which the-

oretical constructions are composed, experience is not governed
by logical necessity. On the contrary, it is radically contingent.
In fact, until reflection imposes a certain order upon it, experience can even seem chaotic and meaningless.

The choosing, doing, and suffering that compose the real
experience of life often precede the thematized understanding
of what we are doing and why. For example, the instinct of many
women religious to abandon the instruments of separation from
other people in the Church and society such as special dress, titles, dwellings, and customs led to seemingly radical changes in
religious lifestyle well before the move was explicitated in terms
of Christian solidarity with other lay people in the Church, fidelity to Gospel ideals of equality and simplicity, repudiation of
the elitism and privilege of pseudo-clericalism, the psychological
importance of affirming one's sexuality and individual identity,
and the crucial role of freedom and responsibility in the achievement of human maturity. In similar fashion, several kinds of experience converged to move many religious women out of
traditional institutional ministries and into non-convent living
situations before the task of theoretically justifying these moves
was undertaken.

As women religious have undertaken the task of theorizing
about their lived experience their reflection has been characterized by a tentativeness that contrasts sharply with the apodictic
certitude and clarity of the post-Tridentine theology of religious
life. The formulations of women religious tend to be expressed
as provisional thematizations that are open to revision in the
light of ongoing experience. Nor is this provisional quality seen
as a stage which will be superseded after a suitable period of experimentation by a definitive and relatively unchangeable theology. Attempts on the part of certain Church officials to
declare an end to the "period of experimentation" and to usher
in an era of "stability" are viewed by most women religious as
unrealistic.[3] Change *is* the stable characteristic of experience.
Consequently, the reflection upon experience will be ongoing
and the theoretical articulation of the structure and meaning of
that experience must remain provisional.

This does not mean that women religious lack confidence
in their ability to read the signs of the times in their own expe-

rience or to articulate it in meaningful ways. It simply means that they have come to acknowledge the historical character of all experience and therefore the partial nature of even the best human knowledge, the relativity of their own positions, and the real limitations on human freedom. Consequently, they tend to avoid trying to define their state of life, to state its static essence, and to formulate its univocal theology. Rather, they try to describe what they are living, to articulate its meaning in dynamic evangelical terms, and to surface a plurality of viable theological positions in regard to the issues and problems they face.

The second characteristic of women's post-conciliar reflection on religious life has been its *collaborative* character. The rapidity of the development of this characteristic is almost startling. Just twenty years ago it was uncommon even for most of the members of a single congregation to be involved in the consideration of major issues affecting their own life together. Such deliberation was entrusted to a select group of capitulars which was usually not especially representative of the rank and file and who met only every several years. Today many congregations are involved in total participation annual assemblies and maintain ongoing representative bodies for the processing of ordinary business. Even formal chapters are highly representative and usually open to at least the observation of all members.

But the collaborative nature of the reflection on the life and mission of most congregations has expanded well beyond their own membership. Women religious collaborate widely not only among themselves and across congregational boundaries but also with male religious, with the clergy, and with lay co-ministers. And in the process of evaluating data and articulating positions they call upon not only theologians and canon lawyers but also sociologists, psychologists, economists, group facilitators, political scientists and specialists from a variety of other disciplines.

In summary the content, the method, and the results of the theological efforts of women religious have changed radically in the years since Vatican II. The primary subject matter upon which religious have trained their reflective energies has been their own lived experience rather than theoretical or legal formulations concerning their life. The method of reflection has been inductive rather than deductive and widely collaborative rather than hierarchical. The results have been highly articulate but provisional formulations of the meaning and directions of various forms of religious life in the contemporary situation rather than systematic treatises defining the unchanging nature of religious life as such.

In my opinion, it is the two characteristics of women's reflection on religious life, namely its rootedness in experience and its collaborative character, which account for the choices of literary genre in which the results of this ongoing reflection have been articulated. Women religious have tended to produce articles and short studies on issues that have assumed particular importance for certain groups or for religious generally because of particular events occurring in Church or society. They have also tended to carry out widely representative consultations on important issues, to commission studies of the resulting data by competent professionals in a variety of disciplines, and to publish the reflections of the specialists along with summaries of the data.[4] The theoretical work of women religious is found in a variety of periodicals, in collections of essays, on tapes of conferences, and in the circulations of inner and intra-congregational networks. No full-scale theology of post-conciliar religious life has been authored by a woman and I doubt that one will be in the near future.

THE SHAPE AND SCOPE OF THE PRESENT WORK

In light of what has been said so far no one will be surprised that the present book makes no pretension to be *the* or even *a* theology of religious life. Although all of the essays are written within a certain horizon of reflection that has become gradually more explicit in my mind over the past two decades, and which will be relatively clear to the reader if she or he perseveres to the end, they are all marked by the occasional, provisional, and collaborative characteristics that have stamped the ongoing reflection of women religious over the past twenty years.

With the exception of this introduction all of the essays originated as talks or articles addressing specific issues for particular audiences at definite moments in the recent history of religious life. Most of them were efforts to respond to the requests of various groups for resource material on particular issues with which they were dealing, and they were composed either within the context of structured group reflections or in dialogue with others working on the same issues. Although all of the essays have been revised for this volume on the basis of experience gained in the interval between their original formulation and the preparation of this book, nothing in the book represents the isolated and, as it were, "untested" theorizing of a single religious.

No attempt has been made to homogenize the style of these essays nor to delete occasional repetitions which occur from one to another. On the contrary, I have deliberately preserved the specifying characteristics of each essay, explaining the circumstances of its composition in a brief prenote. The essays were composed between 1975 and 1985 and reflect not only the evolution of my own reflection but also some of the shifts in focus and the variations in the concerns of American women religious over the past decade.

As will be clear from the notes which introduce each chapter of this volume, none of these essays was written in isolation. While I bear the responsibility for the contents of this book, the credit for whatever of value it contains belongs to many groups and individuals with whom I have had the privilege of discussing my reflections on religious life over the past two decades. It would be impossible to acknowledge all of them by name, and in mentioning some of them here I wish to express my deep appreciation to all who have in any way contributed to these reflections.

Particular gratitude is due to my own religious congregation, the Sisters, Servants of the Immaculate Heart of Mary, within which I have learned what religious life means. I wish to thank in a particular way our community leaders, Sisters Anna Marie Grix, Margaret Brennan, Mary Kinney, and Carol Quigley, who have provided me with the encouragement, material support, and opportunity to pursue this work. Two other congregations whose support and friendship have been especially important to me are the Sisters of Charity of the Blessed Virgin Mary and the Brothers of the Society of Mary. The Leadership Conference of Women Religious, by repeatedly inviting me to

participate in their reflective processes, has stimulated much of
my thinking and writing on religious life.

Thanks are also due to the administration of the Jesuit
School of Theology in Berkeley for granting me two semesters
of leave for research and writing; to the Sisters of Charity and
their staff at El Pomar Renewal Center in Colorado Springs and
to the Oblates of Mary Immaculate and their staff at Oblate
School of Theology in San Antonio for providing me material
support, a quiet and comfortable atmosphere for work, and
their friendship during these semesters.

I would also like to acknowledge with deep gratitude the
contribution to my living of and reflecting upon religious life
that the friendship and ongoing dialogue with many individual
religious has made. In particular I want to thank Joseph
Bracken, S.J., Anne Brotherton, S.F.C.C., Mary Ann Donovan,
S.C., Dorothy Feehan, B.V.M., Cornelius Hubbuch, C.F.X.,
Ruth Loftus, I.H.M., Mary Milligan, R.S.H.M., John Mulligan,
S.M., Kathleen O'Brien, I.H.M., Clare Ronzani, S.N.D., Robert
Schmitt, S.J., and Kristin Wenzel, O.S.U. A friend and compan-
ion in the spiritual life who will not read this book, but to whom
I owe much more than can be expressed in words, is William
MacBeath Brown, C.S.B., who died shortly before this manu-
script went to press.

It is a special pleasure to be able to express publicly my deep
respect for and gratitude to John S. Cummins, Bishop of Oakland, California, for his interest, intelligent criticism, and un-
failing support. It is a privilege to work in the diocese of a pastor
who so respects and encourages the intellectual life and especially theological scholarship.

Last, but by no means least, I want to thank Jill Marshall
whose intelligence, humor, and perseverance in the production
of this manuscript exceeded not only my just deserts but even
my fondest hopes. Only Jill knows how much this volume is due
to her efforts. My thanks to her and to all those whose help has
not been acknowledged explicitly here but who have contributed in one way or another to this endeavor. If these pages encourage anyone in the living of religious life or stimulate further
reflection upon this gift to the Church of Jesus Christ they will
have more than accomplished their purpose.

Part One

RELIGIOUS LIFE IN CONTEMPORARY EXPERIENCE AND REFLECTION

Chapter One
WOMEN RELIGIOUS
AND THE TASK OF RENEWAL

The following essay is the revised text of a conference given to the English-speaking members of the International Union of Superiors General at their headquarters in Rome, February 4, 1975. The topic with which these major superiors were concerned was that of the self-renewal, or self-evangelization, of women religious which they saw as essential if religious congregations were to play their appropriate role in the renewal of the Church. It was published in French under the title "Auto-evangélisation des religieuses," *Vie Consacrée* 47 (1975) 267–277.

Evangelization, as we have been painfully brought to realize in recent years, does not take place in a vacuum. It must take place not only within, but in terms of, the concrete conditions of those to be evangelized. Consequently, if we wish to talk about the self-evangelization or self-renewal of women religious we must begin by trying to understand the concrete conditions of our lives which call for evangelization and which invite us to renewal.

I would like to call attention to that condition of contemporary feminine religious life which I think has the most far-reaching and demanding implications for our efforts at self-evangelization, namely, what might be called our frontier position in the Church. The frontier is the growing point. It is the point which has everything behind it and nothing except possibility in front of it. It seems to me that women religious are the one group in the contemporary Church who, as a group, are in such a position. I emphasize that I am speaking of women religious *as a group* because there are, unfortunately, still congregations which have resisted the conciliar invitation to growth and many individuals even within progressive congregations who have stagnated or regressed in the face of contemporary

11

challenges. But as a group women religious probably do constitute today the most creative element within the Church.

The frontier position of women religious is not a situation
we consciously created nor one which should provoke any complacency among us. It is, however, one of serious, indeed of almost frightening responsibility. I would like to indicate a few of
the factors which have helped to produce this situation because
I think it will help us to realize the gravity of our responsibilities
to the universal Church and through the Church to the world.

A first factor is that until about ten years ago women were
not admitted to Catholic theological schools. The felt need
within some far-seeing congregations for theological formation
for their members led not only to a short-lived experiment with
sisters' colleges and juniorates but, much more significantly, to
many sisters receiving high level theological formation at Catholic and non-Catholic universities. Consequently, a significant
(though not yet adequate) number of women religious have
been theologically formed in a context which included lay people, men, and non-Catholics. They have studied theology in a
setting in which theology rubbed elbows both with real life on
and around the campus and with other disciplines, especially
the social sciences, the arts, and education. In short, women religious trained in theology in the past ten years have received,
in general, a more integral and integrated theological formation
than most of their male religious and/or clerical colleagues in the
contemporary Church. This healthier theological formation has
been bearing fruit within many religious congregations in a
more balanced spirituality and a more open and creative approach to world and Church problems.

A second factor is that, until very recently, the direct participation of women in professional pastoral ministry has been
structurally impossible. Consequently, the members of most apostolic congregations have exercised their ministry through
such professions as education, the health services, and social
work. The result is that most women's congregations, even small
ones, have a variety of professional skills and differing viewpoints within their ranks as well as considerable experience on
the part of their members of collaboration with colleagues outside their own congregations. The efforts of some dioceses to

begin to form their younger clergy in various professional fields is still in its infancy whereas, in many women's religious congregations, it is a *fait accompli*. This professional wealth within the ranks is a source not only of creativity in ideas but of effectiveness in action.

A third factor is that most religious congregations have sent some or most of their members, for various lengths of time, outside the bounds of the dioceses in which they have their headquarters. Whether this sending has been for ministerial or for educational reasons it has resulted, not infrequently, in the exploding of the limited viewpoints characteristic of people who grow up, are educated, and work within a single diocese during their whole lives. Religious have *seen,* and what they have seen has been poured into their community consciousness, giving even the average sister an awareness of world problems and of the universal Church which is often broader than that characteristic of the local Church and its diocesan personnel.

A fourth factor is that women ministers within the Roman Catholic tradition have been excluded from ordination and consequently are not responsible for the administration of the sacraments. This has left them, paradoxically, in a position of relative freedom in the development of their ministries. Because it is indirect and unofficial, the sister-minister's effect on sacramental practice has attracted less frightened reaction from lay people or Church authorities. Furthermore, the sanctions which can be applied to non-clerical ministers for creative experimentation are not usually of the type which can put the minister "out of business." The result is that the less constrained experimentation of many women in ministry has generally been more concentrated on good to be achieved than on trouble to be avoided. In general, women's religious congregations have been the most creative element in ministry at least in the past ten years. This is evident in the fields of education and cross-cultural mission as well as in direct spiritual ministries and in active commitment to social justice.

Finally, I would mention what might be facetiously called the "Avis mentality" among women in the Church. Because women have always been "number two," women "try harder." They have not been able to become complacent, to assume that what they learned during formation dispenses them from further education. Sisters in forward-looking congregations are meeting-attenders, workshop-goers, session-makers. Summer school, refresher courses, night classes, and weekend training sessions have been almost as much a part of the average sister's life as liturgy or ministry. For this reason religious congregations have stayed more in touch with new developments and approaches, especially in the social sciences, theology, education, and the arts. This is definitely having its effect on our approach to both the spiritual life and the apostolate.

The results of all these factors are many and various. I would like to point out one result which, as I see it, gives the dominant shape to the type of self-evangelization or self-renewal which we must carry on if we are to meet our responsibilities to the Church and through it to the world.

Women's religious congregations have already gone farther than any other group *as a group* in the Church toward grasping the radicality of the contemporary crises in the areas of spiritual renewal and social justice. Furthermore, many women religious as individuals, and consequently many congregations as congregations, have realized that there is an intimate inter-relation between these two areas. The concern for developing an apostolic spirituality which is really in touch with the contemporary crisis in the interior life and with the contemporary crisis in social justice is a concern that has arisen primarily from within women's religious congregations. It is rapidly becoming the focal-point of renewal efforts in almost every thinking group in the Church, and certainly in every group from which any significant contribution can be realistically expected. The implications for self-evangelization of this frontier situation in the Church in relation to the interface of spiritual renewal and social justice involvement are multiple. Let me point out the three implications which, in my opinion, are the most serious and urgent.

First, as women religious we must accept the responsibility which has come to us through a combination of circumstances which we did not create. We must accept the fact that, to a large extent, as goes women's religious life in the next decade, so goes the Church. If, on the one hand, we recoil from the really radical renewal of the spiritual life which a truly contemporary apostolic involvement demands, or, on the other hand, give up in despair before the enormity of social evil in which virtually every institution including the Church itself is implicated, there is a real possibility that the Gospel will be rendered void for many of our sisters and brothers. However, if we accept the challenge of the long journey inward that is the contemplative search for God shorn of rigidity and distracting frills, and of the long journey outward that is a single-minded and passionate commitment to social justice, the Church could well become even in our lifetime a sign of hope and liberation in a world of almost universal oppression. But women religious, especially those most deeply involved in contemporary society, must also accept the fact that being on the frontier means being largely self-reliant. The paths are not marked for us because they have not yet been walked. This means that we do not have, and cannot waste time and energy pining for, a guidance which will relieve us of risks and secure us against mistakes.

This brings me to the second implication for self-evangelization: the need for serious intellectual and spiritual formation for all of our members and the specialized formation, especially in theology and the social sciences, of some members of every congregation. We must have within our ranks sisters who can serve as resource persons in the important decision-making processes which the next decade will increasingly require. The time is past when we can import, from outside women's religious life, the expertise necessary to chart the future. Indeed, we must accept our share of responsibility for providing not only for ourselves, but for our lay co-workers, our brothers in the clergy, and the institutional Church, the expertise needed to help the Church become a more evangelically simple, poor, non-coercive servant of the oppressed. And the serious formation of our general membership is necessary to insure the informed and generous consensus which is the only viable basis of group apostolic effectiveness in an age in which the autocratic use of authority is finally beginning to become obsolete.

But the general intellectual formation of all our members and the specialized formation of some of them will only create another potential (or actual) oppressor unless it is accompanied by a spiritual formation which is increasingly radical. By "radical" I mean going to the roots, not going out on a limb. As we find ourselves with ever increasing attractive options in ministry and with ever fewer outside guides or valid guidelines we find ourselves in increasing need of spiritual wisdom. We must be able, as individuals and as communities, to discern not only between good and evil but between good and better. Our community choices are, not infrequently these days, between dangerous growth and slow suicide. The stakes are increasingly higher as our resources, both personnel and finances, are diminished in quantity and our options increased in number and variety. The spiritual maturity which will not only survive these choices but make them a road to personal growth and corporate apostolic effectiveness is not something we can have for the wishing or by superficial experimentation with spiritual novelties. Spiritual maturity is essentially a radical interior freedom polarized by a single passionate love. In our case that love is Jesus, gloriously reigning but suffering intensely in his members. There are no gimmicks which will make one free or teach one to love. The central means to Christian holiness is transforming contemplation lived within a vital ecclesial context. We must find the way to enable our members to become genuine contemplatives in a world that seems to leave us neither time nor quiet even to think.

Finally, a third implication of our frontier position is that we cannot wait for others in the Church to blaze the trail in active commitment to social justice. As long as one person is not free we are all slaves. As long as blacks, or native Americans, or Hispanics, or the poor, or women, or migrant workers, or the hungry, or the immigrants, or any other group are oppressed and marginated, we are all in the power of the Evil One. As long as any human being is not free, he or she is not in a position to respond to the Gospel, and as long as we tolerate or contribute to that person's oppression we have snuffed out the Gospel's light for him or her. The active and effective commitment of our members to social justice is going to continue to shake up religious congregations as nothing else except contemplation itself can shake them up. Our willingness to risk our very institutional existence and personal well-being in the service of the freedom of our sisters and brothers is the measure of our self-evangelization today.

If religious congregations are in a frontier position in the Church, community leaders should be in a frontier position in their respective congregations. It is becoming increasingly evident that it is to religious congregations in general and women's congregations in particular that the Church must look for the development of a completely new model of authority, one which will maximize the responsibility and creativity of every individual member in the quest of God and of social justice. If religious are going to be renewed, that is, brought to spiritual maturity expressed in effective apostolic commitment, religious life must become a school of freedom. The entire Church needs to find an evangelical model of authority, one in which coercion has no more place than it did in Jesus' call to follow him, in which dominative power is as foreign as it was to Jesus nailed to the cross for our liberation, but in which loving service unto death by those in authority renders each member more free, more responsible, more creative, more single-mindedly devoted to Jesus' great task in this world: I have come that they may have life and may have it to the full (Jn 10:10).

Chapter Two
TOWARD A THEOLOGICAL
THEORY OF RELIGIOUS LIFE

The material in this essay was developed over the period from 1976 to 1981 as lectures and conferences given to the religious of the dioceses of Spokane, Los Angeles, Oakland, San Jose, and Milwaukee; in classes on religious life taught at the Jesuit School of Theology in Berkeley, California and at St. Norbert's College in DePere, Wisconsin; and in special sessions shared with the members of various congregations, especially the Sisters, Servants of the Immaculate Heart of Mary of Monroe, Michigan, and the Sisters of Charity of the Blessed Virgin Mary of Dubuque, Iowa.

I. THE PROJECT OF THEOLOGIZING ABOUT RELIGIOUS LIFE TODAY

Thinking theologically about the meaning of religious life today is a significantly different kind of project than it might have been at the beginning of this century. Probably the most basic difference consists in the fact that the contemporary theologian cannot realistically start with an "essential definition" of religious life of which different canonical forms are accidental variations and from which such phenomena as secular institutes and non-canonical communities can be clearly distinguished.[1] Canon law may make juridical distinctions among various forms of "consecrated life" but contemporary theologians no longer draw theological conclusions from legal premises because they no longer assume (if they ever did) that canon law is a theological synthesis. Consequently, developing a theology of religious life today is not a deductive process of drawing out the implications of an *a priori* definition; nor is the result of theological reflection on religious life a relatively static synthesis which can be used as a prescriptive guide for the living of "true" religious life.

18

On the contrary, the theology of religious life today is most adequately understood as an ongoing project involving three constantly interacting moments: description, interpretation, and evaluation. The first moment consists in the attempt to describe as comprehensively as possible what people are actually living as religious life today. This description will include such traditional forms of religious life as that of cloistered monastics, canons regular, mendicants, regular clerics, members of the so-called apostolic congregations, and hermits and consecrated virgins. But it must also include the life of members of Secular Institutes who make vows or promises but do not live in communities, and members of Societies of Apostolic Life who live in community but do not make public vows.[2] And it cannot exclude the life of members of newly organized non-canonical groups like the Sisters for Christian Community. In other words, a theologically adequate description of religious life as opposed to a juridical definition must include the life experience of all those individuals and groups who understand themselves as religious and live accordingly. This designation is inadequate for various reasons, but it is an attempt to articulate the fact that a variety of individual and communal lifestyles in the Church have in common something which distinguishes them from "secular" life (also an inadequate designation) and relates them to one another by what we might call a "theological family resemblance." It will be part of our task in this essay to try to articulate this distinction and this resemblance a little more adequately.

The task of description is further complicated by the fact that "pure forms" of religious life are far less common today than they once were. The cross-fertilization of groups and spiritualities has led to considerably more likeness than difference among, let us say, Benedictine, Dominican and Mercy sisters even though, strictly speaking, they respectively represent monastic, mendicant, and congregational forms of religious life. On the other hand, there is an enormous difference between cloistered Carmelites and active Dominicans who should, as mendicants, look more alike if the historical distinctions of forms of life that undergird certain legal distinctions corresponded to lived reality. It would be difficult to discover much real difference between the day to day experience of male Maryknoll missionaries who are, strictly speaking, not religious but members of a Society of Apostolic Life and that of the members of most apostolic congregations of religious men such as the Redemptorists. An adequate description of life cannot draw the kinds of sharp distinctions that are possible in law.

Finally, there are a number of developments occurring in our own day which cannot easily be handled by any of the available traditional categories pertaining to religious life but which are plainly happening within the bounds of that phenomenon or movement which we call religious life. Among these new developments are mixed communities of men and women, communities which have admitted members from more than one Christian denomination, and communities which have admitted as associates married couples and other individuals who do not intend to make religious profession.

Obviously, the task of describing "religious life" is far more complex than that of defining it juridically. But since all of the above factors are part of the present lived reality of religious life the theologian must take all of them into account in some coherent way. To admit that the descriptive moment is essential to the theological task is already to take a theological position. It is to see the theological project as one, not of deciding what may and may not exist or happen, what may or may not legally be called "religious life," but to discover the meaning of what is actually being lived. As will be clear, the pursuit of this theological objective may well result in the discovery that some of these contemporary developments are genuinely incompatible with religious life. But such an evaluation will not be the result of applying an *a priori* legal definition to lived experience. It will be the result of the investigation and articulation of the meaning of religious life as it is embodied in the experience of committed religious and a judgment about the coherence within that meaning of certain contemporary developments.

The second moment in the project of theologizing about religious life is *interpretation*. This is the most properly theological moment, and the most creative one. Here the theologian attempts to discover and coherently formulate the meaning of what is being lived as religious life in terms of the framework provided by Christian tradition and most importantly by the normative articulation of that tradition in the New Testament. Since most of this essay will consist in carrying out this second step we need not pause to explain it further at this point.

The third moment in the theological project is *evaluation* or the attempt to make some well-founded and defensible judgments about the adequacy in terms of the Gospel of what people are living as religious life. Evaluation is not necessarily chronologically subsequent to description and interpretation. Indeed, it may well be the process of evaluation, whether spontaneous or carefully structured, which leads to the raising of the kinds of questions which initiate interpretation. For example, the growing conviction of many religious women in the period beginning just prior to Vatican II that some, if not many, longstanding practices in religious communities no longer proclaimed Gospel values (if indeed they ever did) certainly helped launch the radical rethinking of religious life that has been going on for the last two decades. And, conversely, it is the evident Gospel quality of the life and ministry of certain groups which do not fit canonical criteria of religious life that has raised the question of how appropriate or valid those legal criteria actually are. In other words, the three activities of the theological process are not three steps of a scientific method but three constantly interacting moments within an ongoing reflection.

If the theological project is substantially as we have described it we can expect the results of this activity to have certain characteristics. First of all, because it is an inductive process beginning in a praxis which is always developing, we can expect that the resulting synthesis will be a theology constantly in revision rather than a once-for-all construction. Furthermore, the theology of religious life will be understood to include both the reflective moment in the actual living of religious life, an activity that is informally and continually carried on by all serious religious whether or not they have been formally educated as theologians, and the formal articulation of more comprehensive theory by professional theologians attempting to bring to common awareness in the public forum interpretations of religious life which are adequate to the experience of religious.

Secondly, we can expect that different theologians primarily concerned with different forms of religious life and working within different theological frameworks and different cultural situations will develop different theologies of this reality.[3] In other words, it is unlikely that we will ever again have *the* theology of religious life in the univocal sense that was once embodied in the *Catechism of the Vows*. Just as we have today various ecclesiologies, christologies, and soteriologies, so we will have various theologies of religious life. This pluralism need not involve contradictions but it will certainly lead to different emphases and foster a variety of developments in contrast to the imposition of virtual uniformity on all religious by a univocal theology such as that achieved in the wake of the Council of Trent and the revision of Canon Law in 1917.

However, if pluralism of interpretation need not imply contradiction it does necessarily imply limitation. Contemporary theologians, no matter in what area they are working, no longer aspire to the kind of comprehensive, univocal, and perennially valid synthesis of a Thomas Aquinas.[4] We are too conditioned by our developed historical consciousness to believe that any standpoint allows for a comprehensive view or that any formulation can transcend the cultural and linguistic limitations within which it is articulated. Our insights into religious life, however true, will always be partial and in need of ongoing revision.

If the theology of religious life is and will remain an ongoing project whose results must always be provisional because limited, one might be tempted to ask if the effort of formal theologizing is really worthwhile. Should we not content ourselves with sincerely living according to our lights and reflecting informally among ourselves on those aspects of our experience which seem problematic at any given moment? I can see two major reasons for expending the effort to develop a theology of religious life, even a theology in constant need of revision. The first is that theological reflection, even when it does not afford us certainty, does give us clarity, and in our confusing and rapidly changing times such clarity is a major source of coherence and conviction in our attempts to live religious life. Secondly, theology is a basically contemplative activity because the subject matter of theological reflection is the mystery of God and all those lesser mysteries that mediate God's presence and action in our lives. Religious life is one of those mysteries, and to contemplate it with theological precision is an activity which brings joy and strength to anyone who loves the life and has committed herself or himself to living it.

II. THE VATICAN COUNCIL'S IMPACT ON THE THEOLOGY OF RELIGIOUS LIFE

Those who have concentrated on the explicit teaching of the Second Vatican Council[5] in regard to religious life, that is, on chapter six of *Lumen Gentium* (Dogmatic Constitution on the Church 1964), *Perfectae Caritatis* (Decree on the Appropriate Renewal of the Religious Life 1965), and the two documents published after the Council to implement and/or explicitate the latter's teaching on religious life, namely, *Evangelica Testificatio* (Apostolic Exhortation of Paul VI On the Renewal of the Religious Life According to the Teaching of the Second Vatican Council, 1967) and *Venite Seorsum* (Instruction on the Contemplative Life and on the Enclosure of Nuns issued by the Sacred Congregation for Religious and Secular Institutes, 1969),[6] cannot fail to wonder how these documents could possibly be responsible for the immense ferment of renewal in religious congregations of women. Chapter six of *Lumen Gentium,* probably the best contribution from a theological point of view, is far from revolutionary; *Perfectae Caritatis* is an uneven document mixing rather courageous calls for renewal with a very traditional approach to many aspects of religious life. *Evangelica Testificatio* was, in general, a theological step backward toward preconciliar understandings of religious life[7] and *Venite Seorsum* was undoubtedly one of the most repressive documents to emanate from the Vatican in modern times. Nevertheless, the Council launched a full-scale renewal of religious life, the dimensions of which undoubtedly far exceeded both the expectations and the intentions of the Council fathers.

The real impetus for the renewal of religious life did indeed come from the Council but not through its explicit statements on the subject. Two insights from the Council teachings have had a foundation-shaking impact, especially on the life of women religious. The first is the affirmation which is fully explicitated in chapter five of *Lumen Gentium* entitled "The Call of the Whole Church to Holiness." In this chapter the Council explicitly affirmed that all Christians are called "to the fullness of the Christian life and to the perfection of charity," indeed that "one and the same holiness is cultivated by all who are moved by the Spirit of God."

Religious life, at least since the thirteenth century, has been defined as a higher life, the life of perfection, a superior vocation not given to all Christians. Religious were those who bound themselves to the observance of the "evangelical counsels" whereas ordinary Christians were bound only to the observance of the commandments. The Council undermined in a definitive way this understanding of religious life and, although the Council itself and its implementing documents relapse repeatedly into "superiority" language,[8] post-conciliar religious had to begin to relinquish their self-definition in terms of *de jure* as well as *de facto* superiority in relation to other members of the Church.

Religious as well as lay people could easily understand that it was not only theologically offensive but practically inhibiting of the full spiritual life to define lay people as those called to an inferior form of Christian life. Furthermore, contemporary biblical scholarship had undermined the very concept of New Testament "counsels" meant for some Christians and not for others. Nevertheless, the surrender of the definition of religious life in comparative terms created an enormous vacuum in the theological understanding of that life as well as leading to frightening practical consequences for many who had long understood themselves in terms of such superiority. What could motivate people to add difficult obligations to their already arduous Christian commitments if doing so was objectively no better than not doing so and if the resulting lifestyle was not, at least in principle, superior to others? And if religious life were not a superior and fragile form of life that required protection from outside contamination, what real reason could be offered to the world for the elaborate structures meant to keep religious from interacting freely with other Christians? In short, how were religious to understand themselves and explain their lifestyle to others without recourse to the fundamental premise that religious life was a higher form of Christian life and commitment?

The second foundation-shaking contribution of Vatican II to the rethinking of religious life was the Council's reversal of the centuries-long adversary stance of the Church in relation to the world. From the opening address of the Council fathers to the entire human family rather than to the Catholic faithful, through the most significant of the Council's documents, *Gaudium et Spes* (Pastoral Constitution on the Church in the Modern World), the Council expressed its conviction of the solidarity of the Church with the whole of humanity. The Church is a community which "realizes that it is truly and intimately linked with humankind and its history" (*Gaudium et Spes* #1).

Religious, for the first time in history, were caught in a profound contradiction concerning their own relationship with the Church. Religious have always understood their life as a kind of intensification of the general Christian commitment. They are the most radical representatives of what the Church sees itself to be. Consequently, as the Church has for centuries distinguished itself from "the world," presented itself as a "perfect society" over against that other perfect but inferior society which is the secular state, as the City of God in opposition to the secular city, religious have justified their self-understanding as those Christians who most totally and radically renounce the world and separate themselves, even physically, from it as the logical implication of their "frontline" position in the Church. Separation from the world, renunciation of the secular, even a certain cultivated distance from the so-called "secular" members of the Church itself, has been characteristic of religious life since the days of the desert fathers and mothers. This separation has taken various forms in the course of history ranging from the actual flight from the city to the desert in the fourth century, through the separation by monastic enclosure, to the distance created by means of practices such as dressing differently, living in convents, and following a life pattern that could not be assimilated into ordinary contemporary life.

With the Church's radical reversal of position in regard to its relationship to the world, religious faced an equally radical choice: to surrender their self-understanding as the most eccle-

sial segment of the Church or to surrender their self-understanding as those who renounced the world and separated
themselves from it. Religious could only continue to be at the
very heart of the modern Church if they made their own its
commitment to being in, with, and for the world in solidarity
with all people of good will, Christians, non-Christians, and
even non-believers. But how could religious become truly
"worldly" in this new and positive sense without abandoning not
only the lifestyle of separation from the world but especially that
essential component of the theology of religious life, renunciation of the world through the evangelical counsels?

In practice, American religious as a group (there were notable individual and congregational exceptions, of course) opted
for solidarity with the Church in its abandonment of its adversary stance toward the world. This was not surprising because
post-conciliar religious had been influenced in the years before
the Council by the same historical and theological factors which
had influenced the Council fathers in their move toward solidarity with the whole human family.

The implications for the lifestyle of religious were probably
more disturbing for the average sister than was the theological
revision to which they were related. Perhaps the symbolic linch
pin of the entire movement was the rapid, but wrenching, surrender of the habit which was both the symbol of an implied superiority and uniqueness, and the most effective barrier to the
assimilation of religious to the surrounding culture. The breakdown of cloister in local convents, the widespread repudiation
of anonymous large-group living, the questioning of exclusively
institutional congregational commitments, the development of
relationships of religious across congregational boundaries and
with lay people, the resumption by religious as individuals and
as local groups of certain exercises of personal financial responsibility that had for centuries been exercised exclusively by superiors, and the move toward more representative and collegial
forms of government were only a few of the obvious and radical
lifestyle adaptations which were precipitated by and expressive
of the "return to the world" of contemporary women religious.

The combined effect of these two interrelated theological
developments of Vatican II, namely, the demise of the theology

of superiority and the reversal of the adversary stance toward the world, was far-reaching. The "closed system" of religious life and the sociology of knowledge which it made possible came to an abrupt end. Religious, mixing ever more extensively with their secular counterparts, could no longer live a separate reality in which old world customs and bizarre practices appeared normal while doubtfully Christian attitudes and values were blithely assumed to be part of the call to superior holiness. Young people entering religious congregations could no longer be inducted into a completely separate and self-sufficient social system within which no questions were asked, values and practices were accepted without examination, and assimilation to the group was seen as the highest personal achievement.

But the end of the closed system meant more than the break-up of an ancient self-reinforcing lifestyle. It raised, in an extremely urgent and painful way, the issue of religious self-understanding. What constitutes religious life? Is it in any way different from "lay" life, and if so how? If not, is there any reason for complicating one's Christian life by vows and congregational membership? Furthermore, it was increasingly obvious that whatever answer was given to the question about the foundational meaning of religious life it would have to be an answer that non-religious could also understand since a separate framework of meaning was no longer available to religious. To make sense to themselves religious would have to make sense to the world. This does not necessarily imply that religious life and its values have to be acceptable to the world. But they do have to make sense to the world because the world has become both the framework within which meaning is achieved and the locus of whatever salvific action religious intend to undertake. Nothing less than a full-scale re-examination and rethinking of religious life was called for.

Numerous attempts have been made in the years since the Council to rethink religious life within the framework of theological premises other than those of superior vocation and separation from the world. Some have tried to understand religious life as radical evangelical life or the radical living out of New Testament discipleship as presented in the beatitudes. Others have tried to emphasize the public ecclesial character of religious life. Still others have started from the notion of charism, both that of religious life itself and that of the founder of the particular religious family. Some have seen the life as a kind of institutionalized prophetic or counter-cultural movement, and others have attempted to localize its basic meaning in its public character as witness to the transcendent or eschatological dimensions of the Christian vocation.

From the disciplinary point of view, authors have based their theories in Scripture, ecclesiology, history, systematic theology, liberation theology, and spirituality. What all of these attempts have demonstrated is the richness of the phenomenon of religious life and the fecundity of approaching its meaning from broader points of view than the dogmatic juridical one that had dominated the theology of religious life at least since the Council of Trent.

In the remainder of this essay I will attempt to suggest a basic approach to the phenomenon of Christian religious life in which the phenomenon itself is seen as a relatively widespread human development and the Christian specificity as the characteristic realization, within a single tradition, of this human phenomenon. I will not attempt in this essay to examine in detail the various elements and aspects of the life but simply to answer some of the basic questions we have raised thus far: What is Christian religious life? Why do people choose to live this way? Does the choice make any sense? Why do only some people choose it? How can a lifestyle be understood as special without being understood as superior?

III. TOWARD A THEORY OF RELIGIOUS LIFE

A. *Religious Life as a Movement.*

Religious life is not an "essence," either divinely instituted or deduced from canon law and defined in terms of certain essential notes, which realizes itself in various historical forms. It is perhaps best described as a "movement," which, as we shall see, has existed throughout history, in many different religious traditions, and in a wide variety of forms.

An informal phenomenological effort surfaces at least two

characteristics of movements. First, a movement engages a *group of people who are animated by a common concern*. The group may be small or large; it may emerge at the initiative of a single individual or of a group, or it may emerge spontaneously among many people in different places at roughly the same time; it may engage many aspects of its members' thought and life or only one; it may be highly centralized and tightly organized or it may be very decentralized and amorphous. If we look at characteristic movements of our own time we can see how pluralistic the category "movement" really is. Feminism, the charismatic renewal, the anti-nuclear and disarmament effort, the retreat movement, the Moral Majority, Bread for the World, environmentalism, and physical fitness are all correctly seen as movements. In some of them, we find a high level of commitment touching many areas of the adherents' lives, tight organization, a stress on ideological uniformity, considerable social interaction among the members even to the point of common residence, and hierarchical authority structures. In others, members know of rather than knowing one another; commitment does not necessarily involve ideological conformity, the members being in accord only on the central value of the movement and disagreeing on almost everything else; organization is minimal and authority structures virtually non-existent. But all movements have in common the engagement of people animated and united by a common concern.

The second characteristic of a movement is that it admits of *degrees of participation*. It may well be that this is the distinction between a movement and a formal organization. In an organization membership is formally established, there are usually stages of incorporation, and members can be clearly identified in terms of the degree of incorporation and the type of membership they enjoy. By contrast, people belong to a movement according to the degree of their participation and these degrees often are not formalized. Theoretically, there could be as many degrees of participation as there are members. However, there do seem to be three broad types of participation which can help us organize our reflection on religious life as a movement. First, in any movement which gains momentum there tend to be central or core figures who give themselves to the movement with a totality and exclusivity that makes them recognizable symbols of the movement itself. These people are often the founding figures or major representatives, e.g., Martin Luther King, Jr. in the civil rights movement; Gloria Steinem in the feminist movement; Gandhi in the non-violence movement; Jerry Falwell in the Moral Majority; Dorothy Day in the Catholic Worker movement. These people stand out as core figures symbolizing and animating their respective movements. Sometimes a small group carries this core identity, such as the Ann Arbor and Notre Dame charismatic groups, or the stable members of a Catholic Worker House. In these cases at least the core group becomes an organization.

Secondly, there are members who give themselves to the movement with real commitment and zeal but who retain other non-conflicting commitments. Many committed charismatic Christians do not wish to join covenant communities; many who work actively for peace on a day to day basis as members of Pax Christi or other such movements do not become members of the central organization.

Finally, there are those who give themselves to a movement for a time, either wholly or partially. Some who went to Selma at the height of the civil rights movement continue to support and work within the movement but no longer in a full-time, ultimate risk capacity. Others who have never demonstrated or otherwise become totally involved in the movement have supported it by financial contributions, voting, and personal behavior since its very beginning. Likewise, people have spent years totally involved in a movement such as the Peace Corps and have later left it to go their own way, retaining ties of friendship and support.

Movements, especially those which are relatively small and localized, often institutionalize themselves and become organizations; or organizations arise within the movement which do not necessarily involve all the members. Such organizations may be totally life-involving as is the case with a charismatic covenant community, or partially involving like board membership in Pax Christi. But in any case organization clarifies, limits, and explicitates the conditions and degrees of membership. One is either a member or not; one's stage of incorporation and type of membership is clearly defined and the rights and duties pertaining to that stage and type are clearly delineated. When a movement, or some element within it, becomes an organization it becomes subject to the well-known advantages and disadvantages of institutionalization.

On the positive side institutionalization brings clarity about the identity and roles of members, explicitness about purposes and commitments, stability in responsibilities and criteria for judging the fulfillment of responsibility, effectiveness of leadership and corporate activity, and some assurance about the continuation of the organization in the future. But on the negative side institutionalization jeopardizes the spontaneity and originality of the movement. It risks standardizing commitment and alienating the responsibility of members who leave animation and accountability to the leadership. It often narrows the membership by excluding unconventional types who do not meet standardized criteria of belonging and can ultimately find itself subordinating its original purposes to the need for institutional survival.

I have dwelt at length on this phenomenology of movements because I think it can help to elucidate our actual contemporary experience of religious life. Religious life was, from the very beginning, a movement. Men and women animated by a common concern (the nature of which we must consider later) recognized a certain unity among themselves. The consecrated virgins of the first centuries of the Church, the men and women who retired to the desert as hermits and later banded together in cenobitic or lavral forms of common life, the monastics in the Benedictine tradition, mendicants, canons, clerics regular, members of various apostolic congregations, members of various confraternities, secular institutes, and pious associations, anchorites, beguines, and tertiaries of all kinds belong to the great movement of religious life which stretches from the first century to our own day. These people have lived as solitaries and in community, have made vows or promises or neither, have separated themselves from other Christians or remained fully participating members of the local Church, have assumed special dress and habitat and lifestyle or eschewed such distinctions, have been familial or monarchical or democratic or collegial in their relationships, have made special works essential to their self-understanding or done whatever was at hand to support themselves. Whatever unites all these people is more interior and spiritual than forms of life or types of behavior.

It is also evident that the movement of religious life has admitted, from the beginning, varying degrees of participation from the total life commitment of the desert hermit, through the kind of partial participation characteristic of medieval tertiaries, to oblates and associate members in our own day. Even among the most organized elements there was, for centuries, the distinction between simple vows which admitted dispensation and solemn vows which in principle did not.[9]

Relatively early in its history the religious life movement underwent certain types of institutionalization, and the resulting organizations, namely, religious communities, orders, and congregations, arose. It is important to realize that at no time was the entire movement definitively organized, even though this came very close to being the case after the Council of Trent and especially after the revision of canon law in 1917. At that time strict juridical distinctions were drawn between those who could claim the title religious and those who could not. But as we have pointed out, these juridical distinctions did not change the fact that, theologically, many persons would have to be considered religious who did not qualify for the designation in legal terms. The Daughters of Charity of St. Vincent de Paul are a good example of this phenomenon. They thought of themselves as religious and so did the people to whom they ministered. What is especially interesting in our own times is the re-emergence within the movement of a wide variety of forms of religious life with which the juridical categories cannot deal. The first major development was the birth of the so-called "secular institutes" in the 1940's.[10] Since then we have seen the foundation of non-canonical religious communities, the movement of some canonical groups to non-canonical status, the revaluation of various so-called "lay" extensions of some congregations, and the creation of a variety of forms of associate or co-membership in congregations which previously did not have such "lay" branches. In other words, the "movement" character of religious life is reasserting itself after several centuries of almost total institutionalization. This is causing considerable concern among some religious and those Church officials who have equated religious life with its institutionalized forms and the theological reality with the juridical category. They fear a dilution of the life or even its disappearance in confusion, not realizing that the movement in all its pluriform vitality is the source of the perennial renewal of the organizational realizations of religious life which have the tendency of all institutions toward sclerosis.

In summary, religious life itself is best understood as a movement rather than as an institution or even a collection of institutions. Therefore, in order to understand its theological meaning we must attempt to uncover the "common concern" which accounts for the family resemblance among all these various manifestations of the movement down through the centuries.

B. The Common Concern of All Religious.

It will probably seem facetious to say that the common concern of all religious, whatever form their participation in the movement takes, is *religion*, the relationship with the Ultimate or with the Transcendent. This is not to say that religious are the only people who are concerned with religion, but they are concerned with it in a way that is different. We will examine that difference shortly.

It is helpful for Christian religious to attend to the fact, of which we were not particularly cognizant until quite recently, that religious life is not the exclusive property of Christians. Indian Shamans, Buddhist monks and nuns, certain Jewish Torah scholars who renounced marriage to give themselves to the study of the Law, "holy" men and women in many traditions have come to our attention and caused us to look with new eyes even at some ancient "pagan" phenomena such as Socrates' philosophical circle and Plato's academy. "Religious" exist in practically every religious or philosophical tradition in which personal transformation by communion with the Transcendent is a major objective. As we will see, there are certain characteristic traits of lifestyle which lead us to see an analogy among these "religious" regardless of the tradition they represent but what they all have in common at the deepest level is a certain kind of absorption in the religious dimension of life, however that is understood. It is the quality of the absorption, not the theological specificity of the tradition, which makes the person a "religious."

C. Artists, Intellectuals, and Religious: An Analogy.

An analogy which I have found particularly enlightening in the attempt to understand and explain the central concern of the religious is that of the artist and the intellectual. Like the artist and the intellectual, the religious is a person who is fascinated with one dimension of human experience, a dimension that is important for any healthy and truly human life but which is not the practical dominant in the life of most people. I am not speaking here of what people hold as ultimately important, that in terms of which they would choose if a crisis arose, but of that around which their practical day-to-day life is organized. Whereas the lives of most people are organized around their families, and the work, political involvements, and economic pursuits which support that family system, the artist has organized his or her life around the aesthetic dimension of experience and the intellectual around the life of the mind. The artist is not necessarily the most talented nor the intellectual the most brilliant. People who have not given themselves up to art or to scholarship may well be more gifted in these domains. What makes the artist an artist or the intellectual an intellectual is not merely talent, although that is necessary, but some kind of fascination with or absorption in the aesthetic or intellectual dimension of human experience that "compels" these people to allow that dimension to dominate their lives. This dominant concern relativizes all the other dimensions of their lives such as family, economics, politics, geographical location, friendships, and so on.

The religious in any tradition seems to be one who is fascinated with the religious dimension of human experience, for whom this dimension becomes dominant and who wants to organize his or her life around this dominant religious concern.

Such a person is not necessarily the most religiously talented (although some natural bent toward and taste for religious experience is undoubtedly at work), the holiest, or the most virtuous. But religion, the horizon of ultimacy, the quest for the Transcendent, exercises a fascination in the life of this person that relativizes all the "normal" concerns of human life.

Whether we look at the artist, the intellectual, or the religious we note the tendency to organize life in function of the dominant concern. This usually takes the form of a certain protectiveness of the central concern precisely because the "magnificent obsession" in these lives is not the normal one and ordinary life is not structured to foster such concerns. Consequently, these people tend to seek a certain measure of solitude or separation from the rest of society. The artist's studio, the intellectual's study, the religious' oratory or hermitage becomes a sacred space in which to pursue alone and at leisure a passion which will never appear completely "normal" to the rest of humanity.

This need for separation usually goes further than the blocking off of geographical space and private time. These people tend to develop a lifestyle which will foster their dominant interest. Often enough the lifestyle is strange enough that it interferes significantly with ordinary life and relationships. No normal woman would envy the wife of Socrates, and the disturbed family lives of artists are legendary. Religious tend to avoid marital and parental involvements and often enough even filial obligations altogether. In each case it is the all-absorbing quality of the central concern that leads to the creating around the self of a lifestyle which will foster and protect it.

Finally, all of these types tend to seek out like-minded companions with whom to share this interest whose passionate quality is not easily understood by other people. Frequently only another intellectual can understand the boundless enthusiasm of a thinker for ideas and theories; it takes an artist to understand why a dancer will practice to the point of exhaustion and experience sheer ecstasy in the performance; and religious resonate, even across traditional lines, with each other's religious quest.[11] Whether one seeks a mentor, a spiritual guide, a community, a professional association, or a school, one seeks those who can understand how and why a whole life can be given over to something that does not play this consuming role in the lives of most people.

Artists, intellectuals, and religious are important to any society. They seem called to preserve, foster, and develop those dimensions of human experience that are, in one sense, "nonessential" and in another sense the most necessary of all if human life is to be truly human. Relationships, parenting, achieving economic well-being, organizing society in politically effective ways, in short, personal and collective survival concerns, appear to be of more vital importance within the human enterprise than the seeming luxury of pursuing beauty, truth, and unity. But in the long run survival is only worthwhile if the quality of life in a society is enriched and elevated by the transcendental concerns. The aesthetic, intellectual, and religious concerns which dominate the lives of artists, intellectuals, and religious are just as important to the ordinary person as they are for their devotees. Cultivated people know this, and even though they have not given these values the dominant and organizing place in their lives that the artist, intellectual, or religious has, they recognize the importance of these people and their passions for society as a whole. However, important as these concerns are for everyone in a society, they are also extremely fragile values, usually the first to be sacrificed when survival values are threatened. Somehow nature seems to have provided from the beginning for the protection of these values by producing certain people who invest these values with the survival urgency most people attach to social, economic, and political affairs. However annoyed "ordinary lay people" may get with the personal excesses, the financial irresponsibility, or the impracticality that is sometimes manifested by these "gifted" types, society knows that without them life would be immeasurably impoverished.

However, even as we recognize the importance of these people in society, we must not disguise the fact that there is a built-in tendency to exaggeration or oddity in the personality of the gifted types. There is a baffling tendency for them to be remarkably deficient in the very sphere of their special gift. Artists, the treasurers and creators of the beautiful, are notoriously capable of living in unnecessary squalor and making remarkably sordid specimens of their own lives. Intellectuals are renowned for their absent-mindedness and inability to order their own lives in an intelligent manner. And religious throughout history have been the instigators and executors of some of history's more horrible episodes of human violence. This is perhaps only a limited verification of the Aristotelian principle that the corruption of the best is the worst. But it is important for everyone, most of all the gifted types themselves, to be aware that the gift is not a guarantee of actual superiority in the sphere of one's gift. It is a trust always in danger of perversion to selfish or evil ends.

Artists, intellectuals, and religious are dangerous gifts to the community. They are gifts because of their role in preserving and developing those dimensions of human experience without which we would cease to be human. But they are dangerous not only because of their propensity to pervert the gift, but also because it is easy for them to monopolize these values and thus alienate them from the other members of society rather than preserving and mediating them to their fellows. Unfortunately, others in society often connive with this elitism and even encourage it. They are happy to let the religious pray for them and the intellectuals think for them while they attend to the more engrossing concerns of ordinary life. The more isolated and elite the gifted become, the greater their tendency to overestimate their own specialness, to appropriate the values to themselves, and to disdain the complementarity and mutuality which would prevent their own alienation and make possible the genuine mediation of their gifts to others.

If, in the light of this analogy, we now look specifically at women's religious life as it has developed in the Church, we can perhaps account for both its healthy and its unhealthy manifestations. We are speaking here only of religious with a genuine vocation to this life, not of those apparently numerous individuals who entered religious congregations under the unconscious influence of personal, familial, psychological, or economic considerations that had little or nothing to do with the search for God.

The genuine religious is a person for whom religious reality

is not only a central but an absorbing interest. She is not necessarily any holier or more virtuous than her contemporaries
but she is fascinated with religion, with the quest for God, perhaps with ritual, certainly with personal religious experience,
the way others are engrossed in their prospects for marriage
and/or the development of their careers. The desire to structure
her life for the protection and nurturing of this gift leads her to
select a religious lifestyle, usually but not always as a member of
a religious congregation. In any case she will try to build into her
life the space, in terms of time and privacy, for the pursuit of
her interior life and to seek those companions who will understand her involvement and foster its development. The Christian religious whose experience of the Transcendent centers
explicitly in her relationship with Jesus Christ will find the
choice of the celibate state eminently suited to her pursuit of this
single personal relationship whether she articulates this in terms
of the exclusivity of her love for him or in terms of freedom to
devote herself to his affairs.

There has never been any question about the recognition
by the Church, leaders and members, of the importance of religious for the rest of the Church. Nevertheless, it has unfortunately been true that religious have sometimes been
remarkably "un-Christian" in the way they have related to the
other members of the Church community. Charity and filial responsibility have been sacrificed to religious observance; elitism
has been carried to the point of disdain as religious have arro-
gated to themselves privileged status in the community; and
worst of all, they have often so monopolized the values of religion that others in the Church have actually not felt called to
real sanctity, believing "perfection" to be the business of the
professional religious.

The analogy among artists, intellectuals and religious can
also suggest how we might deal with the problem of the "superiority" of religious life in the Church. If we talk in terms of a
gift given by God to some members of the Church which consists
in a special attraction to and absorption in the religious dimension of human experience, we can both affirm the specialness of
the vocation and avoid attributing superiority to either the people thus called or the lifestyle they elaborate for the fostering of

the gift. Like the artist or the intellectual, the religious is the bearer of a special vocation but not a superior one. The religious is not necessarily called to nor blessed with greater holiness than any other Christian. Each believer attains that holiness to which he or she is called in proportion to his or her response. The explicitness of the religious' concern with the Transcendent is important for the whole Church; but it is not any more important than the vocation to Christian marriage. There will probably always be a tendency among humans to attribute superiority to whatever is less common. And there will probably always be a tendency on the part of those whose vocations are less common to arrogate to themselves elite status in the community. Perhaps this is why Jesus so frequently warned his disciples against seeking prestige for religious reasons, competing for first place in the reign of God, arrogating to themselves special titles and positions, adorning themselves with special clothes, or seeking exemptions from the ordinary duties of believers (cf. Mt 23:5–12 and elsewhere).

So far we have been speaking of "religious" in the broadest sense of the term. Such people may or may not join canonical religious congregations, but in the Church most of them do. However, this is where the conception of religious life as a movement can help us to come to terms with some of the non-canonical and even non-communitarian developments in the contemporary Church. As in every movement, there are in this movement religious who are so totally absorbed in and by the search for the Transcendent, the relationship with God in Christ, that it is and must always be for them an exclusive commitment. Such individuals are usually not especially disturbed by changes in the external forms of religious life, for their own primary commitment is not to any organization. They are convinced that if all religious congregations disappeared tomorrow they and others like them would simply refound the life by continuing to live it. It is undoubtedly from among such people that the great founders of religious orders and originators of classic spiritualities have come. We cannot help being amazed at the spiritual itineraries of some of these people who have been members of several different orders in their lifetimes and sometimes have finished their lives officially exiled from their own congregations or even expelled from canonical religious life. They never seem to doubt that they are religious nor to accept the definition or control of their vocation by anyone, however highly placed in the hierarchical structure of the Church.

Not all such religious emerge into public prominence, but every congregation has them and they are frequently a source of continuity and stability as well as of development and renewal. It might be well to point out, however, that such religious types do not necessarily respond to their vocation fully or achieve remarkable sanctity. Nor are they preserved from the day-to-day fluctuations in ardor and enthusiasm that afflict all human beings. They are gifted with a religious interest that can and should lead to real sanctity just as an artistic or intellectual talent should lead to striking production. But as we well know, not all talented people actualize their potential. Some dabble irresponsibly, producing nothing of moment; others use their gift to get by without exerting their best efforts; some actually prostitute it for personal gain or the manipulation of others. Jim Jones is a chilling example of how wrong the religious gift can go. But when all the provisos have been allowed for, it still seems correct to say that the movement we call religious life (still in its broadest sense) is carried in a special way by these individuals who have a special and permanent vocation to pursue the religious dimension of human experience in an exclusive kind of way.

There are many others whose primary but not exclusive life concern is the religious one. They give themselves to it with energy and dedication without totally renouncing other non-conflicting commitments that are also important to them. I suspect that many members of active religious congregations belong to the religious movement in this way. They have integrated a certain number of important commitments into their primary commitment in such a way that the religious commitment inspires the others, and those commitments provide an expression for the central religious concern. In the best of situations there are no serious conflicts among such ordered commitments. But in the real world in which most religious are members of religious organizations, such conflicts can and do develop, and these people must sometimes make agonizing decisions about retaining formal membership in their communities.[12] The genuine religious, even if she leaves the organization, will continue to pursue her religious concern in ways that do not obviate her other commitments.

It seems to be these religious, when they are members of congregations, who devote the most time and energy to the religious institution, its survival and renewal. They are not charismatic refounders so much as they are committed members who prize the potential of the community to support and sustain their own religious commitment but also desire the flexibility of organization that will allow for a variety of compatible commitments. Such concerns are less pressing for the first type who tend to generate the religious life movement rather than to be regenerated by it and who usually subordinate other aspects of life, even ministerial ones, to their religious interest.

Finally, there are those who give themselves totally to religious life (in or outside of a religious community) for a time and who then carry the fruits of this experience into other life commitments, and those who associate themselves with religious life in an ongoing but never total way. For these people the concern with the Transcendent surfaces repeatedly and claims its due, but it never so takes over the life of the person that it becomes the organizing principle.

If religious life, in the broadest sense and not merely in the juridical sense, is a movement, it is only to be expected that there will be members for whom the quest of the Transcendent is a virtually exclusive commitment, those for whom it is the primary commitment among others, and those for whom it is an important commitment that is periodically primary. In this broad sense of the term, the religious life movement could be compared to the civil rights movement or the feminist movement or even to the Christian movement itself. Just as the concern with justice and equality belongs to the very meaning of Christian commitment and requires some kind of active participation on the part of every member of the Church, so the absolute claim of God on every human life belongs to our vocation as Christians and must come to expression in one way or another. Our reason for speaking of some people as "religious" in a special sense is not that any Christian can be non-religious but that this designation captures the peculiar gift by which the religious dimension of human experience exercises a dominant and organizing role in their lives and brings about a permanent, active, full-time commitment to the movement generated by this special gift. When these people, whom we call "religious" in a strictly theological sense, organize themselves into congregations or communities, they situate themselves as organizations within the Church and the juridical question of their canonical status arises.

Most of what has been said so far pertains to religious life as such, in whatever religious tradition, Christian or non-Christian, it arises. But obviously Christian religious life has important distinguishing characteristics which shape it in a recognizable way. When we turn our attention to this Christian specificity we pass from a general theory of religious life as such to the theology of Christian religious life.

All religious are absorbed in the quest for the Transcendent. But for the Christian, the Transcendent has a face. The Christian religion is structured by Judaeo-Christian revelation, that is, by the encounter with the self-giving God through participation in the identity (filiation) of Jesus of Nazareth and his salvific life experience (the paschal mystery) through the gift of the Holy Spirit. This Christian specificity shapes the religious experience of all Christians including the Church's religious.

First, the religious quest for the Christian is necessarily *personal and interpersonal.* Thus prayer is central to Christian experience. No matter how mystical Christian prayer becomes, it is never total absorption, and never simply personal enlightenment. It is always encounter with an Other, One whom we "become" without ceasing to be ourselves.

Second, because of the Trinitarian character of the Christian experience and the universal salvific intention of God's revelation in Christ the Christian religious experience is necessarily *communitarian.* Although there are numerous ways in which the communal dimension of Christian experience can be realized, even in the paradoxical form of the hermit life, the Christian can never espouse in strict literalness the neo-Platonic ideal of being "alone with the Alone." The God of Christian revelation is not the Alone but Emmanuel, God-with-us. And Jesus formed around himself a community of disciples whom he wanted to be one with each other as he and the Father are one so that finally we might all be one in God (cf. Jn 17:20–23). Community, in some sense of the word, is not an optional element of Christian religious life but its necessary context and its ultimate goal.

Third, the Incarnation or self-manifestation of God in the historical person of Jesus marks Christian religious experience as historical, that is, *sacramental or symbolic*. The Christian way to God is not by transcendence into non-materiality but by transforming immersion in history. That which enables this immersion to be truly transforming, both of the believer and of history, is the sacramental life in which the material mediates the spiritual and is transformed by it. Christian religious experience, in other words, is necessarily sacramental and liturgical. Christians are the priestly people whose liturgical activity must sanctify all creation until that day on which Christ hands it over to God who will be all in all (cf. 1 Cor 15:25–28).

Finally, because God's self-manifestation in Jesus was finalized by God's salvific intention into which we are initiated by the gift of the Spirit, Christian religious experience is necessarily *apostolic*. Our task as Christians is not simply to find God for ourselves. It is to further the divine intention of universal salvation. Again, there are numerous ways to participate in the salvific mission of Jesus ranging from the most interior involvement through contemplative prayer to the most active involvement in ministry. But the fact remains that a nonapostolic Christian religious life is a contradiction in terms. Mission belongs to the very meaning of Christian religious life, not because it is religious but because it is Christian.

Now, it is evident that these specifically Christian characteristics of religious life are just as essential to the life of any Christian as they are to that of the religious. Because religious recognize their life as "special," as somehow different, they can be tempted to attach relatively little importance to that which they have in common with other Christians and to attach excessive importance to those practices which are elements of their particular lifestyle. Since Vatican II religious women have become very conscious of the degree to which this tendency has marked their experience. Community devotional prayers, for

example, often took precedence over liturgy; community horarium was more important than ministerial responsibility; charity was sacrificed to practices of silence or enclosure; solitude
and formalized togetherness were more important than friendship and genuine community; sacramental freedom was curtailed by rules and customs; and Christian freedom in prayer
and life was immolated to a rigid authoritarianism in a mistaken
understanding of religious obedience. Without anyone intend-
ing such deformations, being different often came to be more
important than being Christian. In fact, it became so important
that when the differences were minimized by a re-emphasis on
the Christian character of religious life many religious came to
wonder whether there was any point to being a religious if one
"lived like everyone else."

The point of this essay has been to suggest that what makes
religious "different" is *neither* the specifically Christian character
nor the peculiarities of lifestyle that congregations develop but
a need to respond to a particular gift, a special vocation, that
consists in an absorption, for the sake of the whole community
of believers, in the religious dimension of life. That absorption
finds its expression in the lifestyle it generates. But it finds its
meaning in its absorbing search for the Transcendent which, for
the Christian, means the search for union with God in Christ
through the gift of the Spirit. If the expression takes precedence
over the meaning, the result can only be the death of the spirit
at the hands of the letter. But if the meaning retains its priority
it can enliven a lifestyle that will be a gift to the whole Church.
Charity, faith, hope, prayer, liturgy, ministry, and community
are the heart of the Christian experience for all Christians. Thus
what religious and other Christians have in common is far more
real, profound, and important than any differences among
them. Later in this volume, in speaking about profession, the
vows, religious community, and the like we will attend to the differences, the unique expression by which religious respond to
their particular vocation in the Church. For now we want to emphasize the meaning of "religious life" as such and the specifically Christian characteristics of Christian religious life.

Chapter Three
TOWARD A CONTEMPORARY
THEOLOGY OF RELIGIOUS PROFESSION

> This chapter draws heavily upon the research which I did for my unpublished S.T.L. thesis (Institut Catholique, Paris) entitled *The Theological Significance of Virginity According to the Fathers of the First Three Centuries*. The material has since been developed for lectures, conferences, workshops, and courses on religious life.

I. INTRODUCTION: THE RELATIONSHIP OF PROFESSION AND THE VOWS

In recent years religious, and especially candidates for religious life have raised serious questions about the meaning of profession. These doubts have centered upon the permanence of the commitment and upon its content, the three traditional vows of poverty, chastity, and obedience. The former question will be taken up in chapter ten; our concern in this chapter is with the latter.

Among the difficulties that have arisen concerning profession of the three vows, two recur regularly. First, is not religious commitment fragmented, legalized, and narrowed by the triple engagement? Second, do these three vows really express what religious actually live or even what they aspire to live? In other words, the equation of religious profession with the three traditional vows raises questions about the unity and the authenticity of religious commitment.

Many religious are genuinely disturbed when these questions are raised because they feel that such questions threaten the very essence of religious life. Permanent commitment through the three traditional vows has had such an unquestioned role in constituting the religious life that it seems hardly conceivable that the life itself could survive substantive change in this matter. What I will try to demonstrate in this essay is that

45

this conviction about the absolutely unchangeable character of the form of religious commitment is based upon three unexamined and, in fact, false premises: first, that religious profession is strictly synonymous with the making of vows; second, that the traditional three vows have always been the content of religious profession; and third, that they have always had basically the same meaning that they do today. In fact, religious profession is a constant element of religious life but it has not always been expressed by the making of vows. Even after vows became the normal form of religious profession,[1] the same vows were not made by all religious. And even when most religious made the same vows of poverty, chastity, and obedience, the meaning of the vows was not always the same. Furthermore, as we will see, the three vows themselves are not on an equal footing. They are not equally ancient; they do not have equal bases in the New Testament; and they are not equal in theological significance as constituents of religious life.

The equation of religious profession with the making of the three traditional vows is enshrined in canon law and in the documents of Vatican II.[2] The practice of making permanent profession of the three vows has become virtually universal.[3] Since the development of monastic life in the fifth century profession of the three vows (along with other vows in some cases) has initiated religious life, and it has been considered theologically essential at least since the Middle Ages when this position was explicated by Thomas Aquinas in his treatment of religious life in the *Summa Theologiae*.[4] Nevertheless, the experience of religious in our own times has raised questions about this equation of religious profession with the three vows, and the historical facts permit us to re-examine the issue. What historical investigation shows us is that religious profession is truly distinct from its expression in the three vows and that profession enjoys an historical and theological priority over the vows. History also gives us confidence in our re-examination, in the light of our own experience, of the whole question of religious commitment because both the form and the content of religious profession have evolved over the centuries without its losing its essential meaning. If we can discern the inner meaning of religious profession we can both understand its evolution toward the making of the three vows and raise meaningful questions about the appropriateness for ourselves of continuing this form of profession.

II. THE MEANING OF PROFESSION

Profession in some sense of the word has always been a part of religious life, but it has not always been expressed by the making of vows. The profession of faith by which one enters the Christian community, and the profession of mutual self-gift by which two people enter into the state of matrimony, are good analogies for the understanding of the act of profession by which one enters religious life. In all three cases the fundamental meaning of the profession is the formal, solemn, and public declaration of one's profound faith convictions and of one's desire and intention to embody those convictions in one's entire life. The making of promises which give a certain concreteness to the commitment is a natural development. The new Christian promises to renounce sin and live the sacramental and moral life of a disciple; the married couple promise to cherish each other in faithfulness and to support each other in good times and bad; the religious promises to fulfill the obligations of the religious state as these are detailed by the constitutions of the congregation to which she or he now belongs. But the important point is that the profession itself does not consist in the making of promises but in the declaration of one's desire and intention to undertake the new form of life.

III. THE HISTORY OF RELIGIOUS PROFESSION

Before attempting to discern the formal structure and essential content of religious profession it will be useful to undertake a brief historical survey to see how the act of profession, which I will later define as the formal, solemn, and public undertaking of religious life, evolved from the first century to our own times and how it gradually became equated with the making of three distinct vows. Most historians of religious life begin their accounts of the movement with the fourth century desert hermits. In fact, the first religious were the virgins and the widows of the first centuries of the Christian era.[5]

The virgins were Christian women and men who, in the totality of their response to the Gospel, dedicated themselves to the exclusive love of Christ in a life of prayer, meditation on the Scriptures, and good works. Virginity, for them, was neither a negative condition nor an ascetical practice. It was a state of life, analogous to the state of marriage. The virgin understood herself (although there were male virgins, the vast majority of those who embraced this life were women) to be the spouse of Christ, an existential situation which precluded marriage to anyone else. The virgins entered upon this state of life by professing their intention to the bishop who extended to them his special protection. Their situation in the local Church was a public one in the sense that they were recognized as virgins consecrated to Christ who were not to be disturbed in their resolution.

The virgins of the early Church did not make a vow of celibacy in the modern sense of the word. They professed their intention to live the virginal life which meant not only abstention from marriage and all that it permitted and implied but also total, exclusive, and lifelong dedication to Christ and his Church as a wife devotes herself to the love and care of her husband and family. In other words, the virginal commitment was not the disposition of a single aspect of the self (i.e., one's sexuality) but of one's whole life. Although the writers of the early Church insist on the importance of the virgin's physical integrity, this is primarily because this integrity of body is the outward sign in the Church of the integrity of the virgin's faith and love. Celibacy and the chastity appropriate to this state were to the virgin what abstention from adultery was for the married woman.

The widows in the early Church were women who, after the death of their spouse, renounced the possibility of a second marriage and sublimated their circumstantial solitude in a life of service to the Church by prayer and care for the needy members of the community. These women were a recognized "ordo" in the early Church, a group of official ministers with special tasks and status. We do not know if they were ordained but they were publicly and officially enrolled in the order of widows after a suitable period of testing.

Unlike the virgins for whom virginity in the global sense described above was the very substance of their lives, the widows did not seem to center their devotion to Christ so much in the exclusivity of their relationship with him as in their service to him in his members. Their decision not to remarry was partly motivated by the generally negative view of second marriages in the early Church but, since such marriages were not forbidden, the choice of celibacy was deliberate and free. We do not know whether the widows made a specific vow of perpetual celibacy, but it is certain that the obligation of celibacy was considered essential to the life of the consecrated widow. For the widows celibacy was one element in a state of life that seemed to be defined by its ministerial finality whereas virginity was a state of life in itself.

The almost simultaneous emergence in the earliest Church of these two rather different forms of what we today would call religious life is quite instructive on two points. First, both had in common the character of being "states of life" which were entered publicly, formally, and definitively after suitable reflection and testing of intentions. It is the declaration of a binding intention to live the life undertaken and the acceptance and recognition of this intention by the Church which is the earliest form of religious profession.

Secondly, although both involved a commitment to remain unmarried, the commitments were understood quite differently. In the case of the virgins, celibacy and its appropriate form of chastity were an integral expression of the global self-donation that was understood as marriage to Christ. In the case of the widows, celibacy and celibate chastity were an obligation, related specifically to the area of sexuality, and undertaken as one part of a larger commitment that involved other areas of life as well. In other words, for the widows the commitment to celibacy was much like the vow made by later religious which denotes one obligation among others. Down through the ages these two approaches to non-marriage for the sake of the Gospel will continue to exist in the experience of religious, but the distinction was progressively obscured with unfortunate effects for the self-understanding of many religious.

What we see in the comparison of these two earliest forms

of religious life, both of which involved celibacy, is that by
profession one enters the religious state, but that profession
need not express itself in separate vows bearing upon specific
areas of human experience. In other words, while profession is
essential for the constitution of a state of life in the Church, its
form can vary according to the way in which the life state is
understood.

In the fourth century a new form of religious life emerged
in the Church. Men and women, who felt that it was virtually
impossible to live the Gospel in all its fullness in the midst of the
Hellenistic culture in which the Church now participated fully,
fled to the desert where they could live their discipleship with
single-minded intensity. Thus was born the Christian eremetical
movement. In leaving the city to seek God in pure contemplation they sought to strip themselves of everything that could en-
tice the heart, engage the passions, or distract the mind.
Consequently, they abandoned human companionship, sought
to silence their sexuality, and renounced any material goods
which were not strictly necessary for physical survival. Their
motivation and goal were profoundly Christian but it cannot be
denied that these desert hermits were heavily, and perhaps ex-
cessively, influenced by both stoicism and neo-Platonism in their
choice of means. In its most extreme form this kind of religious
life did not last very long. The hermits eventually gathered together in communities and lavrae which eventually gave rise to
classical monasticism.

The form of profession among the hermits was, in many
cases, non-verbal. The person who decided to undertake this
life simply disposed of his or her possessions, broke family and
social ties, traveled to the desert, donned the rude habit of the
hermit, and commenced to live the life. The intention of such
people was recognized by the Church in the sense that their solitude was respected and that they were relied upon for prayer
and sometimes for spiritual guidance. Sometimes, especially as
the life developed and certain hermits were recognized for their
spiritual maturity and wisdom, an aspirant to the life would
come to the desert and apprentice himself or herself to an experienced hermit from whom he or she would learn, as much
by example as by word, how to live this single-hearted search for

God. This "novitiate" ended either with the death of the mentor or with the latter's recognition that the novice was now capable of living the life without further assistance. As far as we know, no particular promises or vows were made by the hermits as part of their entrance into the life itself although some seem to have made particular temporary or permanent commitments to some special ascetical practice such as fasting for a particular period of time, eating only so much bread per day, or working so many hours before resting or eating. If a hermit decided to abandon his or her profession and return to "the world," the departure was signalized by the putting off of the habit and the return to the city. Here again we can see the real distinction between profession by which a person entered the state of life and the making of vows that bear upon particular aspects of that life. To "go to the desert" was to embrace a life of solitude, ascetical self-stripping, and continuous prayer which implied fasting, celibacy, poverty, silence, and work. It was not necessary for the hermit to make separate vows concerning any of these things, for they were all understood to belong to the life itself. If a desert-dweller made a particular vow it was usually to do something quantitatively beyond or qualitatively different from what was expected of all hermits, or to strengthen his or her resolve in some area of special difficulty.

In the fifth century, under the inspiration of St. Benedict in the west and St. Basil in the east, classical cenobitical monasticism developed. This new form of religious life rapidly became the dominant form, and it would remain such for the next seven hundred years. Unlike the previous forms of religious life, monasticism was essentially a communitarian venture. In order to seek God with one's whole heart one entered the monastic family where, under the guidance of the abbot or abbess, one would participate in a common life of prayer and work. It is in this form of religious life that profession came to include the making of explicit vows. The man or woman who had worn the habit and shared the life of the monastery during a period of testing and formation would make monastic profession formally by asking for admission to the monastic family and then promising to remain attached to the monastery, to live in celibacy, poverty, and obedience to the rule and superior, and to labor unceasingly at his or her own conversion. It was this act of profession and its acceptance by the community representative which definitively incorporated the new member into the monastic family.

Monastic profession, even though it involved the making of particular vows, was nevertheless still a more wholistic experience than religious profession of vows came to be in the post-Tridentine period. It was understood explicitly as an analogue and development of baptismal commitment. Like the latter it was the formal beginning of a new life, which, although it entailed the acceptance of new obligations, was nevertheless not to be equated with or reduced to such obligations.

Furthermore, although the vows bore upon certain specific aspects of the monastic's life these aspects were understood as dimensions of a single reality, namely monastic life itself. The monk or nun undertook celibacy less as an ascetical practice for the control or sublimation of sexuality than as the appropriate lifestyle for community living; poverty was not the extreme self-stripping of the hermit but the involvement of the new member in the care, sharing, and use of the monastery's material goods for the sake of the monastic family; even obedience was more an initiation into the system of relationships and the patterns of behavior of the monastic family than an exercise of personal discipline or ascetical submission of will. The characteristic monastic vows, which later forms of religious life did not adopt, were those of stability, i.e., of fidelity to the monastery of one's profession; and conversion of manners, i.e., the ongoing effort to become ever more what one had chosen to be through the unceasing use of the instruments of good works provided by the Rule. Although all of these obligations had their ascetical purposes and efficacy they were not meant primarily as separate practices, but together they described the monastic life in its dynamic functioning.

In summary then, monastic profession, modeled on baptismal consecration, took the form of a statement of desire, a petition for admission, and a series of promises by which the candidate symbolically accepted the responsibilities of his or her new life, followed by the acceptance of the new member by the community. The promises, or vows, were integral to this formal, solemn, and public act of entering the state of life but were still only one aspect of that act, and, in the final analysis, probably not the most important.

In the Middle Ages, especially under the inspiration of Dominic Guzman and Francis and Clare of Assisi, the mendicant form of religious life developed. In this new form of religious life a further step was taken toward the eventual equation of profession with the making of vows. Although the mendicants retained most aspects of the monastic life they introduced a significant alteration by shifting the primary emphasis from community life to the preaching of the Word. By entering the brotherhood (the sisters in this movement were still cloistered and participated in its active dimension through prayer) one did not so much enter a stable monastic family but rather associated oneself with an itinerant band whose primary purpose was to bring the good news to the poor by word and example. This meant that each friar, rather than being borne by the collective life, had to become a kind of incarnation of that life. Thus, more emphasis fell upon the obligations assumed by profession, obligations which one might well have to carry out in the solitude of long journeys far from the strengthening company of one's brothers and the steady rhythm of prayer and work within the monastic enclosure.

A second factor in the increasing emphasis on the vows was the mysticism of poverty developed in the Franciscan movement. For Francis, poverty played somewhat the same role that virginity did for the earliest religious. It was not so much an obligation among other obligations but rather the form of unitive love, the joyful celebration of the mutual self-gift of the religious and Christ. But unlike virginity which, in a society in which virtually everyone married, easily constituted an unambiguously distinctive state of life, religious poverty could never be absolute (everyone requires some material sustenance) but had to be quite radical if it was to differ significantly from the widespread poverty in medieval society. Consequently, despite Francis' own rhapsodic approach to the espousal of Lady Poverty, it rapidly became necessary to spell out the requirements of Franciscan poverty, both for individuals and communities, in considerable detail and to protect them by rules and regulations. The vow of poverty in the mendicant form of life, although the repository of a truly mystical intuition, paradoxically contributed significantly to the understanding of the vows more in terms of obligations undertaken than as symbolic expressions of the life as a whole.

The theological contribution of Thomas Aquinas to this development of the understanding of religious vows as the assuming of distinct obligations should also be noted. In his section on religious life in the *Summa Theologiae* (II–II, 186), Aquinas, in his effort to explain the specificity and ultimately to establish the superiority of religious life in relationship to other forms of Christian life, focused on the individual vows rather than on profession as such. He explicitated the distinction between the "evangelical counsels" which were the objects of the vows and the "commandments" by which all Christians were obliged. The vow was defined as a solemn promise made to God to do something supererogatory and more pleasing to God than its opposite. Thus, the taking on of added obligations became the specificity of the religious state and the touchstone of its superiority to other states of life in the Church. It became ever more necessary to determine exactly the extent and gravity of these obligations and the penalties for their infractions. Each vow now had a specific content obliging under penalty of sin only when certain conditions obtained but challenging more universally by the virtue which it enshrined. This theology completed the development toward the equation of religious profession with the making of specific vows by which one took upon oneself obligations beyond those incumbent on ordinary Christians, thereby establishing oneself in a superior state of life.

In the sixteenth century, with the emergence of still another form of religious life, that of the regular clerics, e.g., the Jesuits, the development of this theology of the vows continued. This new form of religious life assigned an unqualified priority to mission and suppressed all aspects of monasticism, such as cloister and office in common, which impeded total apostolic mobility and involvement. It became even more necessary that each religious be formed as a veritable embodiment of the life, capable of living it fully even if he spent his whole religious life alone among infidels. The obligations and practices of the life were no longer integral elements of a common experience but an individual program for which each religious accepted individual responsibility on the day of profession. He had to know thoroughly, and be ready to carry out unto death, his obligations. Thus the rule had to be detailed, the obligations of each vow unambiguous, and the formation of the individual religious intensive.

Furthermore, the ascendancy of the apostolate naturally focused attention away from poverty, which had had priority among the Franciscans, and toward obedience, which Thomas Aquinas had already defined as the chief vow (*Summa Theologiae* II–II, 186, 8). The missionary, whether he was a teacher, a court advisor, or a country preacher, had to make use of whatever material resources he needed to further the work of the Gospel. Poverty, therefore, was no longer seen as an end in itself, a mode of union with the self-giving God, but primarily as a way of managing the resources necessary for the apostolate. Obedience, however, as the individual's involvement in the command structure which assured the efficiency of the group's missionary endeavor, was the most important virtue and obligation of the apostolic religious. To a large extent obedience lost the flexible form and familial character it had among the members of the monastic family and the democratic, collegial form it had among the mendicants and assumed a quasi-military character and the strictly hierarchical, even monarchical form that already characterized the organization of the Counter-Reformation Church itself. Obedience came to be seen as the central vow of religious life, the one which governed every act of every day and whose practice became the touchstone of religious perfection. The ultimate development of this primacy of obedience was achieved in Ignatius of Loyola's doctrine of "blind obedience," the willingness to call black white and white black if so commanded by superiors. The importance Ignatius attached to obedience, and its intimate connection with the apostolic finality of his order, were aptly institutionalized in the Jesuit "fourth vow," a special vow of obedience to the Pope in matters of mission which was made only by the society's most elite members.

It is interesting to note, however, that even among the Jesuits who placed such emphasis on the obligations assumed by the making of vows and felt a necessity to multiply vows and promises in order to explicitate the obligations assumed, profession retained in a way its more fundamental character as initiation into a life. Only those members who were admitted to "final profession," including the "fourth vow," were considered "first class" members of the society able to hold its highest offices and be entrusted with its most sensitive missions. Even though this initiation came to be seen less as an entrance into religious life itself than as an entrance into the specific order one can still discern traces of the ancient understanding of profession as primarily the undertaking of a life rather than primarily the assumption of specific obligations.

By the time of the Reformation the virtual equation not only of profession with the making of vows but also of the keeping of the individual vows with religious life itself had become so absolute, and the claim by religious to superiority because of their vows so commonplace, that Luther, correctly seeing that this understanding of religious life constituted a denigration of Christian life itself, made the repudiation of religious vows part of his fundamental protest against the Church of Rome.[6] This led to a strong reaffirmation by the Council of Trent not only of the legitimacy and praiseworthiness of the vowed life but of its intrinsic superiority to other forms of Christian life, specifically marriage.[7]

When, in the period after the French and American revolutions, still another form of religious life developed, namely, the congregations of simple vows devoted to alleviatory works of charity and to the Christian education of youth, there was no question in anyone's mind that the religious life was constituted by the vows of poverty, chastity, and obedience. Profession consisted in making these vows and religious life consisted essentially in living out the obligations incurred by them.

What we have traced in this brief historical overview is the gradual transformation, under a variety of historical influences, of the understanding of religious profession, from the *undertaking of a state of life* which, entailing certain obligations, was in no sense constituted by or reducible to them, to an understanding of profession as the *undertaking of these specific obligations* and the state of life as constituted by them. This might, at first sight, appear too subtle a distinction to merit much attention but it actually lies at the heart of the identity crisis through which both individual religious and congregations have been struggling since Vatican II. It is certainly true that most religious viewed their lives as more than a collection of obligations. But while their motivation for living this life was the love of Christ and his Church and their goal was eternal union with him, that which essentially constituted this life and distinguished it from "lower" forms of Christian commitment was undoubtedly the array of special obligations the religious assumed, especially those arising from the vows and lived according to the rule. The excessive rigidity of convent life, within which not only psychological health but charity and apostolic effectiveness were often sacrificed on the altar of legalism, bore eloquent testimony to the centrality that obligations had assumed in the understanding and living of religious life. It is, then, not surprising that both religious and lay people have found it increasingly difficult to comprehend the specificity of religious life now that it is no longer structured by a vast complex of regulations and prohibitions. The emphasis in religious life has shifted away from legal obligations, but it has not yet clearly focused elsewhere. It is this focus we are seeking.

IV. THE FORMAL STRUCTURE OF RELIGIOUS PROFESSION

Let us return now to the definition of profession with which we started. Profession is not synonymous with the making of vows even though they may be an appropriate expression of it. Profession is the formal, solemn, and public undertaking of a state of life. It rests upon the fundamental profession of baptism, specifying that original commitment and giving it a characteristic "shape." We might say that baptism establishes one in a state of being a child of God and member of the Church, and that religious or marital profession involves us in a state of life within which and according to which we live out our divine filiation and ecclesial identity. For the moment we will suspend the question of how the shape religious profession gives to our baptismal commitment differs from the shape marital profession gives to it in order to concentrate on the formal structure of profession itself, whether religious or marital.

First, profession is *formal.* It occurs at a particular time, in a particular place, by means of explicit expressions. Prior to the act of profession one is not formally a religious (even though one might have been living the substance of the life for some time) and after the act of profession one is a religious. This is not a matter of legalism but a recognition of the essentially linguistic character of human experience as such. As human beings we shape our lives by our own wills through the expression of our desires and intentions in acts and words. Of the two, strangely enough, the words are perhaps the more important because it is by what we say that we assign significance to our actions. The pouring of water becomes baptism, the sharing of bread and wine becomes Eucharist, because of the intention we express when we do these acts. Words, of course, are not always oral. The sign language of the mute, the written discourse of the absent lover, and even our silences can express our intentions and desires. But the point is that we shape ourselves and our world by our intentions and desires which we bring into reality by expressing them, in one way or another, so that they can be understood and accepted by others.

Religious and marital profession belong to the category of what linguistic specialists call "performative language," i.e., language which does what it says. To promise, to threaten, to swear an oath are acts by which we *do* something. To make religious profession, or to exchange the marriage commitment, is not just a saying of words but a *doing*, a creation of a new reality. A person who was not a religious becomes one; two people become one family. It is precisely because language has this creative and determinative role in human experience that we formalize our most serious and transformative intentions by verbal declarations whose form is determined, and which are said aloud, officially witnessed, and records of which are signed and preserved. Religious profession is the formal, that is, linguistically explicit, undertaking of religious life.

Second, profession is a *solemn* act. This trait has less to do with the elaborateness of the proceedings than with the gravity of the approach to the act and the ritual character of its accomplishment. Again, we are not primarily concerned with externals but with the reality of what is being done. To give definitive shape to one's fundamental life commitment as a Christian is no light matter. Consequently, we do not approach this decision except after prolonged, serious reflection and adequate testing of its maturity. And it is more than fitting that we ritualize such a weighty act by celebrating it in community. The unwillingness of many people in contemporary society to solemnize the great acts of their lives is a witness, not to a charming simplicity and lack of affectation, but to our increasing inability to take anything seriously in a world of too rapid change and too much instability. Young people are exposed to such irresponsible fickleness in life commitments and such casual acceptance by society at large of this incapacity for fidelity that they can hardly be blamed for not wanting to solemnize in their own lives what may well turn out to be but another brief and shallow episode. Nevertheless, for the Christian, both marriage and religious profession are solemn acts because unless they are meant to be the final and permanent disposition of a life they lack religious substance and meaning.

Third, profession is a *public* act. The term public does not have to do with where the ceremony takes place or how many people attend. It has to do with the assumption of the social consequences of one's acts. By making public profession the religious assumes the responsibility to live religious life in the Church and to be held accountable for how he or she carries out that responsibility. Anyone who wishes to may privately commit himself or herself to remain celibate, to practice some form of poverty, or to obey a freely chosen rule or spiritual mentor. But such people are not religious. A person may freely associate himself or herself with a religious community and live its life in whole or in part, but such a person is not a religious. Neither has publicly entered a state of life in the Church; neither has assumed the social consequences of professing one's intentions in such a way that the rest of the Church has the right to hold one accountable for the fulfillment of those intentions.

The analogy with marriage is quite exact. One who is going steady with a partner, or who is engaged to a partner, or who is even living with a partner, is not in the same situation as one who is married. The unmarried, however deep and intense the relationship, can end the relationship without the permission or offices of the larger society and there are no publicly enforceable financial or social consequences to the relationship. But once one is formally married the union is public. It has social consequences which cannot be avoided. The married person is responsible and accountable for the union he or she has freely established. The same is true for the religious. The person who has made a private commitment can change it without anyone's permission or help; the novice can leave the community at will. But the professed religious is accountable to the larger society of the Church for the state of life he or she has freely entered.

In summary, then, religious profession is not to be equated with the making of vows. Such vows may be the most adequate expression of the desire and intention to undertake religious life, and I will try, later, to make a case for the appropriateness of the three traditional vows. But other expressions are possible, and historically have existed. Again, the analogy with marriage is helpful. In our country people marry by exchanging vows. But in other cultures people marry by changing abode, by offering gifts, or by having sexual intercourse under certain prescribed conditions. The point is that to marry or to make religious profession is to enter definitively into a certain state of life which, while entailing many obligations, is not synonymous with or reducible to those obligations. The obligations flow from the understanding of the state of life. Thus, if marriage is understood primarily as an arrangement for the propagation of the family or clan, polygamy may be seen as an obligation, whereas if marriage is understood primarily as a total, exclusive, mutual self-gift of husband and wife, monogamy becomes obligatory. As we have seen, the understanding of religious life has changed often and quite radically in the two thousand years of its history. When it was understood primarily as virginity or marriage to Christ, community, habit, and common abode were not seen as obligatory, whereas in monasticism these elements were obligatory.

V. THE MATERIAL CONTENT OF RELIGIOUS PROFESSION

We have so far said that by religious profession one formally, solemnly, and publicly undertakes religious life but that, in the course of history, the movement that is religious life has crystallized in a wide variety of forms. This raises the question of whether there is anything in these various forms that has remained constant, anything that creates among them a family resemblance by which we identify them all as religious life. Is there a material content to religious profession as such?

It seems to me that there is such a constant element, namely the commitment to celibacy. But as we have seen, there are two basic understandings of this commitment which are quite different. In what might be called the "nuptial" understanding celibacy coincides existentially with the life itself. Because the person's experience of her or his relationship with Christ is marital in character, the person experiences marriage to another as existentially impossible for him or her. In what might be called the "ascetical" understanding, celibacy is a means to the realization of a or the purpose of religious life, whether this be contemplation, community life, apostolic activity, or eschatological or prophetic witness.

However, this difference in motivation and in the actual experience of celibacy does not preclude what I might call the "state of life" effect of celibacy freely chosen for the sake of the Gospel which both kinds of celibacy bring about. John Lozano in his recent book, *Discipleship*,[8] claims that what distinguishes religious life from other forms of Christian life is the fact that religious life raises to explicit articulation in *lifestyle* that which is common to all Christians, namely, the vocation to follow Jesus by leaving behind all that impedes our discipleship so that we can freely participate in his filial identity and his salvific mission. Although every Christian must be fully disposed to leave all things, and must actually put aside anything which hampers his or her following of Christ, the religious creates a lifestyle of renunciation not only of that which actually impedes his or her following of Christ but of "everything" so that the intention and reality of discipleship may be explicit in the Church and in the world on, as it were, a full-time basis. This renunciation is not necessarily more real or complete than that of any other Christian but it is more explicit and visible, just as the fruitfulness of the union between Christ and the Church is not necessarily more real in Christian marriage than it is in the life of the celibate, but it is more visible and explicit.

It is particularly in the choice of celibacy as a lifestyle that the total renunciation to which Christians are called comes to explicit articulation. Neither poverty nor obedience has or can have the same quality of witness that celibacy does. First of all, both poverty and obedience in some form are incumbent on all Christians. We are all called, as followers of Christ, to steward the goods of this earth so that all people can live decently and realize their earthly and eternal destiny. There are numerous ways in which this can be done, and even among religious these ways vary from the absolute destitution chosen by the desert hermits through the relative affluence of the medieval monastery to the conditional independence in financial affairs of the members of contemporary apostolic institutes. No Christian can amass and hoard wealth while his or her fellows suffer want.

Secondly, poverty, no matter how one builds it into one's lifestyle, can never have the unambiguous quality of absolute realization. Everyone, no matter how devoted to poverty, must make use of material goods in one way or another. Poverty is always relative in practice, no matter how absolute in principle.

Likewise, obedience as the continuous seeking and faithful execution of the will of God in one's life is incumbent on all Christians. From the child yielding to parental authority, through the mutual obedience of husband and wife, to the submission of each of us to the dispositions of providence and the adversity of fortune in our lives, every Christian obeys God in and through the circumstances of his or her life. While religious have created for themselves certain particular structures for the mediation of God's will in their lives they are not actually more subject to the divine will than anyone else.[9] And again, the practice of obedience has varied widely among different forms of religious life.

Secondly, like poverty, obedience can never be absolute. Even the choice of particular structures for the mediation of

God's will is a personal choice. And the one obeying always retains the obligation to judge the conformity of any command with what is already known of God's will. In other words, obedience is always relative in practice, no matter how absolute in principle.

Celibacy alone, among the characteristics of the religious lifestyle, is not incumbent upon Christians as such, is absolute and unambiguous in practice as well as in principle, and literally structures the life of the person by visible renunciation not of what is forbidden but of what is good, thereby articulating the disposition to lay aside everything, the good as well as the dangerous, for the sake of the following of Christ.

Celibacy is the only "evangelical counsel" in the traditional sense of a gift and call not addressed to all Christians. Poverty and obedience, in themselves, are not matters of choice, but celibacy is optional. Poverty and obedience are concerned with ways of handling goods which we cannot finally renounce but must use in some way, namely, material resources and personal freedom. But celibacy is a choice to renounce definitively the possibility of sexual fulfillment in the foundation of a family.

It is celibacy which creates the state of life within which certain forms of poverty and obedience are subsumed and take on their particular significance as part of religious life. Thus, it is by the analysis of the meaning of consecrated celibacy that we gain entrance into the fundamental meaning of the religious state of life within the Church.

Celibacy, no matter which of the two basic motivations energizes it, is the choice not to "build oneself into" the ongoing historical process of this world by the founding and/or continuance of a family. This choice only makes sense, religiously, in terms of identification with a transhistorical reality embraced in faith and unshakable hope, namely, the reality of the resurrection life that we call the reign of God.

In fact, we see that historically the religious state of life has always involved a double-sided commitment. "Negatively" religious commitment has involved the taking of a stance toward "the world" which, if not outrightly negative, is at least reserved. Religious have chosen not to involve themselves at the deepest level, that of producing the future of the race, in the ongoing

historical process of this world. Usually religious have created a
"setting" for this choice in the form of world-distancing or at
least world-challenging behavior. They have "left the world," by
fleeing to the desert or entering the monastery, or by wearing
distinctive garb, or by abandoning their family names, or by
adopting culturally unassimilable behavior, or in various other
ways elaborating upon the fundamental theme of celibacy, the
personal renunciation of total involvement in the destiny of this
world in its intra-mundane history.

"Positively" religious commitment has involved some kind
of active involvement in the transhistorical project of realizing
in this world the reign of God which, although occurring in history, is not produced by history. The virgins of the early Church
embodied the reign of God in their own unitive experience; the
desert hermits sought to bring about the reign of God through
unceasing contemplative prayer; the monastics created that
oneness in community which Jesus, in the Gospel, tells us is the
participation of humanity in the unity of God; the apostolic religious, realizing that much of humanity had not yet heard the
good news, sought to extend the reign of God by their preaching. Celibacy, as the renunciation of total involvement in the intra-mundane dynamics of history, only makes religious sense if
it is the other side of a total devotion to the coming of the transhistorical reality of the reign of God.

Religious profession, whether expressed in the making of
vows or not, is the formal and public undertaking of a state of
life in the Church whose most unambiguous and visible expression is celibacy for the sake of the reign of God. Throughout
history the celibate lifestyle has been elaborated by various types
of world-distancing practices, and the wholehearted devotion to
the realization of the reign of God has been pursued in different
ways depending on how the reign itself has been understood. In
chapter six we will deal, in greater detail, with how the "negative" and "positive" faces of religious commitment might be
understood today. Here we must attend briefly to the question
of the relationship of religious commitment to Christian marriage.

States of life in the Church differ, not hierarchically, but in
terms of which aspect of the Christian mystery the vocation

brings to explicit articulation and clear visibility in the community. This mystery, as well as the vocations which bring it to expression, is paradoxical. Salvation, brought about and revealed in Jesus of Nazareth, is both radically historical, taking place in this world and in the lives of real people, and transhistorical in the sense that it is not produced by this world or the dynamics of human history but given freely by God in God's own time and way. Christian salvation is already realized in the resurrection of Jesus of Nazareth and the present gift of his love in the Holy Spirit, but it is not yet realized and will not be until Jesus comes again in glory to take possession of his own and to turn over the reign to God who will be all in all (1 Cor 15:28).

The life of every disciple of Jesus is characterized by this "already but not yet" paradox. We live the mystery of a salvation that is historical and transhistorical, present already and not yet ours. Christian marriage brings to visibility in the community the radically historical character of Christian salvation. Especially in the generation and raising of children, Christian spouses express the Church's identification with this world and its history. And, as they struggle to express transcendent love in the limitations of the flesh and to raise children of God in the midst of the sinful structures of this world, they experience in manifold ways that the reign of God is not yet come. Religious, on the other hand, by renouncing the joy of building themselves radically into the historical process of this world, express the transhistorical character of Christian salvation, the fact that salvation is not the product of human history but a gift of God. In the experienced love of God, which gives the strength for and significance to this renunciation, they experience the already present reality of final salvation. But just as Christian spouses rely upon the transhistorical character of salvation in which their faith and hope are anchored, and experience through and in their love for one another the present grace of God, so religious remain involved in history and wait in expectation for the coming of the reign which is not yet manifest. In other words, all Christians who live their Christian vocation integrally participate in the entirety of the Christian mystery but, by the lifestyle they choose, they bring to visibility in the Church certain aspects of that mystery that are less visible in other lifestyles.

Here the comparison of Christian states of life with the relationship between masculinity and femininity can be instructive. The latter are two ways of being human. They each equally
and fully embody humanity, but they embody it differently.
Typically, each of the two ways of being human highlights certain aspects and potentialities of humanity without denying or
silencing the others. Similarly Christian marriage and religious
life are two equal and full embodiments of the Christian vocation to discipleship. But each of them highlights, brings to visibility and articulation in the Christian community, certain
aspects of the Christian vocation without negating the other aspects.

The comparison with masculinity and femininity is also
negatively instructive, for just as we have historically tended to
hierarchize the relation between the sexes, assigning superiority
to masculinity in the abstract and to individual males in the concrete, so we have tended to hierarchize the relationship between
states of life in the Church. We have historically assigned superiority in principle to the religious state and superiority in fact
to individual religious. Vatican II authorized a major advance
in the theology of states of life in the Church by neither repeating nor referring to the Council of Trent's definition of the superiority of consecrated celibacy to Christian marriage.[10] This
liberates us to appreciate the specificity of each of the two states
of life without regressing into useless and destructive compari-
sons that have fostered an empty vanity in religious and a vision-
limiting sense of inferiority in married people.

VI. PROFESSING THE THREE VOWS

Having established a distinction between profession as such
and vows, and having shown that the three traditional vows have
not always been part of the act of profession and, even when
they were part of the profession, have not always meant the
same thing, we must finally raise the question of whether or not
the profession of vows, and specifically of the traditional three
vows, is appropriate today. As was mentioned in the introduction to this chapter, serious objections to the current practice
have been raised by religious who have reflected deeply on their

commitment. The question is threefold: Are vows an appropriate form of profession today? Does not the profession of three
vows fragment religious commitment? Do the three traditional
vows really express the commitment that religious make today?

First, let us attend to the question of whether vows are an
appropriate form for religious profession today. It seems to me
that, at least in our western culture, the making of vows or solemn promises is the most natural and understandable form of
life commitment. Just as the state of matrimony is inaugurated
by the exchange of vows and public offices are undertaken by
oaths, religious life is entered by solemn verbal commitment.
The people of our culture understand this form of commitment. It might not be true that a profession of vows would be
appropriate in all cultures, but in ours it assimilates religious
profession to those other public acts which initiate public states
of life and roles in society.

A second question concerns the making of *three* vows. Many
religious have suggested that the making of three vows not only
seems to leave out of consideration much that is important in
religious life, e.g., mission and community, but also tends to
fragment what is ideally a unitary commitment. Certainly the
way the three vows have been considered, both in law and in
practice, in the past few hundred years would support such objections. However, it seems to me that it is possible to rethink the
meaning and significance of the threefold profession of vows in
a way that would obviate these objections.

In the first place, as we have tried to demonstrate in this
chapter, the three vows do not and never have exhausted the
meaning of profession. They are the form by which profession
is made, not its total content. By selecting three poles of religious
commitment we verbally, i.e., symbolically and effectively,
frame the life we are entering; we do not describe it in detail.
When married people promise to be faithful to each other "for
better or for worse, in wealth and in poverty, in sickness and in
health" they are not excluding such important issues as sexual
adjustment and mutual self-gift, the shared raising of children,
fidelity, the acceptance of each other's families, and all the other
important components of married life. They are selecting three
typical and important axes of married life, and by affirming fi-

delity in terms of polar possibilities along each of these axes, they are verbally framing their life commitment. In other words, the "three vows" in the marriage formula are a symbolic expression of the total mutual dedication that entering into marriage involves. In the same manner, religious, in professing the three vows, do not describe exhaustively their life nor do they limit their commitment to the areas designated by these vows. They undertake a life, of which poverty, celibacy, and obedience are a fairly adequate symbolic expression.

But the question might still be raised: Why three? Why not one, such as a vow of membership in the congregation according to the constitutions, or a vow of total consecration to God, or a vow of evangelical life? I think the answer to this question is again best seen in the analogy with marriage vows. Why should the married couple specify health and wealth? Does not the "to have and to hold as my spouse" express the totality of the commitment more globally and less restrictively? What is logically most correct may not be what is psychologically most effective. By specifying two areas in which the ups and downs of marital commitment are likely to be experienced (even though these are by no means the only two such areas and in some real marriages not the most important) the couple bring home to themselves and to the witnesses that this commitment is not a vague ideal but a considered choice of real attitudes and behaviors in concrete circumstances which cannot be foreseen but which have already been anticipated and accepted in advance. What really expresses the totality of the commitment is the "to have and to hold . . . until death do us part," just as what really expresses religious commitment is the "I vow to God . . . for the rest of my life." Poverty, celibacy, and obedience are not the only areas of life that are affected by profession. Sometimes they might not be the most important. But the specificity of the vows expresses to both the religious and the witnesses the concrete reality of this commitment to live daily life in the real world and Church in a certain way.

Finally, there is the question of whether the three *traditional vows* are the ones we should make today. The answer to this question is much more complicated and will be the burden of chapter six. I am of the opinion that the three vows, which have meant various things in various eras and in different forms of religious life, are undergoing a change of meaning today. The change is an expansion in depth and reach. As I will try to show in chapter six, the three traditional vows have a peculiar relevance to our present societal and ecclesial situation and, therefore, a particular capacity to symbolize the total consecration which religious life entails. The three vows, however, are not "equal." Just as "for better or worse" is more global than the references to health and wealth, so celibacy is the determining characteristic of religious life in a way that neither poverty nor obedience can be. Celibacy distinguishes religious life from other forms of Christian life just as taking another person for one's lawful wedded spouse for better or worse distinguishes marriage from other states of life. Nevertheless, the three vows provide three axes around which religious life turns and their profession is a symbolic embracing of that life in its totality.

In summary, the questions that have been raised about the appropriateness of vows, about their plurality, and about their objects are real questions which have been evoked by the narrowness and fragmentation that several centuries of legalism have encouraged. This does not, however, necessarily mean that they should be abandoned or replaced. It might mean, as I think it does, that profession itself and the vows in particular must be rethought for our time.

Chapter Four
COMMITMENT:
LIGHT FROM THE FOURTH GOSPEL

The material for this chapter was originally prepared for and presented to participants in the Los Angeles Religious Education Convention in February 1978. It was originally published in *Biblical Theology Bulletin* 8 (February 1978) 40–48.

Fidelity in commitment is a perennial human and religious concern both because the quality of life of the individual person is largely determined by the types of relationships he or she establishes and because the quality of any society, secular or ecclesial, is a function of the quality of the relationships which constitute it. Nevertheless, it must be recognized that this perennial concern has taken on an unprecedented importance in our own times. Vocational instability has reached epidemic proportions, and if this instability reflects a substantial decline in fidelity to interpersonal commitments, both in principle and in fact, then we are dealing with a significant change in human values, or at least in the motivational force of those values. It is not, however, perfectly clear that vocational instability is directly proportional to infidelity in interpersonal relations or to incapacity for commitment. That instability is often the expression of infidelity cannot be denied. But neither can it be denied that many persons who have, with serious deliberation, responsibly decided to terminate an interpersonal commitment go on to make new, permanent commitments which endure, the quality of which belies any simplistic judgments about the validity of such a course of action.

The ambiguous and disturbing facts of the current situation invite the concerned Christian, as well as the ecclesial community, to reflect seriously and prayerfully on the religious and spiritual significance of commitment. Both Old and New Testaments reveal that loving fidelity is a defining characteristic of the God of the Judaeo-Christian tradition. For the Christian, then, it is the ideal in all interpersonal relationships. But the complexity of contemporary experience precludes any simplistic assumptions about the meaning and implications of this ideal.

The situation invites us to scrutinize the Word of God and to bring to bear upon our questions the light of divine revelation. In doing so, we cannot naively address these peculiarly contemporary questions to the Scriptures in hope of straightforward answers. Our biblical forebears did not have our questions, and consequently they did not answer them. The theological and pastoral impasses to which a non-critical proof text approach to the question of vocation and commitment has led in the past should warn us against biblical fundamentalism, anachronism, and accommodation in this matter. However, although the Word of God is not an answer book for contemporary questions, it is a source of light for all of the perennial religious concerns of humankind. The contemporary question of commitment has a particular form that the Bible does not address, but the concern itself is as ancient as the relationship between God and the human race.

The following pages will be devoted to a consideration of what the Gospel according to St. John can contribute to Christian reflection on the subject of commitment. The space of a chapter is too restricted for even a superficial presentation of what the entire Bible, or even the entire New Testament, offers on this subject. Limiting our reflections to a single Gospel will allow for greater depth. The choice of the fourth Gospel is motivated by several considerations. First, it is historically the latest Gospel to be written (probably between 90 and 110 A.D.) and therefore represents a longer period of Christian reflection on the implications of the Christ-event. Second, John's Gospel is correctly regarded as "the most mature fruit of Gospel composition, and the perfect embodiment of all that 'Gospel' implies by its very nature."[1] Third, because of the historical situation of the community for which this Gospel was composed it is particularly concerned with the question of Christian commitment. In the light of the fourth Gospel's radical reflection on commit-

ment some of our contemporary questions on this subject might
be at least more accurately formulated and therefore stand a
better chance of being more adequately addressed.

I. HISTORICAL SITUATION OF THE FOURTH GOSPEL

The Gospel of John probably received its final form in Asia
Minor and was addressed to a community composed primarily,
though not exclusively, of Jews. It was written at precisely the
time when the growing opposition between orthodox Judaism
and Christianity reached a bitter climax in the excommunica-
tion of Jewish Christians from the synagogue by the assembly of
Jamnia under Gamaliel II (c. 90 A.D.). The importance of this
historical situation for the Johannine community, and thus for
the theology and spirituality of the fourth Gospel, can hardly be
exaggerated.[2] These Christians, living at the end of the first century, faced an agonizing choice between abandoning Judaism,
the religious community of the chosen people, and abandoning
their new faith in Jesus of Nazareth as the Christ (or Messiah)
and the Son of God (cf. Jn 20:31). They faced the conflict of
commitments in its starkest form.

It is difficult for a Christian who has never been a Jew to
realize the magnitude of this choice. The Jewish Christian belonged to Israel, the chosen people whom God had rescued
from slavery in Egypt, to whom God had revealed the divine self
on Sinai and given the Torah, whose prophets had spoken in
God's name, whom God had recalled from exile and had promised a savior, in whose midst God dwelt and to whose cries God
was not deaf. To voluntarily cut oneself off from the community
of Israel, from synagogue worship and observance of the Law,
from rabbinic judgment and table fellowship with God's people
was a radical severance from one's past, one's corporate identity,
one's whole historical understanding of the truth of revelation
and its divine institution in Israel. Many passages in the Gospel
of John are concerned with this painful experience and are calculated to strengthen the Christians in their choice by assuring
them that the true Israelite was not necessarily a Jew nor the Jew
necessarily a true Israelite (e.g. Jn 8:33–40).

Because the problem of Christian commitment was so urgent for the Johannine community the Gospel's reflections on the question are explicit and radical. They are especially pertinent to the contemporary situation because the conversion with which the fourth Gospel is concerned is not a conversion from evil to good or from idolatry to belief, but precisely a conversion from a legitimate but no longer viable religious commitment within Judaism to a commitment to Jesus as Messiah and Son of God which was now seen to be the will of God. The members of the Johannine community were called, by a combination of historical events beyond their control, to transcend the commitment to which they had once been called by God. The conflict involved in this new call was not unlike the conflicts experienced by many sincere Christians in our own times. If anything, it was more radical.

II. THE IMPEDIMENT TO COMMITMENT

There is no evidence in the Gospels that the historical Jesus intended to abolish Judaism, much less to found a new religion.[3] On the contrary, Jesus came precisely to call to salvation the lost sheep of the house of Israel (Mt 15:24). The conflict between Jesus and his enemies (the chief priests, scribes, and Pharisees in the Synoptics, usually simply "the Jews" in the fourth Gospel but referring to the Jewish leadership) arises not because Jesus' message was discontinuous with the revelation of the Old Testament but because the Judaism of the hierarchy, theologians, and other officials had become an impediment to the relationship between God and God's people which they existed to foster.

In the fourth Gospel "the Jews" and "the world," when the terms are used pejoratively, are nearly synonymous. They designate those who refused to receive the Word when he came into the world (Jn 1:10–11). John begins by analyzing the refusal of the truth among the Jews who, in the experience of the historical Johannine community, were the collective embodiment of this refusal. Nevertheless, although John's particular interest in the Jews is a function of his historical situation, his reflection remains universally relevant because the phenomenon of refusal is not limited to any time, place, or people. It is through his meditation on the unbelief of the Jews that he comes to understand the real nature of belief and, therefore, of commitment, whether of Jew or Gentile.

The "Jews" in the fourth Gospel who become the enemies of Jesus are the Jerusalem officials. It should be noted that all those who are presented in the fourth Gospel as accepting Jesus, with the possible exception of the ruler in John 4:46–54, are also Jews or, in the case of the Samaritans, originally Israelites. Consequently, it is not Jewishness in either its ethnic or its religious sense that is the source of conflict. It is, quite simply, a literalistic and idolatrous attachment to the Jewish religious institution which, paradoxically, rendered the officials of Judaism incapable of accepting divine revelation, impervious to the truth. The Jews had become committed to their commitment rather than to God! Jesus came as the one sent by God and they could not accept him. What is most striking about Jesus' conflict with the Jews is that at no point does Jesus call them to anything other than the covenant relationship with God which was the heart of Israel's faith. In each conflict Jesus points to the covenant truth at the heart of the institutional expression, and the Jews prefer to cling to the latter rather than to embrace the former.

A. Temple

In John 2 Jesus drives the merchants and money-changers out of the temple, not because he condemns the temple cult but because he truly understands and loves it. He recalls the Jews to the real meaning of the temple: it is the Father's house (Jn 2:16), the meeting place of God and God's people. The Jews refuse this simple and straightforward statement of the truth and focus, instead, on the right of Jesus to question the current institutional practice. Jesus' right is simply the right of truth to name flagrant infidelity and to demand righteousness. But, because the Jews refuse to confront the mystery of the temple in all its gracious exigency, they are incapable of understanding either the cleansing of the historical temple or the abundant accomplishment of the mystery of the temple in the body of the glorified Jesus (Jn 2:19–21).

B. Sabbath Conflict

The conflict over the sabbath, recounted in John 5:2–18, reveals the same pattern. Jesus cured a paralyzed man on the official Jewish day of rest, even though he could easily have done so on another day, for the man had been at the pool of Bethzatha for thirty-eight years (Jn 5:5). Unlike the Synoptic Jesus, who cures on the sabbath to show that religious observances were instituted for human beings and not vice versa (e.g. Mk 2:27), the Johannine Jesus cures on the sabbath in order to reveal the essential continuity between God's creative activity at the beginning of the world and God's salvific activity in Jesus. When the Jewish officials object to the cure on the sabbath Jesus replies, "My Father is working still, and I am working" (Jn 5:17). The Jews understood the revelation. They immediately tried to kill him because he was "making himself equal with God" (Jn 5:18). The real reason for the Jewish sabbath observance was the imitation of God who rested on the seventh day from the work of creation and who fulfilled that work by making Israel God's covenant people. By entering into the divine rhythm, so to speak, the Jews were to become and to remain sensitive to the revealing action of God which resided not only at the origin of the universe and at the creation of the covenant people but continuously in the life of Israel. But the Jewish officials, by their idolatrous attachment to the sabbath observance had become blind to the meaning of the sabbath and were therefore unable to receive the truth offered to them in the saving work of Jesus in their midst.

C. Officials' Reaction

The Jewish officials are shown repeatedly undermining the openness to Jesus of those who could not deny what they had seen and heard in him. The officers sent by the chief priests and Pharisees to arrest Jesus return saying, "No man ever spoke like this man!" They are rebuked for credulity, for lack of religious sophistication (Jn 7:45–49). If they knew the Law they would not so easily accept Jesus' credentials, namely, that he does the will of God and seeks only God's glory (Jn 7:16–18); they would not be so easily convicted by his challenge to honor the Mosaic Law by judging righteously (Jn 7:19–24); they would not be led astray into believing his promise of living water to those who believe (Jn 7:37–39). To Nicodemus, who pleads with the Jewish authorities to apply the Law justly by at least giving Jesus the benefit of a hearing, they declare that he is already discredited by the Law, for it gives no indication that a prophet will arise in Galilee (Jn 7:50–52). The Jews have decided which indications in the Scriptures are to be heeded and which are to be ignored.

After trying repeatedly to intimidate the man born blind into denying the plain fact that Jesus had cured him, they finally expel him from the synagogue because he, an unlettered and sinful man, had dared to teach them the Law (Jn 9:34). He had simply exclaimed in surprise at their refusal to see the work of God in the action of someone who opened the eyes of a man born blind (Jn 9:30).

When many of the Jews are drawn to believe in Jesus because of his raising of Lazarus from the dead, the chief priests and the Pharisees decide to kill not only Jesus (Jn 11:45–53) but also Lazarus (Jn 12:10–11) who was living evidence that Jesus did indeed do the works of his Father as he had claimed.

In the bitter confrontation with the Jews recounted in chapter 8 (a part of the extended controversy which extends from chapter 5 through chapter 10), Jesus challenged the Jews' claim to salvation on the basis of their descendance from Abraham. The Jews had replaced the interior reality of being a child of Abraham, namely being a believer and doing the works of faith, with the external reality of physical birth from Jewish parents. Likewise, in chapter 5:39–40, Jesus convicted the Jews of preferring the letter of the Scripture to the Word of God. If they had allowed the Word to enter their hearts they could not have failed to recognize the Word speaking to them in person.

What each of these episodes makes clear is the fourth evangelist's understanding of unbelief as the great impediment to salvation. Unbelief is a deep perversion of the spirit which makes a person incapable of accepting the truth because of an idolatrous commitment to something other than God. In the fourth Gospel this idolatrous commitment is called "seeking one's own glory" as opposed to seeking the glory of God. Jesus demands of the Jews, "How can you believe, who receive glory from one another and do not seek the glory that comes from the only God?" (Jn 5:44). In contrast, Jesus can say of himself, "I do not seek my own glory" (Jn 8:50). Rather, he seeks the glory of the one who sent him (Jn 7:18).

In the fourth Gospel "to seek" is a theologically freighted term. It is typical of John to denote fundamental attitudes and dispositions by verbs rather than by nouns. The verb "to seek" denotes the finality-governed dynamism of a person's life. The first disciples who follow Jesus are asked what they seek (Jn 1:38). That which one seeks is the motive force of one's actions, and this explains the radical incompatibility between seeking one's own glory and being open to God's revelation. Only the person who seeks in all things the glory of God can be open to the totally unexpected, even to that which calls into question one's understanding of the most sacred traditions and institutions and relativizes the laws which seem most absolute. Only a total and single-minded determination to seek God, regardless of where the divine beckon leads, can enable a person to move beyond the secure structures of religious institution and allow God to be God, totally unpredictable and unmanageable by human systems. Because the Jewish officials were fundamentally motivated by the desire to preserve their own power and position (cf Jn. 11:48) they had a stake in the status quo which made them incapable of seeing and acknowledging the truth in the signs and words of Jesus when these spoke of something new. They were "blind" in the deepest spiritual sense of that word (Jn 9:39–41).

III. THE MEANING OF COMMITMENT

The unbelief of the Jews is the foil against which the fourth evangelist elaborates the true meaning of Christian commitment, namely, to believe in Jesus. John never uses the noun "faith" but characteristically speaks in dynamic, verbal fashion. The verb "to believe" occurs ninety-eight times in the fourth Gospel in contrast to thirty-four times in the three Synoptics combined. The subtle uses of the various constructions in which the verb occurs constitute an original and radical theology of faith as the essence of Christian commitment.[4]

John uses the verb "to believe" in the absolute, i.e., without an object, twenty-five times. "To believe" denotes a fundamental disposition of openness to the truth which makes the person capable of seeing the glory of God whenever and wherever it is revealed. The man born blind, for example, did not know who Jesus was but he staunchly maintained that only perversity could refuse to acknowledge that God was at work in one who cured blindness (Jn 9:15–17, 30–33). He was still ignorant of the identity of Jesus when the latter found him after he had been excommunicated and asked him, "Do you believe in the Son of Man?" The cured man could only ask, "Who is he, sir, that I may believe in him?" This readiness of spirit is identical with his willingness to accept the cure and to attribute it to the action of God. Such a disposition makes possible the full self-revelation of Jesus, "You have seen him, and it is he who speaks to you." The man replied unhesitatingly, "Lord, I believe," and he worshiped him (Jn 9:35–38). It is precisely this unreserved readiness to accept the truth, this unqualified loyalty to reality, which Jesus tells Martha, prior to the raising of Lazarus, is the condition of receiving divine revelation: "Did I not tell you that if you would believe you would see the glory of God?" (Jn 11:40). It is the disposition of the woman of Samaria who was not deterred, even by Jesus' exposure of her immorality, from acknowledging him as a prophet (Jn 4:19) and seeking loyally to know what the true worship of God required of her. In response to her genuine desire for the Messiah, regardless of the changes his coming might entail for her and her people, Jesus answers, "I who speak to you am he" (Jn 4:26).

The examples could be multiplied, but the meaning of "to believe" in the absolute form is clear from these few. It is the fundamental openness of heart, the basic readiness to see and hear what is really there, the devotion to being which refuses to tamper with reality, no matter how frightening or costly it appears to be, in order to preserve the situation with which one is familiar. The basic disposition to accept the truth is what enables the person, regardless of moral weakness and lapse, regardless of ethnic or religious background, regardless of orthodoxy, regardless of religious education or lack thereof, to be interiorly "taught of God" (Jn 6:44–45). Such a person, no matter how far astray he or she might have wandered, remains tractable and can be drawn by the Father to Jesus (Jn 6:44).[5]

The person who has been taught of God is able to see in the words and works of Jesus the glory of the Word made flesh. It is this seeing which leads the person to "believe in" him. "To believe in" is a Johannine construction, foreign to classical Greek, which appears thirty-six times in the fourth Gospel. John seems to have coined the expression to denote the dynamic interpersonal relationship set up between Jesus and the person to whom he reveals himself. To believe in Jesus is to accept him, to identify with him, to follow him, to grow in discipleship. It is, in brief, to commit oneself to Jesus with that totality of self-giving that is suitable only in relationship to God and the one whom God has sent. By the fact and the quality of one's adherence to this person one is proclaiming that he is the Son of God. This is not a theological proposition, an assent of the mind; it is a life stance which could only be legitimate if Jesus is indeed who he claims to be, the one sent by the Father.

It is this personal and total commitment to Jesus as the personal and absolute revelation of God in this world which enables the believer to formulate faith propositions about him. Eleven times in the fourth Gospel the construction "to believe that" appears, followed by a theological proposition about Jesus. The disciples are the ones who believe that Jesus is the Holy One of God (Jn 6:69), "I am" (Jn 13:19), Christ the Son of God (Jn 11:27), the one sent by the Father (Jn 17:8), the one who is in the Father and in whom the Father dwells (Jn 14:10), the one who came forth from God (Jn 16:27; 16:30). All of these propositions are, from the standpoint of the believer, identical. Although there are various aspects under which it can be considered, the mystery which is central to and all-inclusive of Christian faith is that Jesus and the Father are one. It is this which justifies an unqualified commitment to him, a commitment which cannot validly be made to Law, temple, Scripture, sabbath, hierarchy, tradition, or even the covenant community itself.

The nuanced Johannine exploration of believing as the essence of religious commitment is meant for a Christian community but it is radical enough to be universally enlightening. What God asks of every human being, regardless of time, place, or circumstances, is a loyal openness to reality which is incompatible with "seeking one's own glory." To seek one's own glory is to assign oneself an absolute value in the order of being and action which is fundamentally false. To do this is to close oneself to the truth. The only way one can maintain such an existentially false stance is to invest with absoluteness those factors which support and sustain the illusion. One makes a total commitment to oneself, a commitment which cannot fail, eventually, to conflict with God's claim upon one's life. When God's claim is made it is seen as blasphemy because it is, in fact, a challenge to what the person considers to be the absolute. God's revelation is experienced as darkness and sin. This is the blasphemy against the Holy Spirit in Markan terms (Mk 3:29). In the fourth Gospel it appears as the total blindness of the one who claims to see (Jn 9:39–41) but who has made his or her own vision the measure of the visible.

In contrast, the person who refuses the diabolic temptation to absolutize the self remains inwardly open to reality. God educates the spirit of this person who does the truth. Such a person knows that he or she is not the measure of possibility, and it is this attitude which makes divine revelation possible. If and when Jesus stands before this person, doing the works of God, the person, like the first disciples at Cana, will see his glory and believe in him (Jn 2:11). John, of course, is dealing only with people who have seen Jesus, either historically or in the ecclesial community. Consequently, he regards each person as involved in the crisis situation that dominates the perspective of the fourth Gospel, namely, the choice to accept or reject Jesus. To those who accept him, he gives the power to become children of God (Jn 1:12) while those who refuse him are condemned by that very refusal (Jn 3:18). Although John does not explicitly take into account those who may never have been exposed to the revelation that is Jesus, his treatment of the subject of commitment includes, in principle, all human beings. What differentiates those who come to the light from those who remain in darkness is not their actual explicit exposure to Jesus but their deeds, manifesting their basic disposition of heart. Those who do the truth will respond to the light, whenever and however it shines in their lives. Those who do evil will flee from the light (Jn 3:20). In other words it is one's fundamental commitment to the truth, expressing itself in deeds, which opens a person to God's revelation, however that revelation enters the individual's life.

IV. IMPLICATIONS FOR CONTEMPORARY REFLECTION ON COMMITMENT

Although it is true that the author of the fourth Gospel did not have our contemporary questions about permanent commitment, he was writing for a community facing a crisis of commitment: whether to abandon their hereditary religious commitment to institutional Judaism or to abandon their commitment to Jesus as Messiah and Son of God. John tries to help them deal with this dilemma by examining, in a very profound way, the meaning of religious commitment. Although we do not face precisely the same dilemma, the fourth Gospel's elucidation of the meaning of commitment has important implications for twentieth century Christians who also face the challenge of conflicting commitments.

First, *religious commitments are partially conditioned by historical circumstances.* It was God who had originally called the Christians of the Johannine community to membership in the chosen people, including commitment within institutional Judaism. But the leaders of Judaism had progressively transformed the religion of Yahweh into a commitment to the institution rather than to God. Continued commitment within Judaism became impossible. Fidelity to the meaning of the original commitment entailed abandoning it because of the changed historical situation over which the Jewish Christians had no control. John depicts the historical Jesus accusing his contemporaries of an idolatrous commitment to their commitments rather than to God in order to clarify his community's understanding of their own action as deep fidelity to the covenant. To be an Israelite was to believe that "the Lord is God; there is no other beside him" (Dt 4:35). Consequently, it was precisely in order to remain a true Israelite that the first century Christian had to abandon institutional Judaism.

Second, and very closely related to the first, *the only absolute commitment is the commitment to God in Jesus.* All other commitments, however sacred, remain radically relative in relation to this absolute commitment. Relative commitments can certainly be permanent. It is not only legitimate, but necessary, to shape one's life by permanent interpersonal commitments to which one remains faithful over a lifetime. But if any commitment takes on such absoluteness that we become incapable of terminating it if it should become a real hindrance to our love of God and our growth in Christ, then it has become idolatry. This is easy to understand in theory, but when the conflict is between a sacred and permanent commitment, like that of John's community to Judaism, and fidelity to God in Jesus, the theory can be heartbreaking in application. And the application must frequently be made, as it was by the man born blind, at the price of religious rejection.

Third, *every commitment, insofar as it is authentic, is a relative expression of our absolute commitment to God.* This is the source of the sacredness of our commitments and the justification of their permanence. But it is also consolation in the situation in which a permanent but relative commitment must be transcended. In such a case the deepest reality of the abandoned commitment is not lost, however agonizing the experience might be. The Christians of the Johannine community had to abandon their commitment to Judaism, but the essence of what it meant to be an Israelite remained at the heart of their new commitment to Jesus.

Fourth, *the inner disposition of openness to the truth is ultimately our only protection against self-deception and the tyranny of others.* For the mature person, there is only one real guarantee that one's attitudes toward commitments are valid. A calm and trusting openness to the truth, a loyalty to life and to being wherever they lead, is the disposition of one who can and will be "taught of God." No outside agency, however sacred, can be substituted for conscience trained to the truth. Nor can we ever substitute someone else's vision or interpretation of the truth for our own. The man born blind, Nicodemus, the officers sent to arrest Jesus, and the woman of Samaria are all examples of people who resisted the pressure of "authority" in order to respond to the truth as they saw it. Against the man born blind the Jewish officials invoked the Law of Moses given by God, their own hierarchical authority sanctioned by tradition, and even the man's own ignorance and sinfulness to induce him to betray his experience and its revelatory implications. Both the consciousness of his own limitations and the weight of a lifelong commitment to Judaism favored a surrender to the authority of Law, hierarchy, learning, and tradition. But the man chose to follow the truth that he saw, and Jesus' finding of and self-revelation to the excommunicated man is our assurance of the rightness of his choice. In contemporary terms, conscience remains the sole final arbiter in the case of conflict of commitments. Our fundamental challenge is not fidelity to our commitments, but fidelity to the truth. It is this fidelity which discerns and actualizes our commitment to God in the heart of our choices and which, finally, justifies our relative commitments and strengthens us to live them in hope.

Part Two

THE VOWS IN CONTEMPORARY EXPERIENCE AND REFLECTION

Chapter Five
RENEWING THE THEOLOGY
OF THE VOWS

> The following essay originally appeared as "Vow (Prac-
> tice and Theology)" in volume 17, *Supplement: Change in the
> Church* of the *New Catholic Encyclopedia* (New York: McGraw-
> Hill, 1979) 696–699. It attempts to describe, in its major lin-
> eaments, the renewal of religious life that had been going
> on since the 1960's, and to locate the deeper theological, ec-
> clesial and conciliar roots of this renewal. The reader might
> find it interesting to compare this essay with its predecessor,
> "Vow (Practice and Theology of)" in volume 14, *New Catholic
> Encyclopedia* (New York: McGraw-Hill, 1967) 756–758.

Few institutions in the Church have been as profoundly and
pervasively affected by the spirit and content of Vatican Council
II as religious life. The groundwork for the reform and renewal
of religious life began decades before the Council in the crisis of
significance that followed World War II, but the Council gave
impetus to and legitimized the renewal movement. So extensive,
radical, and diverse has the renewal been that it is virtually impossible to speak of *the* theology and practice of the vows. Although most religious have responded eagerly to the Council's
challenge to renew their life in response to the signs of the times
and according to the norms of the Gospel and the particular
charisms of the diverse institutes (*Perfectae Caritatis* 2), there has
been a marked difference in depth and extent of renewal between male and female religious, between clerical and lay religious, and among national groups. Furthermore, even within
the group which, on the whole, has made the most notable progress in renewal, namely, American women religious, there is a
relatively small but powerful and articulate traditionalist movement which has its counterparts in other countries. These di-
versities must be allowed to relativize the following paragraphs
which will indicate the sources and the main directions of con-

temporary theology and practice of the vows as it is developing among the progressive majority.

I. SOURCES OF CONTEMPORARY THEOLOGICAL REFLECTION

The contemporary theology of the vows is no longer synonymous with, nor generative of, the theology of religious life. Rather, the latter is context and matrix of the former. At least three major sources of contemporary theological reflection on religious life (and therefore on the vows) can be clearly discerned.

A. Primacy of Theology

First, there has been a reversal in the relationship between canonical legislation and the theology of religious life. Prior to Vatican II the theology of religious life in general, and of the vows in particular, was almost wholly derived from canon law. The Council's invitation to religious to renew their institutes led to wide experimentation, much of it contrary to common law and custom. This experimentation rapidly produced a vast body of experience which has become the subject matter of continuing, biblically guided, theological reflection on the meaning of religious life and how it should be lived today. The theory emerging from this reflection is now being critically brought to bear on existing legislation concerning religious life. Thus, theologically criticized praxis rather than canonical legislation is becoming the primary source of the evolving theology and practice of religious life, including the vows.

B. The Ecclesial Dimension

Second, following the inspired lead of the Council, which placed the theological treatment of religious life within the Dogmatic Constitution on the Church (see *Lumen Gentium*, V, 39—VI, 47), religious are developing a deepened sense of the ecclesial character of their life. They have appropriated the implications of the Pastoral Constitution on the Church in the Modern World (*Gaudium et Spes*), in which the Church renounced its centuries-old adversary stance toward the world and reaffirmed its solidarity with all humankind in the task of transforming this world into a just and peaceful context for human life and growth. Religious have, in many ways, outdistanced the hierarchical Church in their practical commitment to the mission of being in, with, and for the world, and in accepting the implications of this commitment for personal and corporate involvement in the cause of social justice. Thus, the emerging theology of religious life tends to speak less about the "works" of institutes (often in the past dichotomized from the "spiritual life") and to speak of the life of the institute as essentially missionary. Religious profession, as a particular actualization of baptism which is the true source of Christian ministry, is coming to be understood less as the assumption of personal obligations and more as consecration for ministry within, and as an expression of, the mission of the institute.

C. The Universal Call to Holiness

Third, the theology of religious life, and especially of profession, is being deeply affected by the revalidation of the universal Christian vocation to holiness (*Lumen Gentium* 39–42). The realization of the incompatibility between recognizing that all Christians are called to the perfection of charity and claiming that religious are called to the "state of perfection" or to an intrinsically "higher life" has led to a progressive renunciation of elitist interpretations of profession and of the use of such status symbols as special dress and titles, special domiciles, and social privileges. This deliberate reintegration of religious into the people of God and thus into the world in which that people is a pilgrim has created a challenge to reinterpret religious life as a way rather than as a caste, and to search for an understanding of the vows that does not imply a separation of religious from other Christians or exalt them above their sisters and brothers in the Christian community.

II. DIRECTION IN CONTEMPORARY THEOLOGICAL REFLECTION

The act of religious profession is currently the object of considerable theological reflection; many question whether religious profession is necessarily constituted by the three traditional vows of poverty, chastity, and obedience.

A. *Religious Profession*

There is a discernible tendency to regard profession, regardless of which vows are made, as the act of consecration by which one enters the religious state. Thus it is understood less as the assumption of a specific set of obligations and more as a personal commitment whose primary effect is to structure the life of the religious by a particular set of stable relations, namely, to Christ, to the Church, and to the institute whose life and mission the religious will share. This type of reflection has led to experimentation with a variety of forms for profession even within the same institute. There is widespread discussion of the desirability of replacing multiple vows with a single, all-inclusive vow that would emphasize the unity given to a person's life by religious commitment rather than the multiplicity of obligations assumed. Finally, without denying that the consecration constituted by religious profession is ideally lifelong and that definitive commitment is possible and life-enhancing for those whose gift it is, there is increasing discussion of the possibility that not every religious profession need be perpetual. It is significant that contemporary reflection on profession is concerned with fundamental issues and not merely with legal or juridical problems.

B. *Poverty*

The theology of evangelical poverty, the object of the religious vow, is rooted in the Gospel values of joyous dependence on God and open-hearted sharing of God's gifts within the human community. In the course of history the understanding of this vow has varied widely. In modern times it has been understood as obliging the religious to renounce the independent use and ownership of all material goods. In practice, this renunciation was expressed by obtaining the permission of superiors for the use of whatever material goods were necessary for life or work.

Contemporary reflection on and practice of poverty is being deeply affected primarily by two factors. First, there is the psychological fact that total dependence upon superiors for one's material well-being is experienced by many religious as trivial in itself, unrelated to evangelical poverty, and conducive to immaturity and irresponsibility. The second factor is the increasing awareness on the part of many religious of the extent and severity of real destitution in the world and a consequent sense of inauthenticity in claiming to practice poverty while enjoying a disproportionate share of this world's goods and virtual freedom from material insecurity. These factors have led to considerable modification in the practice of poverty. Members are participating more directly and extensively in the handling of the finances of their local communities and institutes and assuming increasing responsibility for the ordinary economic affairs of their own lives.

These two factors have also had a profound influence on the theology of religious poverty. Many religious are coming to see the vow of poverty as a public commitment to responsible stewardship of the goods of the earth and to the struggle for a just economic order in which an equitable sharing of limited resources will hasten the end of the oppression of the poor by the rich. The implications of such an understanding of poverty reach from voluntary simplification of personal and communal lifestyles to individual and corporate participation in the politics of social justice.

C. Chastity

Chastity, or celibacy freely chosen for evangelical reasons, has been explained theologically in many ways in the course of history. Most of these explanations are considered unsatisfactory today because they involve, explicitly or implicitly, a negative attitude toward sexuality and a denigration of marriage as a Christian vocation. The practice flowing from such theologies, though admirable in many respects, is often seen today as overly characterized by fear, guilt, and repression and as leading to serious affective underdevelopment in many religious.

The contemporary realization of the importance of sexuality in human life and of the irreplaceable role in affective growth of friendship with members of one's own and the other sex has led to a serious revision of both the theology and the practice of religious celibacy. This reflection has been influenced by the increasingly open discussion of sexuality in general, and particularly of homosexuality and of the exclusiveness of the relation of sexual expression to monogamous marriage. The focus of attention, both theologically and in practice, is still largely on personal development, the improvement of the affective quality of community life, and the consequent growth of religious in interpersonal effectiveness. Increasingly, however, religious are realizing the corporate significance of their chosen lifestyle as a witness complementary to that of Christian marriage. They are tending to see their celibacy less as a renunciation of marriage and more as a commitment to growth in love dedicated to the development of a world characterized by unselfish service and mutual care.

D. Obedience

In modern times obedience has been the vow whose theology and practice has had the greatest impact on the daily life of religious. Although it represented a sincere and at times heroic effort to discern and fulfill God's will in imitation of Christ who was obedient unto death, the traditional practice of obedience, which responded to the superior's will as the will of God, tended to diminish the responsibility of the "subject." The contemporary renewal of the theology and practice of religious obedience has been fostered by many factors, among the most important of which are the following: the realization of the psychological underdevelopment that often results from the lifelong surrender of personal decision making and responsibility; the insight into the moral immaturity which often results from the possibility of regarding another as ultimately responsible for one's choices and actions; the sociological data on the superiority of shared leadership over hierarchical authority in voluntary societies; the positive political experience of many societies with democratic government; the relativizing in many institutes of an excessive task-orientation which led to an overdependence on the efficiency of command-obedience relations and the subordination of persons to work. Most important, perhaps, has been the theological realization that the Spirit speaks through all the members of the community and that to assign the role of "speaking for God" to a single member is to impoverish the community's efforts to discern the will of God. In the last analysis, the theological viability of the principle of hierarchy is being brought into question. This probably accounts for the extreme strain that developments in the area of obedience are causing.

In practice, and despite explicit official opposition, many institutes, especially of religious women, have moved steadily away from hierarchical organization. They have adopted participative procedures for the conduct of government, democratized elections, desacralized and in some cases abolished the role of local superior, instituted congregational policies which allow individuals in consultation with community leadership to choose their own ministerial commitments, and made leadership accountable to the membership as well as vice versa.

At the basis of these developments in practice are profound theological convictions about the dignity and equality of persons, the inalienability of personal freedom and responsibility, the right of every individual to justice, and the irreplaceable value for community life of full participation by the members. Many religious envision the building of communities in which authority is the function of truth and is neither confused with power nor buttressed by force, in which justice is the climate for mutual service, and in which all the members participate fully, freely, and equally as a prophetic participation in the Church's mission of liberation and reconciliation.

In summary, the theology and practice of the religious vows is in a state of rapid and profound transformation. This transformation is a function both of cultural evolution and of the theological awakening of the twentieth century. The understanding and practice of the vows is moving away from an emphasis on the assumption of obligations and toward an emphasis on commitment to personal spiritual growth and to participation in the world-transforming mission of the Church.

Chapter Six
TOWARD A CONTEMPORARY
THEOLOGY OF THE VOWS

No essay in this volume has been as widely discussed as the following one. Between 1976 when its first tentative outline emerged as part of the Contemporary Theology of Religious Life Project of the LCWR until 1982 the material has been presented and discussed in lectures, workshops, classes, and consultations throughout the United States. It was presented to the religious of the (arch)dioceses of Northern and Southern California, Greensboro, NC, Milwaukee, WI, and Providence, RI; to the National Sisters Vocation Conference and the National Assembly of Benedictine Prioresses; to members of many congregations including the Christian Brothers, The Sisters of Notre Dame de Namur, Sisters, Servants of the Immaculate Heart of Mary, Sisters of Charity of St. Augustine, Dominicans of Newburgh, Sisters of Charity of the Blessed Virgin Mary; in courses on religious life at the Jesuit School of Theology in Berkeley, CA, Newman Theological College in Edmonton, Canada, and St. Norbert's College in De Pere, WI. The original version was published in *Journeying Resources* (Washington, D.C.: Leadership Conference of Women Religious, 1977), pp. 14–27.

I. INTRODUCTION: THE TASK

This chapter is entitled "*a* theology of the vows" in order to call attention at the outset to the difference between the Gospel reality of religious life and the human effort, called theology, by which we seek to understand and articulate that reality. There will never be a totally adequate theology of religious life (or of the vows), but the inadequacy, and at times even the falsity, of our understanding and articulation cannot destroy or diminish religious life as a gift of Jesus Christ through the Spirit to the Church. Nevertheless, the efforts we make to understand religious life and to make it understandable to our contemporaries profoundly affect the human experience and expression of this gift in the Church and in the world. The glory of theology is its ministerial relationship to the ultimate truth of revelation, and the poverty of theology is its never to be overcome inadequacy and relativity in relation to the truth which it seeks to serve. The present theological effort, therefore, is nothing more than *an* effort to rearticulate the meaning of the vows for our own time.

The history of religious life clearly reveals two important facts regarding the vows: that religious have always made public profession of some kind but not always of vows as such,[1] that the specific vows professed have not always been the same ones,[2] and that the meaning of the individual vows has varied in different religious families, periods, and places.[3] This suggests that it is not only permissible to re-examine the meaning of the vows as they are being professed and lived by twentieth century American religious, but really necessary to do so if we are to remain faithful to the tradition of religious life in the Church.

No one who experienced Catholic life prior to Vatican II would deny that the ecclesial context of contemporary religious life is massively different from that of pre-conciliar times. The single factor in the conciliar reform and renewal which has most profoundly affected religious life would seem to be the position taken by the Council on the relationship between the Church and the world. The Pastoral Constitution on the Church in the Modern World *Gaudium et Spes* represents a real change and development of doctrine which is complex and which should not be treated with naiveté. But it would not be inaccurate to say that in Vatican II the Church abandoned an essentially defensive and antagonistic attitude toward the world and assumed a stance of acceptance, involvement, and solidarity.

The Council's joyful affirmation of the reality and significance of the Incarnation for the Church was profoundly evangelical, but it placed religious life under the necessity of completely reformulating itself. Religious life, at least since the fourth century, has understood itself almost as an institutionalization of the world-transcending dimension of Christianity.[4] The first expression of this world-transcendence (which so easily and so often became world-denial) was the flight from the city to the desert. Later, flight was transmuted into the separation effected by cloister. Still later, when physical cloister gave way under the pressures of the apostolate, a subtle but effective substitution replaced grills and walls with a total subculture that made religious simply unassimilable in any ordinary human situation except those in which they were officially representing the hierarchical and institutional Church to the laity.

The Church, by expressing its slowly matured and radically new conviction that the world is not the enemy but the raw material of the reign of God and that, therefore, the Church is and should be in, with, and for the world, participating in its struggles for the transformation of humankind, has made an institutionalization of world-transcendence (to say nothing of world-denial) not only useless but illegitimate. Religious, whether they like it or not, must be in, with, and for the world as the Church now recognizes itself to be. This has enormous implications in the practical and in the theoretical domains. The practical implications are becoming evident in the lifestyle and ministry of religious. But the gap is widening between an official theory of religious life that is still largely pre-conciliar[5] and a practice which is based more on *Gaudium et Spes* than on *Perfectae Caritatis*.

One of the major results for religious of the Council's launching of the Church into the modern world has been the crumbling of the institutional structures which have enabled religious life to function as a "closed system," running on an independent, if not contradictory, track from "the world." In former times within their own communities and institutions religious could define reality as they wished and the definitions were unquestioned. Religious could say, for example, that poverty means dependence by permission and is perfectly compatible with corporate wealth and personal comfort, or that true freedom is found in abdication of one's personal will to that of a superior who, even when wrong, speaks with the voice of God, and no one questioned the truth of these positions. Religious could decide which apostolic works they were going to do and no one challenged their priorities.

The crumbling of the structures which effectively separated religious from the rest of the Christian community as well as from secular society has made it virtually impossible to maintain the closed system. The subculture of religious life is disintegrating. What religious do and say is no longer safe from telling criticism by the larger society. The criticism makes sense to many religious who themselves can no longer take seriously the 1950's definitions of the vows or accept unquestioningly the priority of ghetto-serving and institution-preserving corporate commitments.

Furthermore, it is clear to anyone who looks fairly at the situation that the efforts being made by non-religious and even by non-Christians to create a better world are often at least as effective in goal, content, and methods as the efforts of religious. Religious are not the only people interested in the salvation of the world, and in some cases a long history of world-denial has made them less capable of grasping the world-transforming vision of Vatican II and less adept at implementing that vision than people who have participated all their lives in the world process that most religious renounced at an early age.

The closed system is dissolving and religious are more and more caught up in the mainstream of society and culture. Two results of this situation condition any contemporary consideration of the vows: (1) to make sense to themselves religious have to make sense to their contemporaries in the world (which is not the same thing, necessarily, as being approved of by the world); (2) to survive as religious in the mainstream it is imperative that religious articulate a new relationship to the world which is neither a surrender to absorption nor the continuation of an adversary stance.

II. THE CONTEXT: A THEOLOGY OF PROFESSION

As we have already noted, religious life has always involved profession, but profession has not always taken the form of vows and the vows professed have not always been the same. Consequently, the question of the meaning of the vows should be set in the context of the more basic question of the meaning of religious profession. Whatever vows are made and whatever their content and meaning is seen to be in any period, place, or congregation, they are and must be the specific expression of the general intentionality of the act of profession.

Profession is the act by which a person dedicates herself or himself to God in Christ by permanent commitment in religious life, i.e., it is the formal undertaking of this form of Christian life. By this dedication the person is consecrated to God in a particular way different from the consecration effected by marriage vows. Giving to one's life the particular structure that is religious life means two things: (1) leaving behind or aside other possible structures (the "negative" dimension); (2) freely tending toward growth and maturity in the way chosen (the "positive" dimension). The classical expression of these two dimensions has been "leaving the world" and "tending to perfection." The first meant renunciation of the world and the second meant attending to one's personal sanctification and to the salvation of souls either through prayer or through the apostolic work of the congregation.

Obviously, "leaving the world" and, to some extent at least, an individualistic and/or institutional "pursuit of perfection" are difficult to harmonize with a conciliar understanding of what Christian life is all about. This raises a perfectly legitimate question which will not unsettle anyone who is somewhat familiar with the long and varied history of religious life. The question is simply: How can religious profession be understood and explained today in terms which are faithful both to the basic meaning of profession as commitment to Christ in religious life and to the contemporary spiritual experience of both the dimensions of that commitment?

What *stance toward the world* does one take by entering religious life today? Clearly, by refusing to "build oneself into" the familial, economic, and political structures of the surrounding society the person has taken a somewhat independent stance. It is not one of "flight" or of "separation." But it is also not one of simply belonging. It is, ideally, one of prophetic presence. Some people have referred to it as a counter-cultural stance. Whatever we choose to call it, we mean that religious try to maintain a certain personal and corporate liberty in regard to the basic structures and dynamics of the world, a liberty which will enable them to bring to bear upon its forms and activities the evangelical values, i.e., the spirit of the beatitudes,[6] which is essential for the transformation of the world. The specific relationship between the individual religious and/or congregation and the particular structures and activities in their sector of the world may be one of condemning outright evil, criticizing the inadequate, clarifying the ambiguous, cooperating with the good, or some combination of these. The important thing is that religious attempt to structure their lives in such a way that they have the necessary liberty to relate prophetically to the world. Prophetic presence requires contemplative insight and courageous action. These, it might be argued, are the contemporary analogue of flight or separation from the world.

To what do religious *positively commit themselves* by entering religious life today? Perhaps we could say that they commit themselves to the great work of transformation that began with the Incarnation and which takes its meaning and structure from that central salvific event. Personal transformation in Christ is certainly integral to this commitment but in the experience of the contemporary religious the transformation of the world and all its people is equally integral and in no sense a "secondary end." This entire process of transformation in Christ is seen as essentially communal, and "community" cannot be defined as exclusively institutional togetherness nor as exclusively congregational. On the contrary, the contemporary religious demands both a more authentic community life within the congregation and a deeper community involvement with those who are not members of the congregation.

In summary, religious profession today is essentially what it has always been, a dedication of the person to God in Christ within religious life. It continues to involve the adoption of a particular stance toward the world which is not simply one of belonging to the world on its own terms, and a commitment to a particular positive seeking of life in Christ. What has changed is the understanding of both dimensions. The adversary stance toward the world has given way to a prophetic stance. The commitment to seeking personal perfection and the salvation of souls has become a commitment to the transformation of all things and people (including oneself) in Christ. It is in the context of the meaning of contemporary religious profession as the initiating act of religious life that we can raise the question about the contemporary meaning of the vows.

III. THE SPECIFICATION:
A THEOLOGY OF THE VOWS

Most religious today profess the traditional vows of poverty, chastity or celibacy, and obedience. By means of these vows both dimensions of religious profession, the prophetic stance toward the world and the commitment to the transformation of the world in Christ, are specified. The traditional three vows locate this specification in the attitude and behavior of the religious in the areas of the three major dimensions of human life (possession, affectivity, and power) which are simultaneously the three major areas of human interaction which structure the world (economics, social life, and politics). Traditional theology of the vows has already attended to the first aspect, the capacity of the vows to direct one's personal energies toward God. But it is only contemporary reflection which has highlighted the potential of the vows for enabling the religious to play a significant role in the transformation of the structures of the world through an evangelical contribution to the major areas of human interaction. Furthermore, the more one reflects on this latter aspect the clearer it becomes that the two aspects, while distinct, are not separate, any more than the prophetic stance toward the world and the commitment to the transformation of all things in Christ are separate. This awareness of the integrity and wholeness of the religious project is perhaps one of the major contributions of contemporary experience to the understanding of religious life.

A. *Poverty*

When the twentieth century American over the age of forty tries to think about material goods she or he has to be aware of the kaleidoscopic transformations in the economy that have taken place in two generations. From an economy of scarcity which reached agonizing proportions in the depression era through an economy of abundance that the post-war generation incarnated in a throw-away culture we have come to a realistic appreciation of our present situation in an economy of finitude.

Material resources are not infinite, and we will either use

them responsibly or we and/or the next generation will not have the means to live at all on this planet. This realization has changed our attitudes toward material goods. Goods are resources, and that means they are to be used *for* and not just used *up*. Furthermore, not all of the projects which resources can serve are equally worthwhile and, since the resources are not infinite, choices have to be made.

Religious were not the first, much less the only, people to realize that as a cosmic community we must undergo a conversion in the area of attitude and behavior toward material goods, from an attitude of mindless exploitation to one of responsible stewardship. Not far behind this realization came the conviction that the inequity of distribution of material goods and the resultant domination of the poor by the rich is an intolerable source of the edge-of-doom situation in which we live. In other words, the human race is beginning to see that the establishment of a sane and healthy relationship between finite material resources and the quality of life for all people is crucial to the survival of the race and of the planet. How to establish such a relationship, given the obvious headstart of institutionalized selfishness, exploitation, crass irresponsibility, and domination, is a staggering problem.

If the religious vow of poverty is going to make sense today, even to religious themselves to say nothing of other people, it cannot continue to be understood as a private reality operating in the closed system that the religious subculture once constituted. It has to relate the religious enterprise to the enormous human project of organizing material resources for the creation of a genuinely human world. Religious poverty has to clearly cast the weight of Christianity into the balance on the side of responsible stewardship, institutional reform, and the liberation of the poor. But even more importantly it should help to surface and explicitate the potentially evangelical values in this world struggle for a human economy and contribute an evangelical dimension where none yet exists.

To build the evangelical dimension into the contemporary economic struggle does not mean simply to baptize with piety what is already going on. It means to contribute to the effort not only by cooperation, criticism, or condemnation but by a mode of behavior which arises directly from a Gospel poverty of spirit, itself the fruit of a profound experience of God's gift to us in Jesus. The contemporary religious who experiences all as gift will transcend not only the excess of having, but perhaps also the facility of giving, and find a Gospel mode of sharing. To be preoccupied with having means to dispossess others. Outright giving, in our society, often places the receiver in the position of a grateful subordinate. To share means to enter into relationship with the other on the basis of recognition that the other has a right to participate in the gift of God to all people, that we have no right to more than we need when another is in want. Sharing is more than the equitable distribution of goods. It is a recognition of our common life as creatures of the same God and a concrete living of that common life.

It is not easy to work out what the vow of poverty means in today's world. In principle, it means to participate prophetically in the human effort to convert the race from exploitation to responsible stewardship, to liberate the poor by an equitable distribution of goods, to create the economic structures which will effectively relate finite resources to human ends. But it also means to model a sharing of life through a sharing of goods that expresses a Christian experience of poverty of spirit. In the concrete it probably means a re-evaluation of holdings and life-styles and an abandonment of the privatized exclusivity of the religious subculture. To work out the details of such an approach will not be easy. But a poverty of this kind, which renounces both the childish irrelevance of an artificial dependence and the romanticism of a useless and unreal imitation of the destitute and concentrates on alleviating misery while building the structures of human solidarity, can make sense to the religious who vows poverty today. And although the world will undoubtedly not always like what religious are doing in this area, it will at least have to take it seriously.

B. *Celibacy*

The vow of celibacy was once the least problematic of the three. It regulated affectivity by almost total denial, if not outright repression, and its obligations were perfectly clear. It was relatively simple to maintain this situation as long as religious life remained a closed system. But today celibacy has to be thought about in the context of the affective revolution that characterizes our time. This revolution includes not only run-away eroticism and its negative corollaries but also a valid liberation of both women and men from sexually stereotyped roles and lifestyles, the movement for the rights of sexual minorities, the struggle for the liberation and equal rights of women. We are midstream in a major cultural conversion from a basically one-sex, male-dominated society (and Church) to a two-sex society characterized by responsible mutuality. The person who vows celibacy for evangelical reasons is in a unique position to contribute to this positive transformation of society.

It has already become relatively clear that celibate women, especially when organized in religious communities, are in an extraordinarily good position to challenge male domination and to foster the emergence of women as equal collaborators in every sphere of life and work. Despite the long history of sacramental subjugation and ministerial exploitation of religious women within the Church, it is a fact that, both individually and as groups, religious women constitute an educated, disciplined, productive, and relatively independent force which is exercising a genuinely prophetic role in the Church and in society. Unmarried women generally have had both more opportunities for developing competitive competencies and more affective and social freedom to experiment and take risks in achieving personal and corporate effectiveness. Religious have the added advantage of corporate resources and outlets for maximizing such possibilities.

A parallel phenomenon is observable among religious men. Despite the locker-room ethos that all-male living tends to create and the chauvinism that was systematically bred into many male religious as a protection, on the one hand, from sexual delinquency, and, on the other hand, of male supremacy and the status quo in the Church, religious men (especially in non-clerical congregations) are rapidly emerging as a major force in the struggle for a new, sexually balanced Church and world. They have more opportunity than most of their married colleagues to meet and work as equals with talented women and more psychological space to come to grips with their own problems in the area of relationships with women.

Although religious are playing a genuinely prophetic role in the affective transformation of society, many men and women celibates find it much more difficult to tackle their own personal affective transformation. Intimacy, with people of their own or the other sex, is unfamiliar territory for many religious. Much of the affective energy which was sublimated into compulsive work for so many years is hard to tap for the development of loving relationships with other individuals and within community. A long indoctrination in avoidance of deep relationships with those outside the community has made it unusually difficult for many religious to enter freely into close friendships with non-members. Lack of experience with their own affective responses causes upsetting reactions when religious who have allowed themselves virtually no affective expression since early adolescence find themselves suddenly in a two-sex world. Vocational disasters have been frequent enough in the last few years to give even the non-scrupulous some pause. Nevertheless, one senses a general commitment among women and men religious to their own sexual and affective maturation and to the creation of loving communities which bodes well for the future of religious life.

Again, it must be remarked that religious are latecomers to the affective revolution that is underway in our society. Religious celibates are being called to participation and cooperation in a positive dynamism which is at work in our culture. But if the participation of religious is to be evangelically prophetic it must be based on a deep religious experience of being loved by God in Jesus and an experienced personal fulfillment in returning that love. The Gospel purity of heart which religious can bring to the affective transformation of the world and the Church is more than just the expression of a well-developed personality. It is the expression in interpersonal and community relationships of an affectivity that has been radically healed, purified, and liberated in the intimacy of a profound personal and communal prayer life.

In the area of celibacy, as in that of poverty, the vow will make sense to the contemporary religious if it leads the person toward personal transformation in love and allows the person to participate meaningfully in the emergence of a new, whole, and loving world characterized by equality, responsible intimacy, and mutuality. What this means in the concrete is less easy to determine. The renewal of community life has been underway for some time and seems to be the first expression of a new understanding of celibacy. It would seem that re-evaluation of totally one-sex formation programs and apostolates is also necessary as well as some experimentation with less isolated living patterns for adult religious. Individual and corporate efforts to break down patterns of male dominance and to establish patterns of equality and collaboration would seem to be an integral part of what vowed celibacy today is all about.

If celibacy comes to mean not simply sexual denial but a total commitment to the creation of a genuine world community and, within that global enterprise, a commitment to becoming an ever more loving human being, it will not cease to be baffling to a world largely structured by selfishness, or offensive to the proponents of unrestrained eroticism, but it will have to be taken seriously as a significant human venture.

C. Obedience

It has become almost a cliché to speak of the crisis of authority and obedience, not only in religious life but in the Church and society at large. This is the context of any contemporary discussion of the vow of obedience. The crisis is much deeper than some proponents of a restoration of the *ancien régime* would like to think. It is not simply that those in authority are exercising authority badly or that those who should be obeying lack faith, humility, or some other virtue (although both are sometimes true). It is that the principle of hierarchy, which is the nerve of both secular and religious obedience as they have been traditionally understood, is being radically questioned and the principle of participation is supplanting it in more and more sectors of life. Because it has traditionally been thought that the Church is hierarchical by divine institution and that nothing can or will ever really change this, many people simply do not attend to the real nature and seriousness of this changing perception of the nature of human relationships.[7]

A hierarchical organization of a society is one in which some members are thought to be really, intrinsically, personally, and relatively permanently superior to the others. However the person came to be in the superior position, whether by conquest, birth, appointment, election, or some other way, his or her authority is thought to be a personal participation in divine authority, and, therefore, to be divinely sanctioned. The basic principle of hierarchical organization is that all legitimate authority comes from God and thus that obedience to this authority is a sacred duty. In chapter eight we will undertake an examination of this premise and try to show the inadequacy of its traditional use. In religious communities the sacralizing of authority has been carried to its extreme in the notion that the superior literally holds the place of Christ, speaks in the name of God, and communicates the will of God for the subject, even when the superior's command is objectively wrong (provided it is merely wrong, not sinful).

A participative organization of a society is one in which all members are understood to be intrinsically equal. If, for the good of all, someone is given a position of authority, it is provisional, temporary, limited in scope, functional, and non-sacralized. The person is first among equals in a particular domain of community life but not the representative of God to the others in an exclusive sense. Obedience in such a context is not so much submission as cooperation, which is every bit as demanding as submission if it is taken seriously. The members of the group never abdicate personal responsibility either for themselves and their own actions or for the group as a whole.[8]

It is important to realize that the distinction being drawn here is not between monarchy and democracy, as some seem to conclude as soon as the traditional hierarchical model is questioned. Both monarchy and democracy can be hierarchical, and both can be participative. The real difference is not in the form of government selected, but in the belief regarding the nature, source and location of authority. If the authority is thought to be somehow God's authority communicated directly to and exercised as a personal possession by the superior in regard to those who do not share in God's authority but submit to it, the system is hierarchical. If the authority is thought to be the community's authority (divine or human in its source) which the community chooses to exercise through one or many of its members, the system is essentially participative. In the former case the terminology of "superior" and "subject" is completely accurate. In the latter there is a real and fundamental equality among the members which is not negated by the appointment of someone to an office and which makes the use of superior/subject terminology both offensive and inaccurate.

To an ever greater degree societies are rejecting the hierarchical principle as a valid way of understanding or organizing social and political life. It is part of the worldwide rejection of domination and espousal of liberation and self-determination, a dynamic that surely owes a deep debt to New Testament revelation. It is the fruit not simply of the desire of people to control their own lives and destinies but also of a fundamental conviction regarding the intrinsic equality of all persons and of a growing sense of the inalienability of personal responsibility.

Members of the Church and religious are not immune from these currents of contemporary experience. In many ways the efforts to understand and practice collegiality constitute a move away at least from the monarchical understanding of hierarchy and toward a more participative practice. Many religious communities of women, and some of men, have largely abandoned, in practice if not in theory, the hierarchical understanding of religious life. This process is being intensified by the alignment of religious as individuals and as groups with the liberation efforts going on about them. They are absorbing the theory and practice of liberation theology and adjusting it to the North American scene. The implications for the organization of the local and universal Church, as well as of religious life, are difficult to ignore.

Obedience is certainly the vow which presents the greatest challenge for the development of a contemporary theology of religious life. It seems to run counter to the most important and positive social movements of our times. If, however, the fundamental intentionality of obedience can be reappropriated by contemporary religious, it is not inconceivable that obedience will make a prophetic contribution to the struggle for liberation. The only reason religious make a vow of obedience is that it seems to them the best way to promote their own true freedom. They have been convinced that in God's will is true peace, within ourselves and among ourselves. Religious obedience in its deepest roots is a dedication to freedom, not to subjection or servitude. It is as true today as it has ever been that true freedom is to be found in union with the will of God, even if religious, along with the rest of the human race, are coming gradually to see that obedience to God cannot be handled as simply as a traditional theology of obedience would suggest.

What religious can bring to the worldwide struggle against domination is a deep hunger and thirst for justice based on their own spiritual experience of liberation in Jesus Christ. Religious are people who know that justice and holiness are finally identical, and that justice is not merely the way humans can and should relate to one another. It is, first of all, a capacity to relate to each other as brothers and sisters which is given to us by the God who created and redeemed us all.

It might be suggested that religious should be on the cutting edge in the development of new forms of community life and organization structured by and for justice. Here, if anywhere, it makes sense for the members to trust one another and thus to be able to abandon all forms of domination, coercion, intolerance, and forced conformity. Religious communities are social groups in which the equality recognized among the members is explicitly seen to be equality not only as human beings but as creatures and children of the same God redeemed by the same Christ. Religious should offer a prophetic witness that it is possible for a group of people to live together in love and justice celebrating their own freedom and equality in the very act of celebrating God's absolute and respectful reign in their lives. Their community life and organization should explicitate the relationship between seeking God's will and experiencing human freedom (which has always been the real meaning of religious obedience), between accepting responsibility for oneself and putting one's life at the service of the other and of the common good (which is the Gospel meaning of maturity).

If to vow obedience meant to commit oneself to a personal quest for freedom and holiness in a community context and to involve oneself in the broader human quest for the liberation of all people both by a prophetic challenge to structures of domination and by a constructive participation in the evolution of new models of community, the vow would make sense not only to religious but to their contemporaries.

The practical implications of such an understanding are already being worked out by some communities. The quest for personal freedom demands a different kind of initial formation in which choice situations are multiplied rather than suppressed, in which responsibility is heightened rather than diminished, and in which subsequent evaluation is individualized and intensified. It requires a much deeper personal prayer life, different and better forms of spiritual direction, and a commitment to lifelong formation.

Participation in the wider human quest for liberation will demand, first of all, a serious re-evaluation of community structures. It calls for the abandonment of all forms of domination and oppression within communities, a refusal to appeal to coercion and use of power to induce conformity, the development of freedom of assembly and discussion, the abolition of prior censorship, and the establishment of due process. In other words, as the 1971 Synod of Bishops candidly recognized in regard to the Church, our witness to justice and the quest of human liberation will not be credible until injustice and the last vestiges of totalitarianism have been rooted out of our communities.[9]

The institutions which religious own, direct, or serve also raise the challenge of justice and freedom. The justice of hiring policies, the recognition and protection of the rights of employees and clients, and the integrity of investment policies are among the justice concerns which touch the religious community directly. But the concern for justice and liberation cannot stop with the community or its institutions. The financial and personnel commitments of religious congregations must express the priority assigned to the quest for justice. As the same Synod of Bishops put it, "Action on behalf of justice and participation in the transformation of the world fully appear to us as

a constitutive dimension of the preaching of the Gospel. . . ."[10]
Religious obedience has always been understood as a quest for
true freedom and as the way in which the individual religious is
integrated into the congregation's apostolate of preaching the
Gospel. It would seem that, at the deepest level, this is still what
it means. What has changed most perhaps is our understanding
of freedom and of what it means to preach the Gospel. As religious interiorize new understandings in these areas and incorporate them into their understanding and practice of the vow
of obedience, the vow itself can become intelligible to their contemporaries and more significant to religious themselves.

IV. CONCLUSION: CHALLENGE FOR THE FUTURE

It would seem useful, at this point, to summarize this rather
lengthy essay which has tried to argue that it is possible to reinterpret the traditional religious vows in a way which would be,
on the one hand, consistent with the tradition and, on the other
hand, more in touch with contemporary experience. The crisis
regarding the vows arises in large part from the fact that religious life, like the life of the Church itself, has been resituated
by Vatican II in, with, and for the world. One result of this re-
situation is that religious life is no longer a closed system operating in isolation from or in opposition to an alien and even
hostile world. Religious life in general, and the vows in particular, can no longer make sense to religious themselves if they
are seen as totally irrelevant to the world and to the process of
transformation that the world is undergoing.

Traditionally profession of vows as the act initiating religious life has meant assuming a particular religious stance toward the world, namely renunciation, and committing oneself
in some way to one's own salvation and that of the neighbor.
Profession today seems to have basically the same meaning. By
this act of self-dedication the religious assumes a certain prophetic stance toward the world, a critical but involved one, and
commits himself or herself to the transformation of the world,
including himself or herself.

The vows, as we have tried to show, can be seen as ways not
only of giving prophetic witness against the chief perversions of

the basic human energies of possession, affectivity, and power, but also of committing oneself to fostering the most positive forces of transformation at work in the world. They can be ways of integrating the evangelical dimension into the struggle to convert society and to transform the world into a human and ultimately holy habitation for human beings. They can constitute concrete modes of fostering the movements from exploitation of material resources to responsible stewardship in a finite universe; from a male-dominated, selfish, and hedonistic society to one structured by mutuality and oriented toward responsible intimacy; from a social order characterized by domination and coercion of the weak by the strong to one in which people participatively and cooperatively seek the maximum of freedom and justice for every person.

Practically, this selective cooperation of religious with the major positive movements in our society will demand a re-evaluation of traditional commitments and a redirection of personnel and material resources. Religious will be less frequently operating and staffing institutions which parallel equivalent secular institutions and more frequently cooperating in ventures they do not control but must influence in virtue of competence rather than of ownership.

Even more importantly, it will demand a different type of formation and professional preparation of candidates. Twentieth century religious will not have the advantages or support of the sociology of knowledge and conviction that living in the total institution provided in the past, and they will be able to influence the larger society only to the extent that they have something to offer personally and professionally.

Finally, contemporary religious life demands a new type of leadership which sees itself as enabling rather than dominative and which knows that genuine moral authority is coextensive with competence and not to be confused with jurisdiction.

Religious life is at the crossroads. Many are asking whether it will survive. Whether it retreats into the ghetto and attracts rigid, frightened, and structure-seeking dependency types, or moves forward to meet the challenge of prophetic presence and creative involvement in the world and attracts freedom-seeking, radical types, it will probably survive. In fact, one might hypothesize that there are more weak than strong people in any society and that, if survival is the question, the chances for quantitative increase of the ghetto congregations is actually better. But the question is not simply one of survival in the sense of duration. It is a question of meaning. Will religious life continue to be a significant evangelical force in the world? The answer to that question is much less certain, and it will depend on the vision and courage of those who can reimagine religious life for a new age.

Chapter Seven
CONSECRATED CELIBACY:
ICON OF THE REIGN OF GOD

The material in this chapter has been developed over a period of fifteen years in discussion with religious communities and in courses on religious life. Most recently, the final sections were presented in a session at Oblate School of Theology in San Antonio, Texas, May 31–June 1, 1984; at the Summer Scripture Seminar, Mundelein, Illinois, June 24–25, 1984; to the Thirty-Plus Club of Cleveland, Ohio, November 19, 1984.

I. INTRODUCTION

For two reasons consecrated celibacy is unique among vows professed by religious. First, it is the only vow whose content has been a constant factor in all forms of religious life throughout history. From the time of the consecrated virgins and widows of the first century to our own day religious life has always involved a commitment to lifelong celibacy. Second, celibacy is the only one of the three vows whose object is, strictly speaking, an evangelical "counsel" in the sense that it is a response to an invitation not addressed to all Christians. Although poverty and obedience are structured differently in the life of the religious than they are in the life of a married or single Christian, religious are certainly not the only Christians to whom the evangelical challenges of poverty of spirit and obedience to God are addressed. Consecrated celibacy, in other words, is the defining characteristic of religious life.

However, although all religious have professed lifelong celibacy, history makes it fairly clear that there have been and still are a variety of explanations or motivations for this choice given by those who profess it. Religious celibacy has been explained as marriage to Christ, freedom for contemplation or for the ministry, eschatological witness, counter-cultural stance, or condition for prophetic community life, among others. It seems to me, both from my study of history and from discussion with many religious about their own experiences, that the various motivations for and explanations of consecrated celibacy fall into two general categories.

The first category, which probably includes a very small number of contemporary religious, is consecrated virginity understood in a mystical/nuptial way as marriage to Christ. For the consecrated virgin non-marriage is the form of total personal dedication to Jesus, just as marriage is the form of lifelong personal dedication to another human being. Abstaining from sexual relationships is part of the total life-stance but by no means the major, much less the defining, characteristic of this stance. Chastity for the consecrated virgin involves abstaining from sexual relations just as chastity for a married person involves abstaining from sexual relations with anyone other than one's spouse. But chastity hardly exhausts the meaning of virginity any more than sexual fidelity exhausts the meaning of marriage.

Difficult as it may be for most people, including most religious today, to understand this conception of consecrated celibacy as nuptial experience, it is important not to negate this explanation, for the nuptial experience of virginity is not only the first celibate experience described in ecclesial literature but it is also the experience of some religious today. However, there is no question about the fact that this type of consecrated celibacy has been opened to misunderstanding by certain historical developments.

First, there is the problem with the terminology. The use of the term virginity rather than celibacy for this form of religious life is appropriate if it is properly understood. Virginity, because it refers literally to a state of never having been married or having had sexual relations with anyone, suggests the totality of the self-dedication which includes not only the whole of one's life from a temporal point of view but the entirety of one's capacity for love. But, as the Fathers of the Church insisted from the beginning, consecrated virginity had to do essentially not with the physical but with the spiritual condition of the person making the profession. Physical virginity was eminently appropriate as a sign of the content of the profession, and perfect continence after profession was required, but not being physically a virgin at the time of profession was not an absolute impediment to entering this state of life. Nonetheless, as the situation developed it seemed preferable not to raise the question of the sexual experience of the religious prior to entrance, and all religious made profession of celibacy rather than of virginity. While this may have been a prudent, and in many cases a kind, move on the part of the Church, it removed from the vocabulary of religious life the linguistic means of recognizing an important experiential difference between those who chose lifelong celibacy as the very definition of their life, as an "end" in a certain sense, and those who chose it as a means to the accomplishment of some life project seen to be more global, such as a life of ministry or of counter-cultural witness.

A second unfortunate historical development which obscured the validity and significance of the mystical/nuptial experience and interpretation of consecrated celibacy was the unreflective use of the texts and symbolism pertaining to consecrated virginity in the formation and ceremonials of all women religious. The use of bridal gowns and veils in reception and profession ceremonies, of marital euphemisms in the sections of rules and constitutions dealing with the vow of chastity, and of sentimental spousal language in spiritual literature, because it did not reflect the real experience of most religious, was seen as superficial at best and offensive at worst. Few religious today are comfortable with nuptial language about religious commitment, partly because it does not reflect their experience and partly because of the memory of its use in times past. Again, it is unfortunate that this historical development has deprived those whose experience of virginity is indeed nuptial of the symbolism and language that would be genuinely expressive for them. In fact, the mystical/nuptial language has been preserved in the literature of mysticism where it continues to nourish those who can understand from their own experience what is being described.

The second category of explanations of and motivations for religious celibacy, the ascetical/apostolic category, probably includes the experience of most religious today. In general, this type of explanation is given by those who undertake lifelong celibacy, not as an end in itself, that is, as a kind of outward manifestation of an experience of Christ that makes marital union with anyone else psychologically and spiritually impossible, but rather as a means to some spiritual end seen as more global than non-marriage itself but as fostered in some important way by celibacy. Celibacy for these religious is not the only means to their end, but it is an important one which gives a definite shape to their lifestyle.

The ends which celibacy has been undertaken to foster include the life of prayer or contemplation, ministry, community life of the kind that would be difficult or impossible among married members, and various kinds of witness that can be given more easily by an unmarried person. We will have more to say about these ends and their relation to celibacy in section three. For the moment, it is important to recognize that the ascetical/apostolic motivation for celibacy is one of the two main strands in the tradition and that it is the strand to which most contemporary religious, both men and women, seem to belong. Any adequate theory of the meaning of consecrated celibacy must take both these types of celibacy into account.

From what has preceded it should be clear that celibacy is a very complex reality. More exactly, it is a mystery whose richness calls more for contemplation and appreciation than for analysis or explanation. The choice of lifelong celibacy bears upon the most intimate core of human existence. It is a choice that matures in the context of a religious experience of more than ordinary intensity, and it is not always completely separable, for purposes of analysis, from the more global experience of religious life. However, the importance of the decision not to marry is such that it demands clarity and maturity. Hence, it is not surprising that we have often been tempted to analyze the reality and simplify the issues involved in the attempt to make sure that people contemplating such a commitment are perfectly clear about its implications. What I would like to do in this essay, however, is to treat consecrated celibacy not as a problem but as a mystery in the hopes that such a treatment will take more adequate account of the complexity and profundity of the subject matter and, for that very reason, be more clarifying of actual experience.

Consecrated celibacy might be helpfully approached through the metaphor of the icon. The icon is not a picture, a portrait, or a photograph. It is an opening on mystery. It renders present, in limited scope and concrete material, that which is neither limited nor concrete but richly mysterious in its spirituality. For that reason the icon can never be "deciphered." The most famous icon of all, the fourteenth century "Holy Trinity" of Andrei Roublev, has been discussed by experts for centuries, and it is still not possible to establish which of the three figures represents the Word and which the Spirit.[1] This inability of the experts is not due to their lack of knowledge but to the fact that the icon is an icon—it renders mysteriously present the mystery that is its subject. The dynamic of intra-Trinitarian life is simply beyond our capacity for clear analysis. The oneness of the three in their unity and distinction is the stumbling block which confronts us in our contemplation of the icon because it is integral to the mystery that the icon renders present. This does not mean, of course, that the iconographer understood the mystery and hid its meaning in his product. On the contrary, Roublev was only able to paint the indecipherable icon because he was possessed by the intractable mystery.

Religious celibacy is a kind of existential icon. A person, possessed in some way by religious reality, produces something in the material of his or her life which even he or she will never fully understand. And the existential text, the icon of the celibate life, both reveals something of the mysterious experience and, at the same time, withholds the totality of its meaning. Different people, equally sensitive, contemplate the icon and interpret it differently. And the meaning is enriched as the icon is brought into different historical and cultural settings and interpreted by different people. The material artifact, the celibate lifestyle undertaken for religious reasons, remains basically the same. And its fundamental meaning, its identity as a response to a Gospel invitation, remains the same. But its being lived by different individuals as integral to their own religious experience allows different facets of the mystery to appear, like the shadows and depths that appear in the icon as different lights play upon it. In what follows we will let the lights of Scripture, history, ecclesial experience, and contemporary concerns play upon this ancient icon.

II. A WINDOW ON THE MYSTERY: MATTHEW 19:12

Matthew 19:12, the so-called "eunuch text," has traditionally been regarded as the biblical basis for the Christian vocation to consecrated celibacy. Recent biblical criticism, however, has raised serious questions about the validity of this position. The text reads:

> For there are eunuchs who have been so from birth, and there are eunuchs who have been made eunuchs by human beings, and there are eunuchs who have made themselves eunuchs for the sake of the kingdom of heaven. Let the one who is able to receive this, receive it.

This text is the conclusion of the passage which begins at 19:3 and is wholly concerned with the issue of divorce and remarriage. When Jesus declares that neither divorce nor marriage to someone divorced is permissible, the disciples conclude that this is such an extreme demand that it would be better not to marry at all. Jesus replies, "Not all can receive this saying, but only those to whom it has been given" (19:11) and then adds the eunuch text. Because of its context Matthew 19:12 must be understood as part of the teaching on divorce and remarriage. It is not a separate logion on celibacy which stands alone.

There are two interrelated questions which must be answered in order to ascertain the meaning of this text and what it might have to do with consecrated celibacy. The first is what the text means in the context of Matthew's Gospel. The second is what the logion itself means since, for various reasons, it would seem that this saying comes directly from Jesus rather than from the evangelist who used it in the context of the divorce controversy.[2]

A number of suggestions have been made by exegetes about the meaning of the text in its Gospel context. Three which seem to have some cogency are the following:

(1) The eunuch text refers to the continence of those Christians whose marriages have ended in divorce and who must, in fidelity to the Lord's command, remain henceforth unmarried.[3]

(2) The text refers to the continence required of the Christian who was married to a converted pagan and whose spouse returned to his or her pagan culture leaving the Christian, still validly married, alone.[4]

(3) The text is an *a fortiori* type argument. The disciples have responded to Jesus' teaching on the indissolubility of marriage by declaring that it is virtually impossible. Jesus responds that it is not impossible; on the contrary, there are even people who have renounced marriage altogether. But just as the ideal of Christian marriage is not assimilable by all, but only by those to whom it is given (namely, Jesus' disciples), so the vocation to celibacy because of the reign of God is understandable only to some (namely, Jesus' disciples).[5]

In my opinion, the third thesis is preferable, although all three are plausible. It seems clear that the eunuch text must be understood as somehow integral to the argument about the indissolubility of marriage. And it seems equally clear from the structure of the logion that the "eunuch because of the kingdom" is to be understood by analogy with those congenitally impotent (those who are eunuchs from birth) and those who have been castrated (those made eunuchs by others). The absoluteness of the incapacity for marriage in these two cases suggests that the eunuch because of the kingdom is not simply someone who, having enjoyed marriage and remaining capable of it, would be free to marry again if the divorced spouse died, but who practices continence for religious reasons. The text suggests an absolute and irrevocable decision not to marry at all, a decision based on some kind of "incapacity" which is here explained as *dia tēn basileian tōn ouranon,* "because of the kingdom (or reign) of heaven (i.e. God)." Furthermore, one who has "made oneself" a eunuch has freely chosen this state, which is not the case if one has been morally obliged to it by the circumstances of a broken marriage.

The suggestion that the eunuch text could be an *a fortiori* argument for continence by those whose marriages have ended in separation or divorce makes good sense of both requirements, namely, interpretation in terms of the marriage context and regarding the state of the eunuch for the sake of the kingdom as a free, absolute, and irrevocable choice. Furthermore, it is at least possible, historically, that the evangelist was using this argument in a demonstrative way. There may well have been, by the time this Gospel was written (c. 70 A.D.), Christians in Matthew's community who had chosen celibacy for the sake of the Gospel. Justin Martyr, who also cites this saying of the Lord but in slightly different form from Matthew, records that there were men and women virgins in the Christian community who had lived this way to the age of sixty or seventy.[6] Justin was writing around 110 A.D., so the virgins to whom he referred had made their choice before the year 70. Furthermore, Paul recommended celibacy to Christians in general in 1 Corinthians (7:32–35) which was written in the middle of the first century. Consequently, if celibacy for evangelical reasons was already being practiced by some among the first generations of Christians, Matthew's argument would have had a concrete referent which other Christians could not gainsay. His argument would be, "If some of the members of our community can renounce marriage altogether for the sake of the Gospel, those who are married can be faithful, and those whose marriages have ended in separation or divorce can remain continent." The heroism required to observe the teaching of Jesus on the indissolubility of marriage is no greater than that asked of those called to celibacy because of the kingdom.

Our conclusion, then, is that the eunuch text, as it stands in Matthew's Gospel, is about celibacy freely chosen for evangelical reasons. Whether the celibacy described as "because of the kingdom" is a hypothetical example, the continence demanded by the breakdown of a Christian marriage, or (as we have suggested) the real state of life of some of the Christians in the community who are here being used as an example and encouragement to their married fellow Christians, the context of the text is the divorce controversy and the subject is Christian celibacy.

This brings us to our second question, namely, what did this saying mean originally, before Matthew used it in his passage on marriage and divorce? There are a number of reasons for holding that this saying comes from Jesus himself.[7] It is hardly imaginable that the first generations of Christians, whether of Gentile or Jewish origin, would have considered celibacy an ideal. In particular, although celibacy seems to have been practiced at least for a time by the members of certain Jewish sects, it was not only not considered an ideal in mainstream Judaism but was even considered reprehensible.[8] And the eunuch was a religious outcast.[9] The notion of celibacy as a religious and spiritual ideal is so original in relation to Jewish tradition that it is difficult to imagine the first generation of Christians developing it "out of whole cloth," that is, without some incentive from the teaching of Jesus himself.

Secondly, the crudeness of the image of the eunuch makes it even more difficult to imagine that the evangelist would have invented this saying and placed it on the lips of Jesus if Jesus had never said such a thing. It has been convincingly argued that "eunuch" was a term of derision directed at Jesus himself by his enemies.[10] Jesus was accused of being a glutton and drunkard (cf. Mt 11:19), of associating with sinners (cf. Mt 9:1), of being a country bumpkin with no prophetic credentials (cf. Jn 7:52), of being a blasphemer (Lk 5:21), of being possessed (cf. Jn 8:48), perhaps even of being illegitimate (cf. Jn 8:41). His usual tactic was to turn these insulting epithets into commentaries on his person and work. If Jesus, because he was unmarried, was derisively called a eunuch, it is quite plausible that he accepted the insult and turned it into a statement about himself. But what is the statement? Jesus would be saying that he had made himself a eunuch (that is, one who is incapable of marriage) because of the kingdom of heaven.

The first problem in understanding the statement of Jesus concerns the interpretation of *diá*. It can mean "because," referring to that which brings something about. Or it can mean "for the sake of," referring to that for which something exists or is done. Kodell argues that *diá* is basically causal, and because Matthew always uses *diá* in the causal sense the word should be interpreted causally in this text.[11] But this only tells us how *Matthew* understood and/or used the expression. It does not tell us what Jesus meant. In fact, the ambiguity of the construction is probably to be considered, if not deliberate, at least fortunate.

The reign of God can well be considered both the cause and the goal of Christian celibacy. Kodell suggests that for Jesus, his experience of the kingdom was such that it caused him to remain celibate. But it might also be the case that it was his concern to announce the kingdom, to establish it, that caused him to remain celibate.

In the first case, the explanation of Jesus' celibacy would be in terms of intense religious experience, that somehow Jesus' experience of God established him in a state of life that was completely original in relation to his religious tradition. We can ask what that experience was and why celibacy was the result. Was it the imminence of the kingdom which made marriage inadvisable? Or was it the totality of the demands of the kingdom which excluded other concerns? Or was it that Jesus' experience of God was so perfectly unitive, so utterly absorbing, that it precluded any other exclusive union? We will never know the answer to these questions.

In the second case, the explanation would be in terms of his mission—that Jesus' sense of urgency about the preaching and establishing of the reign of God which he believed to be "at hand" so consumed his life energies that he could not settle down in the role of husband and father. His need to be "about his Father's business" (Lk 2:49) had become not only the dominant but the only concern of his life. Again, we will never know just how Jesus experienced his mission or what it suggested to him about his lifestyle. The celibacy of Jesus is the first icon of the reign of God. The direction of interpretation is given in the practice itself, but the meaning exceeds our interpretive powers and yields itself only to continuing contemplation.

If it is the case that Jesus himself is the source of the saying about celibacy freely chosen because of the reign of God and that he himself was its first subject, we can draw several conclusions. First, this would explain both the crudeness of the metaphor of the "eunuch" and its maleness. The term was directed at the man Jesus by his enemies and taken up by him in response.

Second, it would also help explain the closing line, "Let the one who can receive this, receive it." The Greek term *chōreō* means "receive" or "make room for." In this passage it is used

both for those who can "receive" Jesus' teaching on the indissolubility of marriage (v. 11) and for those who can "receive" the
teaching about celibacy (v. 12). Obviously, the referent in v. 11,
in the context of Matthew's Gospel, is all Christians who in this
respect are being challenged beyond the natural law and even
beyond the Law of Moses (vv. 7–9). It would seem that the par-
allelism indicates that v. 12 also refers to all Christians. Jesus says
that *some* have made the choice of celibacy, but that *all* are challenged to "receive" or "make room for" this saying. This does
not imply that all Christians should choose celibacy for themselves, but that all must accept it as a valid Christian vocation.
This would be an injunction particularly important for a community such as Matthew's composed largely of Jewish converts
to Christianity, especially if some Christians in the community
had already chosen celibacy. Celibacy was not an acceptable life
choice according to the Law; marriage was the duty of every
Jew. But Matthew presents Jesus as challenging all Christians to
make room in their minds and hearts for a radically new religious life choice: consecrated celibacy. Verse 12 has often been
interpreted as a statement of the superiority of celibacy to marriage on the ground that celibacy is a call not intended for all
Christians but addressed only to an elite. There seems to be
nothing in the Gospel to justify any such ranking among Christians, and a great deal to argue against it (cf., e.g., Mt 23:5–12).
If the foregoing interpretation is correct, Jesus does not say that
celibacy is superior to marriage. Matthew presents Jesus as saying that celibacy is a valid Christian choice and that it is to be
accepted as such by all his disciples.

Third, and most importantly, it would make Jesus himself
the first in the new dispensation to choose celibacy and the
source of its justification as a valid Christian lifestyle. In view of
the non-acceptance of celibacy in Judaism and the arguments
against it on the basis of nature, experience, and, more recently,
psychology, it is important that Christian celibates be able to
claim that Jesus himself validated this choice by word and example. This should not lead to the conclusion that since Jesus
was celibate, celibacy is the superior way to be a Christian, any
more than we should conclude that because Jesus was a male, a
Jew, a carpenter, a Caucasian, that these are normative ways to

be and to live. The problem about celibacy is not whether it is a choice superior to other vocations, but whether it is a valid choice at all. Marriage needs no such dominical sanction because it is written into our very nature and into the Law of Moses. Celibacy does require such sanction because, in very important ways, it runs contrary to the demands of human nature and to the Jewish tradition from which Christianity emerged.

In concluding this section let us turn for a moment to the implications of the foregoing exegesis of Matthew 19:12 for the two categories of Christian celibates which we discussed in the introduction. We spoke first of the "virgins" or those celibates who understand their celibacy as the outward expression of an intense religious experience best described as marriage to Christ. They experience their baptismal union with Christ as so totally absorbing that marital union with anyone else becomes a psychological/spiritual impossibility. Jesus announced the *kingdom or reign of God;* but the early Church announced *Jesus* as the Christ because they understood that the reign of God had arrived in him and would be fully realized at his return in glory. The virgin's adherence to Jesus as sole and total life concern is well expressed as celibacy "because of the reign of God." The virgin's life is consumed by Jesus who is the reign of God already present in this world, just as Jesus' life was consumed with the reign of God that he preached.

The second category of celibates were referred to as those who choose celibacy for ascetical/apostolic reasons. Again, we do not know whether the "because" in the Matthean logion is causal or final. The reign of God which has come in Jesus is, nevertheless, not yet fully realized either in us or among us. There are those who choose celibacy because it is the most effective way in which they can participate in the final establishment of that reign, its final coming in themselves and among all people.

The felicitous ambiguity of the *diá* in Jesus' saying underscores the iconic quality of Jesus' own living of celibacy. Whether the eschatological foundation of consecrated celibacy is understood as realized or as future, it is clear that Christian celibacy is an evangelical mystery, a charism inaugurated in the Church by Jesus himself. As long as our understanding of the meaning of the "reign of God" is incomplete, so will be our understanding of consecrated celibacy chosen "because" of that reign. We do not fully understand what Jesus meant by the reign of God. But as the community of his disciples journeys through history we see different meanings in this tensive symbol of the fullness of salvation.

III. CONSECRATED CELIBACY IN THE CONTEMPORARY CHURCH

If religious celibacy is, as we have tried to suggest, an icon of the reign of God, it follows that each generation of Christians will find, in their contemplation of it, meaning ever ancient but ever new. Some of the meanings will be more evident and more compelling to those who have experienced their own call to consecrated celibacy as a mystical absorption of their life in the mystery of Christ; other meanings will be more readily accessible to those whose choice of celibacy is oriented toward the coming of the reign of God in history. In this section I would like to explore, very briefly, two ways of looking at celibacy that have been meaningful to some people in our own time. These are not the only meanings that this icon yields. Nor are they necessarily the most significant. But they are examples of an ongoing contemplation of this existential mystery that is lived in the heart of the Church and they are offered as a stimulus to both celibates and other Christians to explore in prayer the meaning of this state of life in the community.

A. Making the Paschal Mystery Visible in Time

From the earliest days of the Church's existence martyrdom and virginity were regarded as particularly striking and exemplary participations in the death of the Lord. In some way virginity and martyrdom were seen as essentially identical, both being reversals in the life of the Christian of the victory of sin and death in human life. In the Old Testament the two symbols of the power of sin were childlessness and death. These two realities were essentially identical, for what death cut off for the individual, childlessness cut off for the people. Jesus accepted into his life both celibacy and death and abolished their ancient meaning as the victory of sin by transforming them into the victory of eternal life.

The Christian community will never finish its work of contemplating the meaning of the death of Jesus. By it he entered into our sinful existence, established solidarity with all suffering humanity, forgave his enemies, did ultimate battle with the forces of evil. But there is something else about the death of Jesus which throws some light on the paschal significance of virginity as martyrdom.

Death as a human reality is the end of personal existence. It ruptures the most intimate relationships, rings down the curtain on life work and achievement, erases our presence from this world. Because it is the end of life the Jews understood it as the effect of sin. God is life and whatever is in union with God lives. To die is to lose touch with God which is the very definition of sin. Jesus entered into the experience of human death; what he did with death is what changed everything.

It is important for us, no matter how difficult we find it to do so, to realize that Jesus underwent the experience of death as every human being must. We tend to imagine that he had read the script ahead of time and knew that as soon as the curtain went down on the Calvary act he could "un-die." This is not what the Gospel tells us. Jesus was terrified of death, begged to be spared, and experienced the absolute abandonment by God that the human experience of separation from life entails (cf. Mk 15:34). Every person who faces death stands at a crossroads. One road is marked with the sign of human wisdom which tells us that death is the enemy that will finally win; that death is the descent into nothingness, the end of all our loves and all our works. The other road is marked with the sign of faith. Faith defines death as the final passage from this world to God, the moment of total loving surrender of ourselves into the hands of the God whom we do not see but in whom we believe.

Jesus stood at this crossroads at the moment of his own death. All those around him, and his own inner experience of abandonment, urged him down the road of human wisdom toward the death of ultimate despair. Jesus chose the road of radical faith. He transformed his death from defeat at the hands of finitude and evil into the ultimate act of self-gift, thereby changing forever the significance of death itself. But why, we might ask, was his death a more total expression of his self-gift to God than was his life? Obviously, it wasn't—but it was a more immediate and visible expression of what his life had been. The ultimate character of the death-decision arises from its unequivocal irreversibility. Jesus, at the moment of his death, had no tangible assurance that there was anything (much less anything good) on the other side of his last breath. Both everything and nothing were equally possible. To choose God in the face of the very real possibility that there was no God who could save him from death was an act of radical love which was infinite in intensity and extension, which was unambiguously clear, and which was absolutely irreversible.

John's Gospel calls the death of Jesus his glorification. The full revelation of who Jesus really was, as Son of God, was visible in his death as self-gift in love to the one he called his Father. Nothing further could be revealed; the revelation could be no clearer. The resurrection was the manifestation to Jesus' disciples of the meaning of his death. The glorified Jesus bears in his body the wounds of his death because his glory is the beauty of his death. By dying of love Jesus reversed the meaning of death for all those who could and would die as he had. The martyrs were the prototypical followers of Jesus because they died as he did, commending themselves in faith and love to Christ as he had offered himself to God.

Celibacy in the early Church was considered the strict equivalent of martyrdom. Not to marry, not to found a family, is a choice not to build oneself into the future of the race, not to immortalize the self in the only way known to human wisdom. It is to make one's own death final from the human point of view. Such a choice is total in its intensity and extension because it takes in the whole of one's own life and of one's possible progeny. With terrifying clarity and absolute irreversibility one chooses what can only be seen, from the human point of view, as death. There is no verifiable assurance that there is any value in this act, that there is anything on the other side of this death. Just as the death of Jesus involved a rupture with all that he knew, humanly, as life, so celibacy involves a rupture with our own power to live on in this world.

Just as the death of Jesus was merely the execution of a criminal to many who witnessed it or heard about it, so the choice of celibacy is meaningless and bizarre to many of our contemporaries. But to those who had eyes to see, to the centurion at the foot of the cross who saw how different this man's death was from the many others he had witnessed, to the beloved disciple who saw blood and water flow from the pierced side and knew that that stream would fertilize the whole earth, this death was the revelation of divine glory. The Church has always had eyes to see in the choice of consecrated celibacy a striking representation of the death of Jesus in all its human suffering and mysterious divine glory.

Part of the vocation of the religious in the Church is to manifest the glory of death freely chosen in faith as passage to God. All Christians must die; and the challenge of each is to transform death into life by transforming what comes as necessity into an act of ultimate freedom, the final act of love. Religious, by their choice of consecrated celibacy, raise that Christian choice to striking visibility in the Church. Vatican II proclaimed: "The religious state . . . foretells the resurrected state and the glory of the heavenly kingdom" (*Lumen Gentium*, VI, 44). At least it is possible that such be the case. It was the quality of Jesus' death that made it revelatory, that made his dying a glorification. The clarity of the witness of religious celibacy depends on the quality of the life religious live.

B. Consecrated Celibacy as Facilitator of Ministry

From the time of St. Paul celibacy has been proposed to Christians as a way of freeing themselves to participate wholeheartedly in the quest for personal holiness and in the ministry of the Church. This is at least part of the theoretical justification offered for mandatory celibacy for the clergy. In our own times there is much that demands a careful re-examination of this approach. First, it is clear to many people in the Church, especially to some of the clerics involved, that celibacy not only does not facilitate ministry in the lives of some people but that it constitutes a substantial obstacle to their ministry. Second, it is abundantly clear from Christian experience that married ministers, both Protestant ordained ministers and Catholic non-ordained ministers, are no less effective and are often more effective in ministry than their celibate colleagues. But aside from these experiential arguments against the universal validity of such a position, there are theological reasons for questioning it. To maintain that celibacy makes one more available for God or more free for mission is to maintain that matrimony is an impediment to holiness and to ministry. This is a theologically untenable position. Matrimony is a sacrament, the very sacrament which manifests the mystery of the Church itself as nuptial union between Christ and his body (cf. Eph 5:25–32). That which sanctifies both the marriage partners and the Church itself cannot be considered an obstacle to either holiness or ministry.

Secondly, deeply embedded in this falacious argument that the celibate is more apt for holiness and for ministry than the married person is a profound and un-Christian suspicion of sexual intimacy. Sexual intimacy between married Christians is not only not an obstacle to intimacy with God; it is a divinely ordained, indeed sacramental, means to the experience of the love of God and is the normal path to human affective maturity which grounds the capability for love of God and neighbor. Christianity has a long history of semi-Manichean fear of the flesh, of women, of intimacy, of sexuality. This aberration has had particularly noxious effects not only on the theology of marriage but also on the theology of consecrated celibacy, and it would seem that part of the task of reimagining celibacy as a value in the Church today is a definitive repudiation of these un-Christian fears and their destructive implications.

Having disassociated ourselves, however, from these inappropriate arguments, it is important to raise the question of how the choice of celibacy "in view of the reign of God" is to be understood. If marriage is not an impediment to our seeking of the reign of God, in what sense can celibacy be considered a facilitator of that quest? First of all, it seems fairly clear from human experience that there are some people whose characteristic way of devoting themselves to any goal or task involves a certain exclusivity. There are artists, intellectuals, social activists, professionals of all kinds, who either have not, or should not have, married. For them, their work is all-engrossing and they cannot give themselves to both their work and a family. Invariably, in such cases, it is the family which suffers. Perhaps the classic example of this type of person is Socrates whose poor wife is the patron saint of those who have been abandoned without being divorced. Gandhi is a modern example of someone who perhaps should never have married or had children. But one has only to consider others, such as Coretta Scott and Martin Luther King, Jr., to realize that the incompatibility between total involvement in a life project and complete devotion to and responsibility for a family is temperamental rather than necessary. In short, for *some* people celibacy facilitates ministry by removing competing concerns, but this is so because of their own personalities, not because of the nature of celibacy, marriage, or ministry.

However, this practical incompatibility between some people's involvement in ministry and their involvement in a family does not exhaust the significance of celibacy chosen for apostolic reasons. Celibacy is a choice of solitude as a lifestyle. And this lifestyle brings to visibility in the Church something which must be true of every Christian and of every minister, namely, the final solitariness of each of us in our relationship with God and the ultimate totality of the claims which the reign of God makes on each of us. When the celibacy of a minister is freely chosen in response to a personal vocation (not imposed by law or as a condition of ministry) it can help to bring to the consciousness of all the ultimate all-sufficiency of God as the center of our lives and the real possibility of finding full personal satisfaction and life meaning in the seeking of the reign of God and God's justice. In other words, there is a certain vital symbolic appropriateness of celibacy as a visible manifestation of the inner meaning of the quest for the reign of God. But this symbolic appropriateness should not be transmuted into necessity or universality. Much less should it be made the basis for reducing the married to second class status in the Church. Every Christian is called not only to personal holiness but also to a participation in the Church's ministry of announcing good news to the poor. Some are called to manifest visibly in the Church the totality and exclusivity of that vocation by a life of consecrated celibacy. Others are called to manifest visibly the faithful love of God that is the meaning of the good news by a life of married fidelity. Each of us needs the witness of the other lest celibacy become institutionalized selfishness or marriage privatized self-seeking. Consecrated celibacy, like matrimony, makes an essential contribution to the Church's self-understanding as mission and self-expression in ministry.

IV. THE CELIBACY OF JESUS AND HISTORICAL LIBERATION

In this final section we turn our attention again to the celibacy of Jesus as it is presented to us in the Gospel, not to ascertain the basic meaning of consecrated celibacy, but to see how Jesus' lifestyle can assist us in reimagining celibacy in the context of the characteristic concern of our own age, human liberation. A contemporary biblical scholar, Robert Funk, wrote:

> The Christ-event gives rise to innumerable futures just because it is a historical event and has to be appropriated historically. *The meaning of the Christ-event is disclosed only in the faith to which it gives rise.* Like the Christ-event faith too is historical. It follows that the Christ-event can be appropriated faithfully only in relation to particular contexts. A single monolithic tradition would yield ahistorical faith and an ahistorical Christ. A historical Christ and historical faith necessarily give rise to a multiplicity of traditions and interpretations.[12]

If this is true of the tradition as a whole, it is also true of particular facets of the tradition, such as consecrated celibacy as a Christian lifestyle.

Jesus, the Gospel implies, was celibate by choice. If our exegesis of Matthew 19:12 is correct, he gave only one indication of the meaning of that choice. His celibacy was chosen *diá* the kingdom of heaven. But neither Jesus himself nor the evangelists give us any specification of the relationship between the celibacy of Jesus and the kingdom of heaven. I have been trying to suggest, throughout this chapter, that this non-specification is not an impoverishment but an invitation to contemplation. Each generation of Christians must ask anew about its meaning. And each generation will inevitably ask in the context of its own historical situation.

Our situation today is one of unprecedented concern with human liberation. The characteristic theological development of our time is liberation theology, whether third world, feminist, black, or South African. What we have discovered through the eyes of the oppressed is that the Gospel is about liberation, not just in the afterlife but in this world. The Gospel is not a support for the oppressive status quo and an opiate for the victimized. It is a call for liberation addressed alike to oppressed and oppressor. If the vocation to celibacy is a Gospel call it must have something to do with this work of liberation, and the relation between celibacy and liberation is to be sought first of all in the experience of Jesus himself.

Jesus' celibacy can only be understood in terms of his own cultural context. It must be set against the background of the understanding of sexuality, marriage, and celibacy in the world of first century Judaism. For the Jew of Jesus' time celibacy was not a choice. Marriage was the duty of every Jew. Children were the real assurance against the final victory of death, both for the individual and for the people. And of a Jewish marriage would be born the Messiah who would finally deliver Israel from sin and slavery.

It was against the background of this monolithic understanding of marriage as fate that Jesus chose not to marry. Among his people sexuality was ordained exclusively to marriage, but Jesus situated himself freely in relationship both to his sexuality and to his future. For him his sexuality was not fate but destiny. His sexuality did not tell Jesus how to be human; rather his humanity defined the meaning of sexuality for him. Perhaps Jesus saw the future of Israel in different terms, not in terms of numbers but in terms of quality of life. Perhaps he knew, somehow, that divine life rather than human offspring is our way of defeating death. In any case, Jesus' choice of celibacy defined sexuality as a zone of freedom rather than as a path of necessity. Jesus did not say that celibacy was superior to marriage; but he did say that marriage was not necessarily either the better way or the only way for an adult human being to seek fulfillment and a future. According to Jesus' praxis, our sexuality does not define us; we define it. Our true identity and destiny are not rooted in ethnicity, progeny, or social role; they are rooted in faith.

A second cultural factor in the situation within which Jesus chose celibacy was patriarchy. In Jesus' world all marriages were patriarchal marriages. The man owned his wife and the relationship between them, however loving it might have been in any actual case, was culturally and religiously defined as one of male domination and female submission. Furthermore, because all were expected to marry and therefore to enter into and perpetuate the patriarchal system, the cultural definition of society itself was hierarchical: men in general were superior to women in general.

By choosing not to marry Jesus chose not to assume the male role in a patriarchal family. He was permanently excluded, by his own choice, from active participation in patriarchy, i.e., in the male domination of women. What we see in the Gospel is the result of this self-imposed exclusion. Jesus considered himself free to relate to all women, not as a married man or as one seeking a wife, not as a single male exercising the privileges of the double standard in the use and abuse of women, but as one person to another. Jesus' culturally strange way of treating women as persons and as equals disturbed his followers (cf. Jn 4:27). So did his choice of women as friends and as disciples (e.g., Lk 24:10–12). So did his acceptance of women branded unacceptable by male standards (Jn 7:53–8:11) and his willingness to be touched by women (e.g., Lk 7:39) and to speak to them in public (Jn 4:27). In a culture which allowed only one way of relating with women, namely, in terms of their sexuality and within a system of domination, Jesus chose a lifestyle which allowed him to relate to women as persons whose reality and value exceeded their sexuality (cf. Lk 11:27–28) and to relate to them as equals.

A third cultural factor in Jesus' situation had to do with the Jews' self-understanding as the chosen people. For the Jew, the key to salvation was membership in the community of Israel, that is, family membership. Family was a supremely important value, and the family in question was the biological family within which alone one could be born into the chosen people.

Jesus was born a Jew. But he repudiated the strictly ethnic understanding of both family and salvation. To be a child of Abraham according to the flesh was not a guarantee of salvation (cf. Jn 8:31–59). It was not family established by sexual relations, but faith manifested in the doing of God's will, that made one a member of the family of God (cf. Mk 3:31–35). Jesus never said that biological family was humanly unimportant, but he did maintain that it was not the key to salvation.

In summary, what does the celibacy of Jesus contribute to our contemporary concern with liberation? First, by his celibacy Jesus freed himself (and his disciples of all time) from the "fateful" understanding of human life that had paralyzed the religious imagination for so long. Sexuality, marriage, family and people, death, are all givens of human experience—but they do not determine us in an absolute way. Sexuality does not necessitate marriage. Masculinity or femininity does not destine us necessarily to dominate or be dominated. Family and people do not determine our inclusion or exclusion from salvation. Death does not define the limits of human existence.

Rather, humanity with all its givens is our destiny. It is an invitation to create an appropriate future for ourselves and for each other. Sexuality is a capacity for freely chosen relationships, relationships with persons of both sexes, relationships of equality, respect, and friendship which may or may not be sexually expressed. Family is our first lesson in the importance of community, but community must extend beyond family. Ethnicity is a grounding in particularity as a necessary condition for transcendence toward universality. Death introduces seriousness and consequence into all our choices. But all of the givens of human existence, most fully symbolized by sexuality itself, are open to our freedom. The celibacy of Jesus is an announcement and a celebration of that freedom. It is not an exaltation of celibacy over marriage, but of freedom over fate.

V. CONCLUSION

The thesis of this essay has been that consecrated celibacy is an icon of a mystery. It is validated but not fully explained by the Gospel as freely chosen, irrevocable non-marriage *because* or *for the sake* of the reign of God. It is an original contribution of the Gospel having no real antecedent in the Jewish tradition. The Christian tradition reveals two major strands of interpretation of the practice of consecrated celibacy: a mystical interpretation of virginity as a nuptial experience of union with Christ; an ascetical interpretation of celibacy as a means to fuller participation in the Church's mission of announcing the reign of God. Various specifications of these two foundational approaches have emerged in the history of the Church and others will emerge in the future. One that might have particular significance for our own time, both as a dimension of the liberty of the spouse of Christ and as a dimension of the praxis of the Christian minister, is the witness celibacy can give to the possibility of the liberation of both men and women from the fatefulness of sexuality. In some mysterious way Jesus transformed the twin symbols of evil, childlessness and death, into symbols of eternal life. In some mysterious way he freed the religious imagination from its imprisonment in fate symbolized by sexuality. The Christian celibate chooses to explore this mysterious revelation by living it as personal lifestyle.

Chapter Eight
RELIGIOUS OBEDIENCE: JOURNEY FROM LAW TO LOVE

The following article was written as part of the final and culminating phase of the Leadership Conference of Women Religious' project "to articulate a contemporary theology of religious life" begun in 1976 and finished in 1980 with the publication of *Starting Points: Six Essays Based on the Experience of U.S. Women Religious* ed. L.A. Quiñonez (Washington, D.C.: LCWR, 1980). It was written at an intensive Writer's Conference where it was repeatedly discussed and criticized by the other five writers and the LCWR personnel conducting the Conference. Since its publication it has been presented and discussed by Region XIV of the Religious Formation Conference, the Bishops and Major Superiors of Men and Women of Indiana, The Leadership Conference of Women Religious at their annual meeting in 1980, the Bishops of the Northwest, the Religious of the Archdiocese of San Francisco, and chapters, formation groups, and consultations in a variety of religious congregations.

Few areas of contemporary religious life have proven as conflictual for religious both as communities and as individuals as that of obedience. While it is undoubtedly true that obedience has never been easy it is probably correct to say that, for most religious prior to Vatican II, it was relatively simple. Obedience meant willing compliance with the commands of superiors and the prescriptions of the rule and/or constitutions.[1] Most religious were not concerned with the distinctions between what was required by the vow and what by the virtue, since the ideal was to obey in all things, and few people who had not internalized that ideal remained long in religious life. Although the rule did not of itself bind under pain of sin, religious were taught that willful infraction of it was rarely without fault. Likewise, the superior's command obliged under pain of sin only when he or she formally commanded in virtue of the vow, but the constitutions of most congregations specified that the superior should be obeyed in all cases, even doubtful ones, unless it was certain that the action commanded was sinful. Religious were assured that every detail of their lives was governed by obedience and was, therefore, the fulfillment of God's will. However difficult or painful it might have been at times to submit, the difficulty usually did not arise from any inner conflict about what constituted the will of God in a particular case. And few religious seriously entertained the alternative of not doing what was commanded.

Today the situation is quite different. Obedience is neither easy *nor* simple. Religious, with increasing frequency, find themselves in the painful situation of sincerely doubting whether they should comply with a certain directive of congregational or ecclesiastical superiors even though there is no question about the legitimacy of the command. Even more agonizing are the situations in which whole congregations find themselves in conflict over ecclesiastical directives.[2]

These conflictual situations are usually articulated by religious themselves as a choice between obedience and disobedience, implying that for them obedience is theoretically and functionally equated with material and formal conformity to the legitimate directives of lawful superiors. The situations in which religious (or congregations) choose to "disobey" are becoming more numerous, and the discomfort these choices provoke arises not only from the conviction that disobedience is morally wrong in itself but also from a realization of the consequences of widespread disobedience for unity and order in Church and congregation.

In what follows I am going to suggest that the simple and unnuanced understanding of obedience according to which a person has only two choices in the face of a legitimate exercise of authority, namely compliance which equals obedience and non-compliance which equals disobedience, needs to be re-examined. The basis for this suggestion is the suspicion that any theological position which repeatedly places large numbers of well motivated and generous people in impossible situations is somehow inadequate. Today large numbers of sincere and generous religious, with increasing frequency, are finding themselves in the impossible situation of having to choose between what they honestly think they should do and "obedience" to legitimate authority. This leads to the suspicion that the inadequacy lies in the traditional theory of obedience (which was reiterated in the documents of Vatican II),[3] rather than in the commitment of the religious. The re-examination of a theological position need not necessarily imply that the theory is false in itself or that it was never adequate. But it does imply that there are significant new factors in the present situation which the traditional theory cannot handle satisfactorily. Just as the invention of nuclear weapons capable of obliterating the human race has rendered the once defensible theory of the "just war" totally inadequate to the present situation (even though still useful in regard to certain aspects of the discussion), so the emergence of religious from the closed and simple context of pre-Vatican II convent life into a complicated involvement in a very complex world has made the traditional theory of obedience inadequate to the present reality of religious life.

In the re-examination which follows there are three foci of reflection. I want to examine first the fundamental value which religious obedience affirms and seeks to foster. Second, I will reflect on the theology of mediation which grounds the position that God's will for the religious is synonymous with the rule and the will of superiors. Third, I will examine the theology of discernment which leads the religious to equate the will of God for him or her with the rule and the commands of superiors. I hope to show that the *fundamental theoretical difficulty* lies in the second area, the theology of mediation; that the *challenge for contemporary religious* lies in the third area, the process of discernment of God's will; that the rethinking of these two aspects *need not negatively affect the fundamental value which religious obedience affirms*.

I. THE MEANING OF THE VOW OF OBEDIENCE

Although it is undeniable that the vow of obedience has played an important role in assuring the good order of community life and the effectiveness of corporate apostolates, these communitarian benefits cannot account for the emergence of this vow as integral to religious life.[4] A vow is not necessary to insure the commitment to the common good and the involvement in common tasks that are intrinsic to full membership in any voluntary society.

The real object of the vow of obedience has always been understood to be the fullest possible union of the religious with the will of God. The effect of the vow was to incorporate all that the religious did into the search for and living out of God's will in which consists all holiness. What the religious does then, in vowing obedience, is to commit himself or herself without reserve to the seeking of the will of God in all circumstances and to fulfilling it with wholehearted dedication not only because one's own holiness lies in this total obedience to God but also in order to extend the reign of God in this world.

Traditional treatments of the vow of obedience (e.g. that of Aquinas in the *Summa Theologiae* II-II, q. 186, art. 2, 5, 6, 7, and 8) present it as obliging religious to a seeking and accomplishing of God's will that goes beyond what is required of the ordinary Christian. Actually, it is very difficult to ground such a contention scripturally,[5] for all disciples of Jesus are called to participate fully in his obedience to his Father's will, even unto death on the cross (cf. Lk 14:27; Mt 10:38–39). None of the biblical texts usually cited to encourage religious in their practice of obedience are actually addressed specifically to any one group of Christians. Wholehearted obedience to God is required of all. Vatican II's explicit recognition of the universality of the call of Christians to holiness, which consists in total commitment to God's will, further discourages religious from regarding their form of Christian life as a higher state or their vocation to obedience as more total or radical.[6]

This leads to the question of how to understand the specificity of the religious vow of obedience. If all Christians are called to a single-minded search for and commitment to God's will in union with Jesus who was obedient unto death, what is the significance of making a *vow* of obedience? How can one vow to do what one is already obliged to do?

One approach to this question consists in interpreting the vow not as specifying *what* religious do, namely, seek and obey the will of God, nor the *degree* to which they seek to do it, namely, as totally as possible, but as specifying the *context* in which they will do it, namely, in a religious community. By entering a particular state in life a Christian places his or her discipleship in a particular setting which determines how it will be lived. Religious are not more obliged to seek and fulfill the will of God than is a married or ordained person. But the context of each is different and this will have a significant effect on where and how God's will will touch the person's life. The married person will seek God's will by taking into account in a particular manner the spouse and children to whom she or he is committed. The religious will seek God's will by taking special account of the community within which she or he is committed. In other words, the vow of obedience does not extend the scope or intensity of obedience to God's will in the life of the religious. It affects the mediations of God's will. Rule, corporate apostolate, community members and leaders enter into the mediation of God's will for the religious in a primary way while other mediations of the divine will, such as family, individual talents, and personal projects are relativized.[7] By the solemn act by which Christians enter a particular state of life in the Church they give a certain very definite shape to their obedience, and that shape is determined by the mediation of God's will that thereby becomes operative and primary in their life. This mediation, in turn, shapes the discernment process by which one seeks to perceive God's will and respond to it.

The point of the foregoing reflections is to locate as precisely as possible our re-evaluation of the theology of religious obedience. The investigation cannot have to do with the substance of the vow, that is, with the object of the vow itself. There can be no theology of religious obedience which does not affirm and foster the wholehearted commitment of the religious to seeking and fulfilling the will of God. Whatever questions we raise, then, will have to do with the understanding of the mediation of God's will that is peculiar to religious life and with the process of discernment through which we respond to that mediation.

II. THE THEOLOGY OF MEDIATION[8]

When we speak of "seeking and fulfilling God's will" we can find ourselves imagining God, ensconced in light inaccessible, contemplating a "divine plan" or a blueprint for our individual and corporate lives and silently challenging us to figure out what is in that plan so that we can carry it out. In this scenario, God knows what we are to do but is not telling. Our job is to somehow "discern" this already decided formula for spiritual success and then to follow it. Obviously if this were the real situation our freedom would be reduced to a game of supernatural "blind-man's buff" played for exceptionally high stakes. This certainly cannot be what obedience to God's will means.

Obedience is really the cultivation of a loving union with God which becomes the ground of all our choices which, in turn, unite us ever more profoundly with God. Consciously united with God we see with God's eyes, judge according to the truth, and choose out of love. In any given situation there may be only one loving thing to do; but in other situations there may be several. It is not always the case that there is one choice which is better than all the others. Nor is it the case that God has pre-judged what we are to do. To seek God's will, to obey God, is to make the most loving choices and decisions of which we are ca-pable with God's help at any given moment. It consists formally in how and why we make a certain choice rather than in what we actually choose (although, as we will see later, the content of the choice is a very important element in the how and why of the choice).

In the final analysis the most perfect source of knowledge of God's will is that profound personal religious experience that we call mystical prayer. Transforming union with God is the only ground for full certitude that we have discovered God's will. Jesus, in his earthly life, seems to have acted often out of such direct personal experience of God. He claimed that the Fa-ther was in him doing his works and that he spoke the words of God (Jn 14:10). Jesus even claimed that he was one with the Fa-ther (Jn 10:30). He frequently acted with perfect assurance, ap-parently certain that he was obeying God, when all the normal indications of God's will, namely, the Law, the religious insti-tutions of Israel, and the Jewish authorities, seemed to suggest the contrary. His cleansing of the Temple (Jn 2:13–22), chal-lenging of the authorities (e.g. Jn 5:17–18), breaking of the tra-ditions (e.g. Mk 7:1–8), association with sinners (e.g. Mt 9:10–

13) testified to a personal access to God's will that gave Jesus himself a remarkable sense of security in the face of challenge and left his contemporaries wondering in amazement at his originality and authority (cf. Mt 7:28–29).

Many of us, however, do not live spiritual lives characterized by continual mystical union with God. In the normal course of events we must seek less absolute indications of God's will. This was certainly the case for Jesus' first disciples. The community sought an indication of God's will regarding Judas' replacement by prayerfully casting lots to decide between the two "finalists" who both seemed equally qualified (Acts 1:21–26). Later, Peter found a very significant indication of the will of God concerning the admission of the Gentiles to the Christian community in a waking dream or trance he had (Acts 10:9–16). In this case the Mosaic Law requiring circumcision seemed such an important mediation of this divine will that only God's direct revelation to Peter was sufficient to ground his decision to set the Law aside and act in the freedom of the Gospel. Later, however, Peter retreated from this courageous Gospel position because he feared condemnation by those who still considered the Law an absolute. And so Paul corrected him publicly and Peter apparently recognized in Paul's admonition an indication of the will of God, a call to conversion (Gal 2:11–21). In other words, the normal way in which most of us seek to know the will of God for ourselves, that is, try to discern what love asks of us in a particular situation, is to seek indications of it in and through human events which we have some reason to think manifest God's purposes to us. This conviction that human realities can manifest God's will to us is the starting point of a theology of mediation as one pole in a dialectical theology of obedience. The other pole is a theology of discernment which will be discussed in the next part of this essay.

In the above examples we see that a variety of human realities, e.g., a prayerful casting of lots, a vision, the Law, the admonition of a fellow Christian, were recognized as mediations of God's will. What is the basis for this recognition? Ultimately this interpretation of human realities as mediations of the divine is grounded in the Judaeo-Christian understanding of revelation. We believe that God participates in human history and consequently nothing in our experience is profane. All creation, and history itself, speaks the glory of God to one who has ears to hear. But only to one who has ears to hear! In other words, the theology of mediation implies a theology of discernment because nothing in our worldly experience is self-evidently expressive of God's will. That means that nothing that happens in our historical experience *has* to be seen as an indication of that will. Whatever seems to the believer to mediate God's will could also be interpreted as a purely natural phenomenon without any relationship to the divine. Furthermore, even if one correctly identifies some human reality as the locus of God's self-revelation she or he could be mistaken about the meaning. It is this intrinsic ambiguity of symbolic (i.e. historical) revelation that calls for discernment and that also leads us to try to establish some criteria for deciding where and how the indications of God's will are actually manifest in our human experience.

Religious institutions are the major way in which human beings try to establish some stable and reliable approach for the discernment of God's will. The Jews regarded the Mosaic Law and the religious authorities who interpreted the Law as the primary mediations of God's will for them. The early Church eventually set aside these Jewish institutions in favor of the Gospel as the primary mediation. By "Gospel" is meant the whole life of Jesus, his teaching, passion, death, resurrection, and the gift of his Spirit to dwell in the community and guide it into all truth. In other words, the true mediation of God's will for the Christian community was Jesus as he continued to live and act in the Church through the preaching of the Word and the celebration of the mysteries of his life.

However, from the very beginning it was clear that not all the complicated situations in the Church's life could be handled adequately by a simple appeal to the Gospel. We have just noted the recourse to secondary mediations such as lots, dreams, the advice of fellow Christians, and tradition to help discover just how the Gospel applied to particular situations in the early Church's life. As the Church expanded to include peoples of a variety of cultures, far distant in space and mentality from the original communities in Jerusalem and Rome, the need for more institutionalized systems of mediation of the Gospel message became imperative. The primary forms of mediation became the deliberations of the community, especially of its officials, and the laws which they gradually formulated. In other words, the Christian community gradually established institutional means of mediating the Gospel to the individual believer or to the community as a whole. Laws, traditions, and customs as interpreted by properly appointed officials became the ordinary loci of the expression of God's will, the ordinary mediation of the Gospel.

The theology and institutionalization of mediation are well-founded in the Judaeo-Christian understanding of symbolic revelation. But this theology is also extremely susceptible to serious deformation. When a mediator ceases to be transparent, begins to present itself rather than what it mediates, it becomes an idol. It no longer functions as the locus of the meeting of God and the human worshiper and becomes itself a god. Rather than being that through which God speaks, it begins to "speak for God" and finally sets itself up as a "vicar of God," one who "takes the place of God" in the life of the creature. The creature becomes incapable of distinguishing the voice of God from its human presentation. The only ultimate safeguard against this subtle deception is the believer's personal religious experience. For the truly holy, their direct personal relationship with God in prayer functions as a touchstone for the authenticity of that which presents itself through human mediation. But for the person whose religious experience is entirely localized in the mediations themselves, who has no direct access to God by means of a mature prayer life, there is almost no way to avoid the idolizing of the mediation. John the Baptist and Jesus were apparently among the few people of their time whose direct experience of God was such that it functioned as a relativizing judgment on the Law, the traditions, and the civil and religious officials of first century Judaism.

The weaker a person's personal religious experience the more dependent she or he is on human mediation of the divine will. In other words, the tendency of the mediators to substitute themselves for God by equating their own will with the divine will meets the need of the semi-religious individual to know the divine will with a kind of mechanical certitude. The resulting unhappy marriage is what we should call legalism but often call obedience. Actually, it is the death of obedience in the desert of alienation. In this case certain institutions, either persons or laws or customs or practices, are purely and simply equated with God's will for the person. Obedience ceases to be the constant actualizing of love in one's judgments and choices and becomes a more or less willing, but lifeless, conformity to law which is indeed without tension or ambiguity but is also stripped of originality and creativity. The individual's personal authority, that is, her or his experience of being the author of her or his own decisions which flow from an inner source of union with God, is alienated and comes to be located in persons and laws with whom the person has only an extrinsic relationship. This alienation takes place so unobtrusively that it is often not noticed. How many pre-Vatican II Catholics surrendered their personal moral authority by "asking Father" what to do and blindly accepting his reply as God's will? How many religious rules counseled the members that "in cases of doubt it is always better to obey [meaning to do what one is told to do] because even if the command is an error, one never errs in obeying"? It is worthwhile to examine this subtle but total subversion of the true dynamic of mediation because the bind in which religious so often find themselves today is the effect on the process of discernment of this deformation in the theology of mediation.

A theology of mediation is grounded in the Judaeo-Christian theology of historical revelation. When a person chooses to shape his or her Christian discipleship within the framework of a particular state of life, such as marriage or religious life, the person is acting on the conviction that this choice is a response to a call from God. If this is true, that is, if God has called one to live one's life in a certain context, one is justified in believing that the realities of that context constitute a privileged locus of God's will for oneself. A married person has a right to trust that his or her spouse and their life together are a privileged locus of the mediation of God's will for him or her; religious have a right to trust that the rule, leaders, members, and mission of their congregation are a privileged locus of the mediation of God's will for them. But a simple mechanical equation of the privileged mediation with the voice of God is not justified. It is always God's voice one must listen for, and there is no absolute assurance that any human reality is always the bearer of that voice. One should indeed always listen to the privileged mediations in one's life with a special attentiveness, but one is not thereby dispensed from personal discernment about whether and to what degree what one is hearing *in this instance* is the expression of the will of God. Sometimes it might not be. In other words, a theology of mediation which dispenses one from discernment is a regression into magic, a virtual consulting of oracles which alienates the responsibility and authority of the one who "obeys" and deprives the "obedience" of its truly religious character.

If it is true that not every utterance of legitimate authority is *ipso facto* the voice of God, what is the touchstone of the truly authoritative utterance? When is the word of the privileged mediator truly the expression of God's will for me? Quite simply when, and to the extent that, it is the Word of God. In other words, what is said does not become the Word of God by being uttered by an authority. On the contrary, what the person in authority says becomes divinely authoritative when, and to the extent that, it is the Word of God. Now, obviously, by the Word of God I do not mean the material text of the Bible but rather the content of the good news of salvation brought to us in Jesus. There is no mechanical test for the presence of the Word in concrete utterances of persons in authority. One can recognize the total absence of the Word in a command that involves sin. But the absence of sin does not *ipso facto* assure us that the command is an expression of the Word of God. It might be either the simple exercise of human authority (which will be discussed below) or even an error. In other words, there is no technique, no rule of thumb, by which we can excuse ourselves from the often agonizing procedure which is the necessary correlative of the human mediation of God's will, namely, discernment.

A command is divinely authoritative, and therefore places an absolute claim upon the conscience, only to the extent that the command is truly the Word of God, the actualization of the Gospel here and now, in and for this situation. We are certainly justified in starting with a positive assumption when the one commanding is exercising legitimate authority and the command given is a legitimate command. But we are not justified in ending there. We do have good reason to expect to find the will of God expressed to us in the privileged loci of mediation which are integral to our vocation. But we cannot turn this expectation into a requirement that God guarantee every act of authority or compensate us for the latter's mistakes by suspending our responsibility for the evil or error involved in our "obedience." In other words, "blind obedience" is magic, not faith. It is an attempt to manipulate God by technique. The simple equation without remainder of the will of the finite mediator with the will of the Infinite mediated is idolatry, not obedience. It is the creation and worship of a strange god.

Before turning to the difficult question of discernment we must touch on one more aspect of mediation, namely, the distinction (which is often obscured) between the command which is absolutely authoritative because it is an expression of the Word of God, and a command which has the relative authority that derives from the covenantal quality of the Christian community, whether Church, family, parish, or religious congregation.[9] Absolute obedience, that is, a person's wholehearted, immediate and interior submission, is the unreserved self-surrender that we call worship and it can be directed only to God. It is what Paul refers to as "the obedience of faith" (Rom 1:5). It is the "obedience unto death" (Phil 2:8) that Jesus offered to his Father.

But there is another, a relative and human, obedience by which we freely follow the will of another because it is fitting to do so. It should perhaps be called "religiously motivated cooperation"[10] rather than obedience, for, in reality, it is obedience only because it is part of our obedience to God which embraces every aspect of our lives.

Within the Christian community, as in any community, some stable order is necessary and that involves an apportioning of duties and responsibilities. Thus, some people in the community will make some decisions in some areas which others will be expected to follow. In a religious community these decisions will often have religious content. They will be concerned with such things as how people are to conduct themselves at worship,

who is to preach and teach, how the sacraments are to be cele-
brated, what religious practices are to be observed and so on.
And the reasons given for what is asked will usually be religious
reasons. There will be a conscious effort to show, for example,
that there is biblical warrant for calling these particular rituals
sacraments and these others sacramentals, for requiring certain
practices, and for instituting certain customs. It is very easy for
such human, religious provisions to appear to the devout believer as all of a piece with the Gospel itself. This certainly happened among Jesus' contemporaries. Jesus frequently pointed
out that the legitimate religious laws and customs that Jewish authority had put in place had become so confused with the Law
itself that the leaders of the people had come, at times, to prefer
their traditions to God's commandments (cf. Mk 7:7–9). In
other words, not everything which is sacred is therefore divine.
Just because a provision is religious in content and is proposed
by religious authority, it does not thereby become the absolutely
authoritative proclamation of the will of God.

St. Paul provides us with a good example of this distinction.
In 1 Corinthians 11:1–16 Paul deals with the question of the at-
tire of men and women taking active roles in the Christian liturgical assembly. He begins, "I commend you because you
remember me in everything and maintain the traditions even as
I have delivered them to you." He then goes on to say that men
should not wear head coverings while participating in liturgy
but that women should. He attempts to give reasons from Scripture and from nature for the appropriateness of this tradition.
In other words, he tries to ground his orders in the sacred. He
wants to assure his readers that he is not being arbitrary but is
trying to provide for order in the community according to religious principles. However, when he finishes his admonition on
the subject of head coverings, he concludes by saying, "If anyone is disposed to be contentious (i.e., over his orders about at-
tire), we recognize no other practice, nor do the churches of
God." In other words, when all is said and done, Paul is making
human provision for good order in the community and calling
upon his readers to conform to his decisions because they are
responsible members of the covenant community. He obviously

expects them to cooperate. But he makes no claims to divine authority in this matter, nor does he threaten divine sanctions for non-compliance.

It is quite otherwise in the passage which follows immediately, 1 Corinthians 11:17–34, which has to do with the very nature of the Eucharist. The subject is the unity of the eucharistic community. After vigorously reprimanding the community for its divisions, he substantiates his position by saying, "For I received from the Lord what I also delivered to you. . . ." He goes on to say that one who eats and drinks at the eucharistic table unworthily "will be guilty of profaning the body and blood of the Lord" and "eats and drinks judgment upon himself." The community is to be converted and act worthily in the eucharistic action "lest you come together to be condemned."

The difference between the two sections of this one chapter is striking. In the first Paul is exercising his legitimate covenantal authority. He expects cooperation. But he in no way intimates that his command is God's command and that it is sanctioned by divine judgment. When, however, he deals with the substance of the Eucharist he makes it clear that he speaks not from his own authority as community leader but with the authority of Jesus Christ whose Word he is proclaiming to the community. He applies this Word to the concrete situation and implies that the application participates in the authority of the Word. Failure to heed this command is to invite divine judgment.

The point here is that it is the content of the command, not the position in the community of the one issuing it, which qualifies some commands as the divine will. It is only when the community authority brings to bear upon community life the Gospel in its integrity that he or she can claim to speak with divine authority, for in such a case it is not the person who speaks but Jesus who addresses his Church through this human mediator. This is the only valid grounds for speaking of one in authority "holding the place of Christ."

Relatively few commands of Church or congregational officials are laden with the authority of the Word of God.[11] Directives about what religious should wear, for example, or how the day should be ordered for prayer, or who should be responsible for community government, or what kinds of dwellings are suitable for religious do not partake of divine authority which calls for the immediate and unreserved submission of absolute obedience. It is not necessary to attempt to invest the exercise of covenantal authority in the Church or congregation with divine authority in order for the former to be considered genuinely authoritative. Rather, it is a great disservice to the people of God to foster such confusion under the misguided conviction that things will be better ordered if people think they owe absolute obedience to all the commands of legitimate authority. Religious especially need to be fully conscious of this distinction. The dilemma which prompts this re-evaluation of religious obedience, namely, the simplistic and dichotomous formulation of the choice one faces once a legitimate command has been issued (i.e., as a choice between "obedience" and "disobedience" to God speaking through the rule or superior), arises from a failure to understand this distinction. It might be helpful if we could restrict the use of the word "obedience" to those situations in which we are faced with the Word of God and spoke of "covenantal cooperation" in those situations in which we are dealing with human authority in a religious context. This is not really practical, however, because in many situations a legitimate command is a mixture of the call to conversion demanded by the Word of God and practical applications or provisions which do not have any necessary relation to the absolutely authoritative claim of the Gospel. This is what brings us to our third area of reflection, the theology of discernment in relation to religious obedience.

III. THE THEOLOGY OF DISCERNMENT

In the foregoing section of this essay I attempted to clarify the crucial distinction between the Gospel, which is the sole absolutely authoritative address made to the conscience of the Christian whether religious or lay, and the entire range of legitimate human authority operative within the congregation because of its nature as a covenant community. I tried to suggest that the legitimate religious authority which is operative in the vast majority of the cases in which religious experience obedience conflicts is relative human authority that does not, by the very fact of its exercise, demand absolute obedience. Deciding how to respond to such an exercise of authority in a given case, that is, what response can be integrated into one's obedience to God which embraces the whole of one's life, is the work of discernment.

In the first section below I would like to sketch, very briefly, how the dialectical relationship between mediation and discernment has traditionally been structured, how and why this structure is being undermined in post-conciliar religious life, and how the dialectic seems to be restructing itself. In the second section I will suggest a biblical model for this dialectic which might prove more useful for some religious than the traditional legal and/or philosophical models.

A. The Evolution of the Dialectical Structure of Covenantal Obedience

By "covenantal obedience" I mean the dialectical relationship between the mediations of God's will, that is, the legitimate institutions of covenantal authority such as rule and leadership, and the process of discernment of God's will by the individual or community to whom the legitimate command is addressed. This structure seems to be a triadic relationship among three elements: life, law and theology. I wish to define "life" and "law" in the most inclusive way possible. By "life" I mean the full range of the person's experience, that is, of his or her conscious existence. By "law" I mean all specific exercises of covenantal authority whether these are written or oral, codified or occasional, general or specific, applying to all or directed to an individual, normative or prescriptive. "Theology" will be understood in two ways. In one sense, theology is the professional activity of the trained specialist who systematically brings Scripture and tradition into dialogue with human experience in historical contexts in order to further the Church's understanding of its faith and the impact of faith on human history. In another sense, theology denotes the informal but disciplined reflection which the serious religious does upon her or his own experience in the light of a prayerful knowledge of Scripture, tradition, and other theological sources. The latter type of theology should be well informed by the former type but it is not the work of the theological specialist as such.

1. *The Traditional Structure:* Until the period of Vatican II the relationship among life, law, and theology was a stable (if not sclerotic!) constellation of virtually unchanging elements. Law had an unquestioned priority over life and theology. It was actually from canon law that religious life derived its forms, its operation, and its very self-definition. The striking uniformity of religious across national and congregational lines in virtually everything considered "essential" to religious life testified eloquently to the priority of law over life. Theology of religious life was reflection on law, i.e., on canon law, official documents, and the particular law of the congregation. The task of theology was primarily to explain and justify the law. It should, of course, be remarked that this priority of law over life and the reduction of theology to care-taker status was not peculiar to religious life. It characterized the life of the Church as a whole.

2. *The Subversion of the Traditional Structure:* It is somewhat difficult to locate chronologically the point at which this stable constellation of unchanging elements began to undergo a certain "shake-up." It certainly began before Vatican II and is definitely still in progress. It is constituted by the destabilizing of the relationship among the three elements. Law has lost its clear priority in relation to life and theology. The previous stable constellation has been replaced by a dynamic tension between life and law which has cast theology into a strange position of priority.

There is no need to describe the developments in the life of religious which began, particularly for women religious in the United States, with the Sister Formation Movement in the 1950's. Much of what developed in the life experience of religious was either actually contrary to the law or so original as to have no real relationship, positive or negative, to it. The tension between what religious were living and what their law said they should be and do caused extreme malaise both in superiors whose role was understood canonically to be that of preserving the community in fidelity to the tradition, and in the individual religious sincerely committed to the life she had vowed and deeply influenced by the understanding of authority and obedience characteristic of the Tridentine Church. Superiors found themselves challenged to lead their congregations into an uncharted future for which present law was inadequate; individual religious experienced the call to venture beyond the limits of what was permitted by common or particular law and often into conflict with superiors.

Religious in conflict situations had no schema within which to situate their conflicts except that of obedience/disobedience in the absolute sense, that is, the schema which I have tried to show is validly operative only in relationship to the Gospel itself. Some religious resigned themselves to being "disobedient" because they felt themselves imperatively called by Gospel values which, for some reason, seemed to conflict with the law. Others, unable to tolerate a self or community image that included what they understood as disobedience, opted for a rigid traditionalism which would allow them to die faithful to the commitments which they had made. For the first group their "disobedience" has become perhaps less traumatic as instances of it multiplied but it has remained somewhat personally conflictual and often deeply divisive of community. For the second group, their own dogged fidelity to an older model of religious life has cast them in a reactionary role that many do not relish and divided them ideologically and personally from the more vital elements in their own communities. What does not seem to have happened on any wide scale is a fundamental questioning, systematically carried out, of the validity of the schema which immediately situates every command of every authority on the scale obedience/disobedience and demands a choice between the two.

The role of theology in the tension between life and law has been varied. Theology in one sense *precipitated* the tension. It was the developments in ecclesiology, biblical studies, and liturgy in particular, along with an increasingly historical approach to theology in general, which led to a thoroughgoing rethinking of their lives by many individual religious and communities and thus to ways of living which were in tension with law. Once the tension began to develop theology was increasingly called upon to *arbitrate* between law and life. Contemporary theology made repeated efforts to justify the claims of life while more traditional theological efforts attempted to rationalize the law. Neither wanted to negate the other. The former was trying to show how law could be revitalized by responding to life and the latter to show that life need not be stifled by law correctly understood and applied. No more eloquent testimony to the failure of this dialogue could be imagined than the draft of the revision of canon law for religious[12] and the immediate critical response to the draft by the Leadership Conference of Women Religious.[13]

I would like to suggest that a more creative role for theology in the present situation of tension between law and life is that of *interpreter,* of creative hermeneut of the tension itself. In this role, the theologian of religious life would attempt to describe and analyze the tension in its causes and to reinterpret the relationship between law and life in function of theologically valid premises, thereby supplying a more useful schema within which to situate the conflictual cases than the unnuanced obedience/disobedience dichotomy.

3. *The Contemporary Restructuring:* Theology is already beginning to operate as creative interpreter of the tension between law and life[14] in the effort to foster the emergence of a new structure which would be accurately characterized not as a stable constellation of unchanging parts but as a moving equilibrium in which life has priority, but in which law, sensitively responsive to life, would play a stabilizing role as repository of conscience-tradition and challenge to fidelity. Law would not be asked to play the role of ideal which belongs properly to the Gospel but to function as protector of rights, reminder of responsibilities, and minimum standard of community identity. Theology, both professional and informal, would function in this structure not as a factor standing outside the tension between law and life attempting to arbitrate between them but rather as a reflective and creative moment within the moving equilibrium of law and life, an illuminating servant of that equilibrium.

The following section will be an attempt to make a biblical-theologial contribution to this moving equilibrium, an attempt to shed light from within on the structure and process of religious obedience understood as the dialectic between mediation and discernment.

B. A Biblical Model for Religious Obedience

We come finally to consider the question of discernment, that is, the process by which the religious (or community), faced with the exercise of legitimate authority, responsibly decides what the proper response to the law (personal or written) is in this particular case. Let us recall the conclusion of the first part, namely, that the absolute choice between obeying and disobeying confronts the Christian immediately and directly only when she or he is addressed by the Word of God. In the majority of cases in which religious face "law" situations in their personal and communal lives the commands in question are not proclamations of the Word of God or its clear application but rather legitimate exercises of human religious authority which derives from the nature of covenant community. Such exercises of authority, we have said, make a relative claim upon the religious and, therefore, it is not helpful to immediately place them within the schema obedience/disobedience which is proper to the absolute claim of God. They must first of all be allowed to fulfill their proper function, which is to *raise* (rather than answer apodictically) the question, "What is the will of God for me (or for us) at the present time and in these circumstances?" Only after the discernment necessary to answer that question has been responsibly carried out can the *answer* to that question (which is not necessarily synonymous with the original command) be placed on the scale obedience/disobedience. Only the will of God, that is, the Gospel claim once properly discerned within the context of the command in question and all those factors to which the command itself is relative, raises for the religious the question: Do you freely choose to obey God?

Traditionally, religious have relied on philosophical, political, sociological, and juridical models to understand how religious law functions and thus how one should respond to it. I would like to suggest that a more enlightening model for Christians in general and religious in particular is the New Testament picture of Jesus' process of discerning God's will in terms of the human mediations which had a privileged role in his life as a Jew. To examine this model we must go beyond the few explicit statements about the law that Jesus made (which have been repeatedly exegeted) and attend to the understanding of law that is operative in Jesus' responses within his life as a whole insofar as the Gospels record it. This is a somewhat risky procedure because it involves the interpretation of some of the most ambiguous episodes in the Gospels. However, I think the cumulative picture is convincingly consistent and can be genuinely enlightening about the Christian process of discerning God's will.

One of the most evident characteristics of Jesus' public ministry is his violation of Jewish religious laws. He not only set aside dietary regulations and purification rituals (e.g. Mk 7:1–8, 14–23), but he quite deliberately broke Israel's most sacred religious law, the observance of the sabbath (e.g. Mk 3:1–6). On the other hand, Jesus seems normally to have observed religious law, even in cases which seemed to justify non-compliance. Jesus arranged, for example, to pay the temple tax (Mt 17:24–27) when he did not have the money and could easily have justified not paying it; he instructed his disciples to practice what the scribes and Pharisees taught even though the latter, because of their conduct, were unworthy of the positions which they held (cf. Mt 23:2–3); he instructed those whom he had healed of leprosy to observe the details of the Mosaic Law in regard to showing themselves to the priest and making the required offering (e.g. Mt 8:1–4); and in numerous other ways he showed a ready compliance with the law of his people.

However, Jesus' non-observance of the law ran the gamut from condemnation of human religious laws as intrinsically perverse (e.g. the case of the law of Corban, Mk 7:9–13), to a suspension of the law in a particular case because of the absolute claim of God's great commandment of love (e.g. the curing of the man with the withered hand on the sabbath, Mk 3:1–6), to a seemingly casual disregard of the law because it was inconvenient (e.g. the plucking of the ears of corn on the sabbath, Mt 12:1–8), to the kind of deliberately provocative violation of the law which we would probably call civil disobedience (e.g. the curing of the paralytic at the pool, Jn 5:1–9), to the actual abrogation of laws which were outmoded and unnecessary burdens (e.g. laws about clean and unclean foods, Mk 7:14–23, and purificatory washings, Mk 7:1–8).

Only two things, it seems, are clear from Jesus' behavior: (1)

that he seemed to accept religious law as legitimate within the covenant community of Israel and that he seemed disposed, under most circumstances, to observe it even when it was not convenient; (2) that he considered all religious law relative and dispensed himself and others from it for numerous reasons, light and grave, while reserving unquestioning and whole-hearted obedience to the single expression of the divine will which he considered absolute: "Thou shalt love the Lord thy God with thy whole being and thy neighbor as thyself" (cf. Mt 22:34–40).

To what did Jesus consider human religious laws relative? Even a partial answer to this question would require an examination of each incident in which Jesus either observed the Law or did not observe it in order to discover what the context shows to have been the reasons for his behavior. We would find such things as the following: sometimes a law should be observed to avoid unnecessary, even though unjustified, scandal (e.g. the case of paying the half-shekel tax, Mt 17:24–27); sometimes it should be observed, even if unnecessary in this particular case, because its purpose is the protection of the safety of the community (e.g. allowing the priests to verify the completeness of a cure from a contagious disease before the person rejoined the community, Mt 8:1–4). On the other hand, sometimes a law which has become rigid and opaque should be broken to reveal its original intent (e.g. the cure of the man with the withered hand in order to reveal that the real purpose of the sabbath was the doing of good, Mk 3:1–6); sometimes it should be broken because it really serves no useful purpose in the present (e.g. fasting when it is not meaningful, Mt 9:14–15); sometimes it should be broken to safeguard a higher value (e.g. Jesus' cure of a woman on the sabbath to demonstrate the supreme value of the human person in comparison with financial resources, Lk 13:10–17); sometimes it should be broken because subsequent revelation makes it no longer an adequate expression of the religious value it was meant to express (e.g. Jesus' allowing himself to be rendered "impure" by touching a corpse, Lk 7:14, Mt 9:25, or allowing himself to be touched by a hemorrhaging or sinful woman, Mt 9:20–22, Lk 7:36–50); sometimes it should be broken because one's personal religious experience makes it clear that one is being called beyond it (e.g. Jesus' going outside the "house of Israel" to which he had been sent by curing the Syro-Phoenician woman's daughter, Mt 15:21–28). This list is not exhaustive. But it should indicate that the number of factors which enter the situation when one is trying to decide what role a relative human command, however legitimate, plays in the discerning of God's will at a given moment is far larger than we have been taught to think. Most religious learned that the only factor which could relativize a legitimate command was "that the action commanded is sinful."

It appears, then, that we cannot derive a readily applicable norm for deciding how to react to the legitimate exercise of covenantal authority by studying the actual choices of Jesus as recorded in the Gospel. What we do get is a sense that each individual case in which the command appears to one as somehow problematic demands a free and honest decision which takes into account not only the legitimacy of the law or command (e.g. whether it is according to the rule, not sinful, and commanded by someone in office) but also all those factors in the public and private situation which seem to be relevant to the discerning of God's will in this particular case.

However, there is another aspect of the Gospel accounts of Jesus' attitude toward religious law which has much more radical consequences, namely, Jesus' solidarity with sinners. In recent years exegetes have examined in great detail Jesus' solidarity with the poor and the oppressed. But Jesus' most notable and deeply disturbing choice was to associate with sinners. To grasp the full significance of this choice we must attend to the fact that Jesus did not merely condescend to be with sinners in order to convert them. He says clearly: "I came not to call the righteous, but sinners" (Mt 9:13; Mk 2:17). Luke amends this shocking saying to read, "I have not come to call the righteous, but sinners *to repentance* (Lk 5:32), but the Markan version, with its scandalous preference for sinners, is undoubtedly the original version.[15] It is not simply that Jesus extended the call to sinners as well as the righteous. Jesus did *not* come to call the righteous at all. He had made a choice between them and had chosen the sinners.

Who are the righteous and who are the sinners in Matthew's

Gospel? We are at first tempted to answer: the righteous are those who keep the Mosaic Law (and its extensions in Jewish law) and the sinners are those who do not. However, the distinction is not quite so simple as it might seem. The Gospels make it fairly clear that the sinners often acted according to the Law (although they also often did not) and that the righteous sometimes broke the Law (although they usually did not). In other words, the real difference between sinners and righteous is not reducible to *behavior* in relation to the Law. The difference is more subtle; it has to do with one's *attitude* toward the keeping of the Law.

The Pharisees were the quintessential "righteous" of the Gospel. What characterized them in their attitude toward the Law was not that they kept it but that they absolutized it as the expression of the will of God for the people, including themselves. They therefore considered it the real norm of one's acceptability to God. In other words, it was not that the righteous never broke the Law but that when they did they considered themselves to have sinned. Likewise, they considered their righteousness to consist in their observance of the Law. The perfect example of this attitude is the Pharisee in Luke's story who thanked God for his righteousness because of his observance of the Law (Lk 18:11–12). In Pauline terms, the righteous are those whose salvation comes from the Law if they keep it and whose damnation will also come from the Law if they do not keep it (cf. Rom 8:1–17; Gal 3:1–29).

When we look at the sinners in the Gospel we do not find them to be unmitigatedly evil. The sinners often did very good and beautiful things. In fact, if they had not habitually observed at least the most essential demands of the Law they would probably have been in Roman prisons, not listening to Jesus, for murder, robbery and the like are also against the civil law! The Samaritan, the publican praying in the temple, the sinful woman who washed Jesus' feet, the dying thief on the cross, were all, in fact, behaving as the Law commanded. What characterizes the sinners, in other words, is not their breaking of the Law, which might not have been any more serious or frequent than the sins of the righteous in any given case, but the fact that they had, in a certain sense, "given up on the Law" as a source of salvation or as a criterion of acceptability to God. Most of the sinners were simply the *am ha eretz,* the simple folk of the land who had neither the leisure nor the learning to be knowledgeable in the Law and who found themselves frequently outside it even when they were not choosing evil for motives of pleasure or profit. Such people had only two choices, to despair of their salvation or to develop a humanly groundless and stubborn hope that God would find a way to save them in spite of the fact that they were and always would be sinners.

It is well worthwhile to explore the spirituality of such people. They are those who believe in salvation but do not believe that it will come from the Law. They are "lawless" in a certain sense. They are "outside the Law," not because they habitually violate it but because it is useless for them to try to keep it integrally. They are those for whom the Law functions to teach them that they are truly helpless, in need of a salvation which the Law cannot provide as Paul says (e.g. Rom 1:8). In other words, the Law can never absolutely assure them that they are doing God's will, that they are "good." They must do their best but trust only in God. They cannot demand rewards or approval from God as their just deserts. They can only receive salvation, if at all, as a free and undeserved gift.

Such people are involved in a kind of existential humility; the only prayer that they can say with any conviction is that which magnifies God for God's utterly prodigal mercy and that which implores God's mercy on themselves. And, by the same token, such people can never condemn anyone else, however much another may look worse than themselves, because they have given up the norm by which to decide who is righteous. If they do not declare themselves either condemned or saved on the basis of their own relationship to the Law, how can they make any such declarations about anyone else? To despise or condemn another is to assume the status of the righteous and to lose one's claim to being among those for whom Jesus came. This is the lesson Jesus gives to the righteous Simon who condemned the repentant woman (Lk 7:36–50).

Such people must remain quite tentative about themselves no matter what they do or why. Whatever assurance they feel in their behavior rests only on their conviction that God sees the heart and its intentions and that God is larger than their heart. They cannot really have any sense of having earned a reward by doing what they should but only of being unprofitable servants of an infinitely merciful God. This does not mean that such people make no judgments about what they should and should not do. They obviously do make such judgments. The blind Bartimaeus decided to call out for a cure (Mk 10:46–52); the sinful woman to enter the house of Simon the Pharisee and wash Jesus' feet (Lk 7:36–50); the thief to ask for a remembrance in Jesus' kingdom (Lk 23:42); Zacchaeus to try to see the teacher, to welcome him into his home, and even to try to be a just tax collector, which was, according to the Law, a contradiction in terms (Lk 19:1–10)! But their decisions are not made to fulfill the Law, even when they accord with what the Law demands. All their decisions, to do what the Law commands or not to do so, stand not under the judgment of the Law but under the mercy of God.

These are the *anawim,* the truly and utterly poor before God. They have no appeal except to God's mercy. They have and need no defense before God because they make to God the only appeal which God is powerless to resist: "Lord, have mercy." This is a cry which cannot be uttered in total truth by anyone who does not see himself or herself as belonging irrevocably to the category of the "sinners." The righteous who has broken the Law can ask for the forgiveness of the offense; but the sinner must ask for the unspecified mercy which must find or create the good in the sinner who cannot find it in himself or herself because he or she has no external norm by which to discern it. It is the Lord who must create in the sinner a new heart and teach the sinner God's way. The Law does not tell the sinner what is pleasing to God; it is the relentless desire to do God's will which indicates to the sinner what is truly God's will. The true sinner, then, can never feel complacency but is engulfed in a never-ending, progressively more peaceful compunction of heart.

Jesus came to call sinners, to express the mercy of God in which the sinners of all time have trusted to the sinners of his time and place. And he expressed that mercy not as a righteous God, nor even as a righteous man! Jesus appears in real solidarity with sinners. He can share table fellowship with sinners because he is truly one of them. St. Paul says that Jesus "was made sin for us" (2 Cor 5:21). We usually interpret this text in a substitutional sense, that the sinless Jesus "took on our sins." But the Gospel suggests that Jesus actually saw himself as one of a crowd of sinners, of those who did not hope for salvation from the Law. The people of his time, both Pharisees and common folk, also saw him that way. He opened his ministry by being baptized with the baptism of repentance (Mt 3:13–15), i.e., by a conversion, a confident turning to God as the only reference point and justification of his adult life.

Throughout his public life Jesus repeatedly broke the Law, although he also usually kept it, and he did not contest the condemnation he suffered for this. He placed himself gladly among the sinners, he ate with them, he chose them as his intimates. When he died, he died as a sinner who had no real defense against the charges of breaking the Law that were brought against him. He had predicted the destruction of the temple; he had broken the sabbath; he had claimed equality with God. In short, he was, by the measuring rod of the Law, a sinner. On the cross he did not appeal to God to vindicate him by taking him down and thereby confounding his accusers. As always, he appealed only to the mercy of God, commending himself in death as he had in life to the God whom he trusted in spite of everything and whom he would not tempt.

Jesus came only to call sinners and he did so by entering into solidarity with sinners, by becoming one of them. He exercised during his lifetime the freedom from the Law that Paul saw as the distinguishing characteristic of the Gospel. But even by Paul's time the first converts were hankering for the fleshpots of the Law, trying to discover norms and laws according to which to justify themselves before God and each other. What Paul warded off among the Galatians (cf. Gal 3:1–5), however, and successfully combated in the new community's dealing with the Gentiles (cf. Gal 2:11–21), reappeared almost immediately and has been the bone of contention among Christians ever since. How are we to understand the Christian's freedom from the Law? There is a constant fear that to be free of the Law is anarchy, renders the community unstable, gives scandal, makes everyone a law unto himself or herself, subverts corporate efforts, and undermines legitimate authority. Paul did not agree. He maintained that the heart of the person who had surrendered appeal to the Law was supremely open to the Spirit who was a Spirit of wisdom, prayer, love, pressing zeal, the very Spirit of Jesus (cf. Rom 8:1–17). Paul thought that the Spirit could be trusted if only he could get his converts to surrender the Law.

What is the meaning of all this for the tension between law and life experienced by the contemporary religious? It seems to me that it suggests that we have often mistaken the direction of our conversion. We are not called to be converted to the Law, whether that be our own rule, the commands of legitimate congregational authority, the prescriptions of ecclesiastical authorities, or even the Ten Commandments. We are called to be like Jesus, truly poor "outlaws," those who do not appeal to any law as the criterion of our justice. We are called to live without the security of abiding by the law even though, as members of a human community we must make laws, and as cooperative people we usually observe them. This means that we cannot necessarily consider ourselves or others "good" religious because we do what the law commands. We cannot necessarily declare ourselves or others "bad" when we do not keep the law. We cannot justify ourselves before God or human authority or even our own conscience. We can only do our best to live the Gospel of love, trusting absolutely in the mercy of God who knows, and is greater than, our heart (1 Jn 3:20). We thus abandon all self-condemnation and condemnation of others as well as all complacency and act in tentative hope out of an ever-renewed love according to whatever light we have. It is not the law which will tell us what is good (or that we are good); it is our constant seeking of the good which will enable us finally to discern what, in our human affairs, is truly God's will.

IV. CONCLUSIONS ON THE SHAPE OF A CONTEMPORARY THEOLOGY OF OBEDIENCE

In these final paragraphs I would like to summarize the argument of this essay in more succinct form.

A. On the Nature of Religious Obedience

The only object of absolute obedience is the will of God, and the call to absolute obedience is addressed equally to every Christian. By the vow of obedience, made in response to a genuine vocation the religious situates his or her total commitment to the will of God in a context of mediation comprised of the persons and institutions of the congregation entered.

B. On the Theology of Mediation

The Judaeo-Christian theology of historical revelation grounds our belief that the will of God is mediated to us by human realities. If our entrance into religious life is the response to a genuine vocation, then the human realities which compose the context in which we live our life, i.e., the religious community, have a privileged status as mediators of the divine will for us.

However, to simply equate the human mediation with the will of God is to create an idol. The alternative to this unnuanced and idolatrous equation is serious discernment which begins with the question concerning the proper response to the law in each individual situation. It is the process of discernment which prevents the alienation of personal authority and responsibility that would turn our obedience into magic.

The first stage of the discernment process is to distinguish clearly between the absolutely authoritative command which is constituted by the clear proclamation of the Gospel and those relatively authoritative commands which are a legitimate exercise of convenantal authority. In the case of the former our response can only be immediate and unquestioning obedience. In the case of the latter our response can only be a careful and responsible discernment of what God's will is for us in this particular situation. The mediation which belongs to our vocational context has a privileged place in this discernment but it does not pre-determine the outcome. The outcome is the result of a prudent adjudication among all the factors relevant to the decision. Only when we have discerned, to the best of our ability, what the will of God is for us in this situation can we proceed to the conscience question of obedience.

C. On the Theology of Discernment

Discernment is the process of creatively mediating the tension between life and law by means of a theologically informed reflection proceeding from a spirituality of freedom. Jesus is the model of this discernment.

It is crucial to realize that the tension between law and life is operative *within* ourselves before it is realized between ourselves and legitimate authority or among groups. This tension arises from our need for approval, for assurance and recognition of our goodness and acceptability. We seek this justification in the law, in the approval of persons in authority, in the security of a "good conscience."

What Jesus shows us is that our freedom and our obedience begin in the realization that all law, however sound, is relative, except the absolute call to love God and our neighbor with all our heart. It is relative to the great commandment of love and relative to the many other factors which, in any given circumstance, have some claim to be taken into account in our decision. These factors may be as light as convenience or as serious as justice. Only the person in question can decide which factors are relevant and how they must function in the discernment process.

The basis of the discernment process is conversion from a spirituality of self-justification by the Law to a spirituality of the *anawim*, a spirituality of total reliance on God's mercy which frees us to risk loving in every situation whether or not we are approved.

In the final analysis the dilemma of obedience does not reside in the structures, congregational or ecclesial, which surround us. It arises in the heart where fear struggles with faith, need for heteronomous approval wars with personal authority, alienation fights against Christian identity. The only solid ground of obedience is freedom, and genuine Christian freedom cannot be bestowed upon us by law, structures, or superiors. Freedom is the gift of God to the person who has given up on the law as justification and given himself or herself up to the infinitely merciful God who is the Father of Jesus Christ. Such a spirituality will not amicably resolve all disputes, nor will it prevent the abuse of authority or the misuse of sanctions, but it will place us, in such situations of dispute and tension, with Jesus whose great command was "Love one another" (cf. Jn 15:12) but whose authority and originality were the wonder of his contemporaries.

Chapter Nine
EVANGELICAL POVERTY:
COMMITMENT TO THE COMING OF
THE REIGN OF GOD ON EARTH

The ideas in this chapter have emerged, more directly than those of any other chapter, from my experience with religious in spiritual direction. It is from these conversations with many deeply committed religious that I derived a sense of the complexity and urgency of this issue and of the newness of the problematic in our own times. The reflections in this chapter were presented formally to the participants in a workshop held at Oblate School of Theology, San Antonio, Texas in May-June, 1984.

I. INTRODUCTION

It is impossible to doubt the sincerity with which contemporary religious are wrestling with the issue of religious poverty. Not only have many individual religious made heroic choices for solidarity with the materially disadvantaged but many congregations have willingly divested themselves of corporate holdings at a time when the financial security of their own members is in jeopardy. Some religious communities have renounced, or supported individual members who have renounced, lucrative apostolates in favor of ministries among the poor which cannot even support the ministers themselves, much less contribute to the support of the congregation. Such far-reaching choices cannot be written off as posturing or faddism. Nevertheless, there is widespread confusion among religious about what poverty means today, what it demands of us, and even about whether it is authentic for middle class Americans (which most religious are) to make such a vow at all.

No one, to my knowledge, has definitive answers to these questions, least of all myself. In this essay, therefore, I propose something much more modest than a comprehensive treatment of this subject. I would like to try to sort out the issues that are involved in a contemporary approach to poverty as the object of a religious vow in order to facilitate creative reflection on the subject by those living religious life in the United States today.

II. WHAT IS POVERTY?

A. Poverty: An Analogous Term?

An analogous term is one which is used of a number of realities to which the term applies in a way that is both somewhat the same and somehow different. For example, "life" is predicated of humans, of animals, and of plants. In each case its meaning is somewhat the same, namely, the power of immanent activity, but the activity of a person and of a petunia are so different that we have to say that the word "life" really means something very different in the two cases. Life is both the same and different when predicated of beings on different levels of the life scale. The danger with analogous terms is that we tend to forget the significance of the difference because we use a single term for realities which are not identical. It is true, for example, that "all life is sacred." But that does not mean that we should let a human being die to avoid killing an animal.

Poverty, it seems to me, is an analogous term. We can speak of a poor person, poor soil, a poor idea, a poor joke, poor taste, a poor excuse; of material, intellectual, spiritual, aesthetic, cultural, physical poverty. It is the primary analogue, the reality to which the term properly applies, which governs the meaning of the term in relation to the secondary analogues. In the case of poverty, the primary analogue is the economic one. Poverty is, first and properly, the lack of sufficient material goods. What the idea of poverty carries into other spheres is the qualification of insufficiency, lack, defect, whether that lack be material or spiritual, literal or figurative.

The question I want to raise is whether poverty of spirit, the virtue of poverty to which all Christians aspire and which religious make the object of a vow, is actually an analogue of poverty, i.e., a kind of poverty, or whether it has another relationship to poverty which is being obscured or confused by a literalist understanding of the term. Poverty of spirit is, after all, not a defect but precisely a virtue. It is not a form of insufficiency but the proper disposition of a person before God. Why, then, is it called poverty and how is it related to real, that is, economic poverty and the latter's genuine analogues?

B. A Phenomenology of Poverty

To avoid all romanticism and unreality we had best begin with a frank description of real poverty. Obviously, the term can be used to cover a broad scale of conditions running from mild want to destitution. But its identifying characteristic is insufficiency. What, then, does "insufficiency" look like? First of all, it means not having enough of those goods which are essential for human life: food, clothing, and shelter. Then, it involves the consequences of these lacks: poor health and inadequate medical care, low energy, no time or energy for anything except survival activity. It means little or no education or cultural development. It means little opportunity or resources for escape from poverty. At all levels poverty is characterized by lack of options. The life of the poor is determined by the insufficiency which governs their world and experience.

When we describe poverty as insufficiency it is clear that a very simple but balanced life in a primitive setting, which by comparison with life in suburban America would seem unbelievably poor, might not be really poor at all. The members of a close-knit tribe might never have heard of the opera or seen a modern hospital. But their style of life might well provide a truly meaningful and fully human experience of individual and corporate existence. In other words, simplicity and poverty are not the same thing. Simplicity is not "mild poverty" or "decent poverty." It is not poverty at all. Poverty involves insufficiency, not having enough of what is necessary for a meaningful human existence, however that is defined in the situation in question.

Once we define poverty in terms of its primary analogue, material poverty, it becomes clear that poverty is an evil. There is nothing about poverty as such which is desirable. Poverty ought not to be sought for oneself or for others. On the contrary, everything possible should be done to alleviate it and eventually to abolish it. The same has to be said for all of the kinds of poverty to which the term analogously applies. Intellectual poverty, social poverty, spiritual poverty, all refer to insufficiencies in important areas of human experience. No such defects are desirable as such. Whatever religious "poverty" is, it is not an analogue of real poverty. We must seek its relationship to poverty elsewhere than in the sphere of proper designation.

C. Poverty as a Religious Virtue

The history of religious life shows that from the very beginning religious have willingly chosen "poverty," by which they mean a relative lack of this world's goods, as an aid in the spiritual quest. In our effort to understand this choice we must be clear that our question concerns the balanced and sane pursuit of this poverty, not the historical excesses which everyone can recognize as such, at least in retrospect.

Two points are immediately clear from a survey of the history of religious life. First, the poverty in question was not genuine insufficiency in regard to essentials; second, the forms of poverty were extremely diverse, one form often contradicting another. In other words, the term was used in a relative sense, and it was not some Platonic ideal or essence but a specific arrangement for a particular situation.

The virgins and widows of the first three centuries lived simply but they were adequately provided for by the early Christian communities in which they lived as esteemed members. The desert monastics of the fourth and fifth centuries sought a life as devoid of material supports as possible but they did not live without the necessities of life. Rather, they so simplified their lifestyle that they were able to live quite well without most of the material baggage that their contemporaries in the city considered necessary. The monks and nuns of the first Benedictine monasteries founded in the sixth century had a very different conception of poverty. The individual monastics had nothing of their own, but the monastery was a prosperous economic unit that provided comfortably for the needs of its members who, in turn, cared for the community's goods with the reverence reserved for God's possessions. The mendicants, founded in the Middle Ages, decided on a corporate form of poverty in which the order possessed no holdings. Therefore, the individual religious had to live by begging or by work. This was an insecure and uncomfortable life consciously modeled on that of Jesus, the itinerant preacher, but, like Jesus, the mendicants were not habitually in dire want. The apostolic orders founded in the sixteenth and following centuries worked out various combinations of corporate possession and personal non-possession in order to pursue their apostolic activities in efficient ways. In various circumstances throughout history individual religious or religious groups did indeed suffer want. But this was never the object of the vow of poverty, and it was always a situation which the religious tried to remedy by begging, by work, or by careful handling of resources. In short, whatever the object of the vow of poverty was, it was not poverty in the primary and proper sense of the word: insufficiency.

As mentioned above, poverty is a relative term. It is relative not only to the standards of and needs generated by a particular society; it is also a relative term in the sense that material possession in any individual or corporate case is situated somewhere on a scale between real poverty (insufficiency) and real wealth (abundance or even superfluity of goods). The closer the situation comes to the pole of insufficiency the more reason there is to qualify it as poverty even if the actual needs of the people involved are being minimally met. In other words, there is a way of using the word poverty which is legitimate even if it is not literal in the sense of denoting real insufficiency. It is in this relative sense that religious have used the word poverty to describe a certain ideal of their life.

This raises the question of what exactly religious are trying to denote about their life when they speak of it as "poor"? It seems to me that there are two things they want to say: first, that they intend to keep considerable distance between themselves and the wealth pole of the material scale; second, that they want to approximate the poverty pole without, however, lacking at least the bare necessities of life. This stance bears considerable reflection. Wealth is nowhere in the Gospels denoted as evil. Jesus says it is dangerous in that it makes entrance into the reign of God difficult, but he does not say that it is evil. On the other hand, there is no question but that poverty is evil. Why, then, have religious seekers of all times and all cultures (not just Christian religious) preferred to approximate a true evil, poverty, rather than a dangerous good, wealth? It is the answer one gives to this question which illuminates the meaning of religious poverty and suggests what its contemporary practice might involve.

III. THE VALUE OF POVERTY

A. Asceticism, Spirituality, and Poverty

Christian religious were not the first spiritual seekers to realize that wealth is dangerous to the spiritual quest. Wealth, at least if it is used for oneself, leads almost inevitably to various forms of luxury or "soft living." Too much eating, drinking, and sleeping (which usually go together), a debilitating pampering of the body, sexual excess, addictive habits, in short, all the elements of the luxurious lifestyle, undermine any kind of spiritual activity, intellectual or religious. People who are serious about the spiritual life have, therefore, always embraced an ascetical lifestyle which, to the luxurious, appears "poor." Christian religious are no exception to this tradition.

As pointed out above, the importance and kind of asceticism in the life of religious has varied depending on the purposes of the form of religious life in question. Some of the extreme physical deprivations of the early desert monastics are probably not suitable for twentieth century apostolic religious. But asceticism is no less necessary. When contemporary religious speak about seeking a "simple lifestyle" they seem to be talking about this ascetical aspect of poverty, about a deliberate choice to avoid a spiritually debilitating luxury.

B. Justice, Charity, and Poverty

Detachment from material goods has a second relationship to Christianity which has always been important for religious. As the philosophers have pointed out, matter is the principle of individuation. Matter is the kind of being that, strictly speaking, cannot be shared. What one person possesses the other must lack and vice versa. Unlike spiritual goods, such as ideas or love, which can be shared infinitely without anyone being impoverished and which, therefore, unite people, material goods divide people into haves and have nots. Jealousy, envy, competition, coveting, stealing, in short, all the bases for injustice, hatred, and war, are provided by material goods. This is not the fault of matter as such; it is due to the fact that material goods are essentially limited and can only belong exclusively to one person or group at a time. The only way to overcome the divisions and struggles occasioned by material goods is to make human decisions to renounce possessiveness in favor of a common project of stewarding the scarce resources of this earth for the good of all of the human family. Such choices are not natural or spontaneous. They represent a triumph of the disciplined spirit over the instincts of sinful humanity.

Christianity is a religion whose central tenet is love, universal love of neighbor based on and enlivened by an unconditional love of God. It is not surprising, then, that Christian religious seeking the fullness of the Christian ideal have taken strong positions on the attitudes toward and the use of material goods which have such a propensity for causing division and hatred. To hold material goods in common immediately eliminates the basic cause of social division: competition for finite goods. But if goods are held in common the basic values of ownership can also be realized: care of the common property and use of it for human purposes. In other words, the kind of poverty religious embraced was calculated to prevent both the dangers of wealth and the evil of real poverty.

Not only does renunciation of individual and private ownership make for peace and unity in the religious community but it disposes the community for love and care of those outside the community. The disposition to share expressed itself, from the earliest days of religious life, in the high value set on the virtue of hospitality. Like Abraham who entertained angels unawares, the Christian religious community held itself in constant readiness to welcome Christ in the person of the stranger. The gradual suppression of this religious virtue of hospitality in favor of cloistered exclusiveness was a development which contemporary religious, especially women, have seriously (and, in my opinion, rightly) questioned in recent years.

Religious not only welcomed the transient stranger but also shared their goods through almsgiving and care of the needy, especially in times of social disaster. Because religious were not hoarding their goods in order to become wealthy they could afford to share whatever they had with those who had less, depending on the God to whom they had given their lives to replenish their stores with what was needed. This sharing extended not only to material goods but to their prayer life, their learning, their cultural achievements, and their spiritual wisdom. Unselfishness is an expression of charity which cannot exist piecemeal. The early monasteries became fountains of social well-being for their surroundings and eventually of missionary efforts to share faith itself with those who had not yet heard the Gospel. As other forms of religious life developed, other forms of sharing were developed. What remained constant was the connection between the renunciation of private property and the pursuit of wealth by religious and their disposition and ability to steward material and spiritual goods for the benefit of all.

In our own times, as we will discuss later, our perception of social suffering and its solutions has changed qualitatively but the basic connection between poverty understood as the renunciation of the accumulation of private property and solidarity with and care for the neighbor has not changed.

C. Holiness and Poverty

So far we have explored the relationship between the choice of religious, on the one hand, to avoid wealth (personally owned abundance) and to approximate poverty (insufficiency), and, on the other, religiously motivated asceticism and the practice of justice and charity. It is not difficult to see why, even though actual poverty is an evil which religious have never sought, poverty is a danger that religious prefer to that of wealth which is so intimately connected with luxury and selfishness. Actual want, with its dangers to health and well-being, does not pose the threat to the spiritual life that wealth does.

But the choice of relative poverty has always had a much

deeper interior motivation than asceticism or even Christian solidarity. Real poverty, actual want, despite its capacity to destroy
people physically and spiritually, has a peculiar power to evoke
pure religion. In the Old Testament this realization dawned
slowly and was elaborated in a kind of spirituality of poverty
which modern biblical scholars have explored and described in
detail as the spirituality of the *anawim,* the "poor of Yahweh."
The poor in the Old Testament were not romanticized nor was
poverty glorified or proposed as an ideal. But what the Old Testament writers came to recognize about the poor was that they,
unlike the rich or even the comfortable, were forced in a sense
to choose between complete despair and a kind of no-holds-
barred dependence on God which was the attitude God sought
in all the people of the covenant. Those with resources of their
own were always tempted to rely on those resources first and to
come to God only when these latter failed. For the well-off, God
was a God of the gaps. But for the really and irremediably poor,
life was nothing but gaps. The really poor could not even keep
the Law and thereby earn God's spiritual favor. They were destitute in every sense of the word. They had to receive God's saving love as purely gratuitous. Thus they experienced God as
God really is and accepted God on God's own terms. They were
the poor, the empty, the lowly whom God alone could fill, exalt,
and satisfy.

In the New Testament Jesus evoked this spirituality of the
anawim as the Christian ideal. "Blessed are you poor, for yours
is the reign of God" (Lk 6:20). "Unless you turn and become like
children you will never enter the kingdom of heaven" (Mt 18:3).
"I have not come for the righteous, but for sinners" (cf. Mt
9:13). Essentially, all of these Gospel maxims mean the same
thing. God can only be God for us when all the bargaining is
over, when we have finally stopped trying to pay our own way
and have come to rejoice in our destitution because the extent
of our emptiness is the measure of God's gift. Jesus says this attitude requires a conversion; indeed it is the most basic conversion of all, the final and total acceptance of creaturehood in the
face of God's Creator-love, the reversal of original sin which is
the desire to be our own God.

It is not the case that one must be actually poor, i.e., materially destitute, morally bankrupt, and/or spiritually powerless, in order to achieve that spiritual condition which is alone capable of receiving the reign of God. Job in the Old Testament was a man who had everything but who never lost sight of the truth that all his blessings were from God who retained the right to withdraw it all at any time and without explanation. The officer in the Gospel whose son (servant) Jesus cured was apparently well-off but possessed an openness to God that amazed even Jesus. Mary, whom Luke canonizes as the New Testament embodiment of *anawim* spirituality by placing the Magnificat on her lips in response to God's greatest Gift, was not homeless or starving; she and Joseph seem to have been modestly situated. Jesus himself, during his public life, was not materially destitute, much less morally lost, and he is the consummate example of the truly poor before God. It is probably because of the fact that, on the one hand, material poverty does not guarantee spiritual openness and that, on the other, one can be spiritually receptive without being materially poor that Matthew amended the first beatitude to read: "Blessed are the poor *in spirit*" (Mt 5:3).

Religious throughout history have taken an attitude toward material goods which is quite faithful to what the Gospel tells us. Material goods are not evil; in fact, all of creation is good. Wealth is not evil. But given the human condition, wealth is extremely dangerous because it almost always entices to luxury, divides us from our neighbors, and leads us into a self-sufficiency which at least partially closes us to the infinite saving love of God. Actual poverty is evil and has a tremendous capacity to degrade the human spirit. But God can offer salvation in the midst of any evil, even death itself. Poverty, therefore, is not an ultimate evil. Furthermore, precisely because poverty is an evil its victims cry out to God for salvation. Thus, there is spiritual wisdom in choosing a condition close enough to poverty to ward off the dangers of wealth and to constantly invite us to acknowledge our true condition as creatures crying out to the God of our salvation with the authenticity that comes from actually experienced neediness. This is the poverty religious seek: not destitution, for to seek such would be to tempt God as well as to abandon our responsibility for ourselves and needlessly to burden our sisters and brothers; but a relative poverty that enables us to experience our creaturehood in all its starkness in order that we might be disposed to accept God's saving love and to extend it to others.

IV. RELIGIOUS POVERTY TODAY

A. *Complications*

The proper understanding and prudent practice of religious poverty has probably never been easy in any age. It is of the very nature of religious poverty, because it has to do with material goods with which we cannot dispense absolutely and whose value is always relative to cultural situations, that it is always a provisional arrangement that has to be constantly re-evaluated and readjusted. As many have learned from experience, whenever religious have tried to "solve" the problem of poverty once and for all by making minute regulations that were to be applied uniformly in all situations, communities have found themselves caught up in rigidities that were at least silly if not downright counter-productive. The rebellion of some contemporary religious against certain practices that are quite valid in themselves, such as proper accountability in the use of money, is perhaps understandable as a reaction against some of the infantilizing practices of the recent past. No one of intelligence wants to revive such practices. At the same time, there is widespread concern among religious that the vow of poverty have some defined and recognizable meaning if we are to continue to profess it.

Our own times are characterized by conditions that make the understanding and prudent practice of poverty even more difficult than in times past. The major difference between our own age and any previous one, in relation to poverty, is our global interdependence at the economic level and our awareness of it.

First, we are aware of the immense variety in standards of living throughout the world and even in our own country. No matter how simple a lifestyle we adopt we cannot escape awareness that it is luxurious by comparison with that of many of our sisters and brothers. Furthermore, there is a wealth built into our existence which we cannot renounce even if we choose to. No one with an education, no one who has ever heard a concert, seen a ballet, visited a museum, or enjoyed any of the social, cultural, aesthetic, recreational, travel, or familial opportunities that virtually every religious has enjoyed can ever be poor in the literal sense of the word. Our inner resources, which cannot be renounced, are a wealth of remarkable proportions that marks us off forever from the truly poor.

Second, we are aware of the immensity of the problem of poverty which makes individual acts of sharing and hospitality seem almost pointless. They are swallowed up in the abyss of human misery like drops in the ocean. And our voluntary renunciation of luxuries, or even of quite legitimate but less than necessary goods and services, does nothing at all to redistribute material goods. The hungry do not eat better because I eat more simply. The naked are not clothed because I buy fewer or less expensive clothes. We are seemingly powerless to affect by our own choices the terribly skewed economic situation which victimizes so many millions of people.

Third, and following from the last point, we realize that the only way to affect the economic situation in which we live is to act collectively upon institutions. Poverty, the evil which is eating up our brothers and sisters in so many places in the world, is not a natural disaster nor merely the result of individual selfish choices. It is a systemic evil that must be dealt with systematically; it is institutional sin that must be dealt with institutionally. Whatever poverty means today, it has to take account of these realities.

B. *Mistakes We Need Not Make*

It seems that the last twenty years or so, even if they have not provided easy answers about the theory or practice of religious poverty, have at least indicated that some paths lead nowhere. It might be worthwhile to briefly catalogue some of these dead-ends.

First, nothing much is to be gained by renaming the traditional vow. From everything that was said in the first section it should be evident to all that "poverty" as the object of a religious vow is a term used in a relative sense. It is neither real poverty (the evil of insufficiency), nor an analogue of poverty (like social or intellectual poverty). Rather it denotes a preference for the scarcity pole of a scale that runs from insufficiency to superfluity. The term poverty has the advantage of being "global" in that it embraces the tendency toward the whole reality of what poverty denotes and away from the whole reality of what wealth denotes. In this sense it is more adequate than partial terms like simplicity of life or solidarity with the poor or community life or hospitality which are subsets of the global stance toward material goods which religious poverty intends. In any case, our efforts will be better spent trying to figure out how to achieve what religious poverty is about than trying to come up with an accurate term to denote it. I doubt seriously that such a term exists because we are really talking about a life-orientation with respect to the material universe as it impinges on personal and social existence, rather than about a particular attitude or set of behaviors.

Second, there seems little point in trying to come up with any kind of uniform understanding of what religious poverty involves or how it is to be practiced. History shows us clearly that different forms of religious life involved quite various understandings and practices of religious poverty. Begging was essential to the mendicant conception of poverty but had little or no place in the monastic form. Community ownership of large holdings was an integral part of monasticism and utterly contrary to the mendicant understanding of poverty.

Today the forms of religious life and even the variations from congregation to congregation make a uniform understanding of poverty virtually impossible. While one congregation is divesting itself of its schools, another may be making the decision to retain possession of its hospitals, and both may be exercising the virtue of poverty with wisdom, courage, and generosity. While it may be possible for congregations, especially smaller ones, to establish some general guidelines about material possessions for their members and some fairly uniform practices of accountability, there is bound to be, at least in large, mobile, apostolic congregations, considerable diversity in lifestyle and practice among the members. This becomes especially complicated when the variety exists among members living in the same house. But some of the extremely painful community experiences of the past few years should have made it clear that little is to be gained and much lost by attempts to standardize the practice of poverty, especially when the attempt is made by those who consider themselves the true representatives of Gospel poverty to their less "radical" fellow religious.

Third, a more subtle stumbling block than the ideal of standardizing the practice of all religious or of all the members of a single congregation is the desire of the individual to find the right formula for herself, the way of practicing poverty which will, once and for all, clarify her decisions. This usually takes the form of resolutions to give up certain types of clothes, food, amusements, or the like. Anyone who has experimented with this solution knows that it usually does not work. As we tried to show in the second section, poverty is practiced by religious for several reasons. There are a number of values we seek simultaneously by means of this virtue and, especially in our complicated times, these values often cannot all be attained by a single practice. Our exercise of hospitality in certain circumstances may conflict with our desire to eliminate certain types of food or drink from our diet for ascetical reasons. Our effective participation in certain political actions for the sake of justice may involve expenditures we would rather not make. The number of possible conflicts is endless. While each of us, no doubt, has to develop certain basic approaches and attitudes and even specific behaviors in the area of poverty to guide our everyday living as religious, there is probably no way to avoid the spiritual "hassle" of continuous decision making and the corresponding need to develop a supple habitual virtue of poverty that gradually equips us to deal with the incessant variety of situations in which we find ourselves. It may well be that one of the most painful experiences of poverty that we have today is our inability to permanently "acquire" the virtue of poverty!

Fourth, imitation of those we judge to be truly "poor" is probably one of the most sincere and yet completely misguided approaches to religious poverty. In the first place, as we pointed out above, it is impossible for those of us who have grown up "advantaged" to be poor in the deepest and most damaging

sense of the word. And whether we mean it or not, there is something profoundly disrespectful involved in freely imitating what
the poor have no choice about. It is almost as if a sighted person
stumbled about in imitation of a blind person in order to demonstrate her or his solidarity with the sightless (or to feel less
guilty about being able to see). Nothing changes the fact that the
sighted person is only pretending and can open his or her eyes
whenever he or she wants to. There is a point in seeking a brief
experience of someone's suffering so that we can more deeply
empathize with the other's pain. But true empathy leads us to
do something about the other's suffering, not to imitate it. And,
finally, there is really no way to decide whom to imitate. Whatever lifestyle we adopt there are others somewhere who are even
more poor. This is not an argument against either simplicity of
lifestyle or sharing the standard of living of those among whom
we work. It is an argument against contrived poverty which
helps no one in the long run.

Fifth, a final dead-end is one which might attract any of us
at moments of real insecurity and self-doubt or when the stakes
of a decision are particularly high, namely, a return to the
alienating and infantilizing practices of our own past. The temptation to avoid decisions by turning matters over to superiors
rather than deciding what is required in our own complicated
situation is one we probably all experience on occasion. Virtues,
as Thomas Aquinas well said, are acquired by being practiced in
challenging situations.

C. The Two Foci of Religious Poverty Today

Religious poverty has two foci for the contemporary religious and calls for two rather distinct, though not unrelated,
types of practice. The first focus is the societal one and has to
do with our individual and corporate impact on the institutional
sins which are making and keeping poor the majority of the
earth's people while the minority becomes progressively richer.
The second focus is the personal spiritual one which has to do
with our own ascetical preparation for and interior exercise of
that openness to God in grateful receptivity to salvation that is
the *sine qua non* of genuine holiness.

1. *The Societal Focus.* Religious poverty is the way religious situate themselves in relationship to material goods, and since material goods are foundational to our relationship with other people, religious poverty is necessarily a social virtue. Today we are much more aware than our forebears could have been that unless some of us begin to act effectively to restructure the way material creation is handled by the human race there soon will be no human race. The economic system of the first world is radically unjust because it is built on principles of unbridled greed, selfishness, and might over right. Furthermore, the environment upon which we all depend is being destroyed by the frankly exploitative approach of post-industrial society. The only way to rectify these situations is to use the political and economic systems to change the whole approach of our society toward material creation. Responsible stewardship based on reverence for God's creation and solidarity among people must replace exploitation, and material goods must be redirected toward human ends. It seems to me, and to many religious, that the first objective of religious poverty today has to be contributing to the restructuring of the economic situation on a worldwide scale. This seems especially so for apostolic religious for whom the call to participate actively in the transformation of the world in Christ is so integral to their religious vocation.

There are innumerable ways in which religious can begin to exercise their vow of poverty in relation to the economic and environmental situation of our time. Congregationally, we can *use our corporate resources* to influence policy and practice on whatever level is accessible to us. Many congregations have discovered the leverage of stock holdings, the power attached to corporate actions, and the influence of property location. These are not matters for one or two people "at the top" but call for the informed participation, even monitoring, of the membership. Reading documents, staying informed, supporting representatives, preparing chapter proposals and enactments, voting, and so on are not easy or pleasant activities for most of us. But they are a responsible exercise of poverty, analogous in our time to the material and cultural enrichment the monasteries of the Middle Ages offered to their impoverished surroundings.

The energetic *exercise of personal civic responsibilities* such as voting, writing to congress people, protesting local injustices, supporting non-violent efforts to influence corporate powers, attending meetings where our presence can help, is a way to help bring about the kind of society in which the poor will begin to attain justice.

Proper *corporate planning for the care of our own personnel* is another unglamorous but important contribution to the future well-being of our society. As a society we are getting older. We can plan for a future in which the elderly will have secure, meaningful, and productive lives or we can ignore the demographic data available to us and let develop a world of underemployed, unfulfilled people dragging out meaningless existences in a world that does not want them.

Another important area of personal and corporate decision making concerns the appropriate and effective *commitment of some of our personnel and resources to direct work with the materially disadvantaged.* For some of us it will be the decision to undertake that work ourselves; for others the decision to support those who do in one way or another. Here we are involved in making decisions according to truth, not according to appearances or for the sake of appearances. Who should go, and where, and for what tasks are difficult decisions that require great purity of motivation and careful discernment.

Direct *involvement in political ministry,* although currently under fire from the Vatican, is a particularly powerful way to influence the distribution of money and services to the poor.

This certainly does not exhaust the possibilities of active involvement in the restructuring of our world in justice and love. These are meant only to suggest that the vow of poverty today calls upon us to do for our time what our forebears did in simpler and more direct ways for theirs. Material goods are an important basis of social relationships, and religious poverty involves the proper handling of material goods. It must, therefore, involve a deliberate and beneficent effect on the social and economic relationships which structure our world.

2. *The Personal Focus.* The notion that involvement in corporate efforts to change the unjust economic institutions of our society belongs to the object of the vow of poverty in contem-

porary religious life may be new to many religious who spent the first decades of their religious life enclosed in the privatized economic system that most congregations were until the 1960's. Poverty was seen primarily as a personal ascetical practice safeguarding community life and encouraging interior dependence on God. But for others of us who have adopted a more global approach to religious life in general and the vows in particular and become more involved in ordinary life in our society and culture, the societal focus of poverty has become central to our thinking and the personal focus of poverty may have receded somewhat from consciousness, leaving behind a vague residue of guilt but nothing clear or compelling for personal behavior.

It is perhaps time to revive our awareness of the intimately personal character of the practice of poverty which must complement societal involvement. I am not suggesting here that we return to such earlier practices as repeatedly asking pointless permissions for daily necessities or traveling without adequate funds. Our times call for different, and certainly no less demanding, forms of personal poverty. Without even hoping to exhaust the possibilities I would like to point out, by way of example, a few areas in which the incorporation of poverty into our personal lives might be meaningful and spiritually fruitful for us as twentieth century religious.

The first area is one most serious religious have been bewitched, bothered, and bewildered by for several years: *simplicity of life*. This is probably the contemporary analogue of the ascetical aspect of poverty practiced in earlier days. Simplicity of life certainly has witness value as a challenge to our culture's operative definition of happiness as "more of everything." Voluntary simplicity of lifestyle says that enough is enough, that material goods should be acquired only to the extent that they are really necessary and not as a frantic defense against mortality or an endless competition with one's neighbors.

But simplicity of life also fulfills an important function in the spiritual life of the individual. As the ancients knew so well, material goods create a clutter in one's life. They require care and repair and replacement and housing and arranging. The more we collect the more we want. The itch to acquire is intrinsically escalating, and unless it is deliberately controlled and curtailed it naturally expands to fill the available space in one's life. We are probably more aware of this by personal experience today than our immediate forebears in the religious life were for the simple reason that we have more control over personal expenditures today and we know how easily the acquisitive instinct can be mobilized. In contemporary terms we are talking about consumerism, the insatiable desire to acquire more and better. We are rightly suspicious of any return to exaggerated gratuitous self-affliction, but experience is rapidly teaching us that there was a solid wisdom in the ascetical tradition. If we want to pray, to be available for God and others, to keep our lives focused on the purposes for which we chose religious life, we cannot surrender ourselves to the current of materialism that carries our culture. As children of an economy of abundance living in the world's richest nation we probably have to make a more conscious decision in this area than people of less prosperous times and cultures.

A second area in which poverty might touch our personal lives has to do less with behavior than with attitude. I am speaking of the deliberate development of the *sense of gift in life*. We live in a culture of achievement and production which believes that people should and do get what they deserve. As Christians we know that this is not so. The infinite bounty of God begins with the gift of life itself and continues with everything that sustains it. Our activity is not so much an earning our way as a cooperating with the Creator God in transforming history into God's reign of justice and love. Building this attitude of grateful response into our lives requires a constant cultivation of faith against the seemingly self-evident "way things are" around us. We each have to find our own way to do this, but one might be the care we take of our own life, the first and fundamental gift upon which everything else rests. The attitude we take toward eating, sleeping, exercise, recreation, stress management, and life-planning can express how we feel about the gift of life, whether indeed we hold it as a treasured gift or regard it as a private possession. Our attitudes toward friendship, that choicest of all human gifts, especially when it competes with "work," can also indicate to ourselves and others whether we place priority on the giftedness of life or on earning our way. The capacity for enjoyment, for the sharing of simple pleasures, for delight in uncontrived beauty, has to be developed in our artificial and overstimulated environment. But these are essentially contemplative attitudes that conduce to recollection of spirit and prayer and that bathe our surroundings in evangelical poverty.

A third area in which the personal practice of poverty might be developed today is one that was not available to many religious in more enclosed times: *hospitality*. To welcome others into our homes and into our lives is naturally easier perhaps for extroverted types, but it is a challenge for everyone because it involves putting ourselves at others' disposal. It means sharing our material goods, something we are more aware of now that we live on finite budgets rather than out of the endless invisible supply of "community funds." But it also involves spending time in preparation and cleaning up, in caring for others in very direct, human ways. Hospitality offers a marvelous experience of solidarity with other people. It involves the active and joyful breaking down of social barriers and breaking open of private supplies. It acts against the hoarding instinct and creates the community that calls into being here and now the future we believe in and which Jesus so often imaged as table fellowship in the reign of God.

A fourth area in which poverty touches the personal life of the contemporary religious is that of *community financial structures*. Most of us no longer live under the rigid systems which literally controlled every penny we handled in days gone by. Checkbooks, credit cards, and cash have become realities in our everyday life, and most of us have discovered that we are quite capable of responsible financial management. But with that discovery has also come, for many religious, an impatience with community procedures such as budgeting, accounting for funds spent, use of community banking systems, having second signers on our accounts, following tax exemption procedures, and especially initiating open consultation on major personal expenditures which involves the real possibility of decisions with which we do not agree. Putting in the time and effort required to live communally from the financial point of view and accepting the restrictions on our own freedom involved in the real renunciation of the independent use of money can be a severe form of asceticism because they are not simply a nuisance factor in our busy lives; they are a daily reminder that we have chosen not to be financially independent agents but to cast our lot with others in community. Like the early Christians we have decided to hold all things in common, and the form that commonality takes today is not so much uniformity of dress or food or lodging but the filling out of forms and the open and willing consultation and even yielding of our own opinions in financial matters which directly affect our own life.

Another area of personal poverty, one that seems to me more and more significant, has to do with one of the most painful aspects of real poverty, namely, *the lack of options.* The real differences between the truly poor and people who choose a poor lifestyle is precisely that the latter choose it, and they can unchoose it if things become too difficult. Even if they never do, the fact that they can assuages the violent determinism that constitutes real poverty. The poor get the worst groceries in their neighborhood stores because the managers know that the poor cannot go elsewhere; they are a captive clientele because they have no transportation. The poor get the worst teachers in their schools because they do not have the option of going to private schools; they are stuck with what they get. The apartments of the poor do not get repaired because, in any case, they cannot move out, and they cannot afford to apply pressure that would get them evicted. The great privilege that goes with resources is having options, being able to alter reality in our favor.

There are many aspects of our lives in which we have choices that the poor do not have. But there are also areas in which we do not have choices. We cannot lengthen our day, and if someone consumes time we had allotted for other purposes there is no reclaiming it. We cannot do anything about weather that keeps us from getting where we need to go. We cannot keep from getting the flu and losing a week of work at a critical juncture in an important project. A delayed plane, an inefficient travel agent who messes up our reservations, a microphone or tape-recorder that does not work, the computer going down, a flat tire, or even a string of red lights at the wrong time are just some of the multitude of situations in which we suddenly find ourselves without options, victims of a situation we did not create. We often feel justified in our rage at these frustrations. After all, we are important people doing important things—and all for the glory of God! But more basically, we are creatures who do not control the universe and who have no more real right to have everything go our way than all those "unimportant" people we call the poor. When we have no options we are poor, no matter how educated or rich or important we may be. When our options evaporate we experience solidarity with the poor, not the conspicuous solidarity of chosen deprivations but the real solidarity of fellow-sufferers in a world we do not control and cannot change.

One of the many areas in which many of us probably experience our lack of options most painfully is precisely that of effective action for justice. We know that most of what we do, in a personal way, will not have much effect on the unjust social systems in which we live. Even worse, we also know that we are constantly implicated in fostering the very systems that we have analyzed as unjust and exploitative. Every time we go to the bank, buy groceries, fill the gas tank, we participate in one way or another in multinational systems which are, at some near or far remove from us, exploiting the poor. The point is, in many areas we really have few or no options either for effective action against or for non-participation in structural injustice. Our frustration matches in some ways (certainly not all) the frustration of our victimized brothers and sisters. What they cannot do for themselves we cannot do for them, and the more we care the more this hurts. The name of that hurting is compassion and it is a fruit of genuine poverty.

A final aspect of the personal practice of poverty that might be mentioned is our *participation in the world of work*. Religious, like the poor, have always worked hard. But we used to work in systems that we more or less owned and operated and that were structured in our favor. Now many of us work in situations owned and operated by others. Many of us have found out what unemployment means, how job insecurity feels, and even what it means to be discriminated against because we are women. We experience powerlessness on the job and the exploitation, often by the Church itself, of our dedication through unjust wages and a refusal to allow us to participate in decisions which touch our lives. These are the experiences of the people in the laboring class in a capitalist society, and again they establish a certain solidarity between us and our sisters and brothers who suffer much more bitterly from the injustices of an exploitative labor system than we do.

Every reader could no doubt lengthen this list, but the point is that our situation is both old and new. It is old because religious have always realized that the attitude we take toward material goods and the behaviors that flow from those attitudes are crucial for the spiritual life. It is new because the historical situation in which we find ourselves, the forms of religious life in which we are involved, and the social and psychological developments that have marked our personal development are vastly different from those of our nineteenth and early twentieth century predecessors. We, like religious of all time, are called to a life of evangelical poverty. But we are also called to redefine that virtue so that it is meaningful in our lives and fruitful for our times and not a dead mimicry of either past religious forms or present social conditions.

V. CONCLUSION

This essay has been an attempt to sort out the issues involved in reimagining religious poverty for the twentieth century. I have tried both to distinguish religious poverty from economic poverty and also to show what its relationship to that economic poverty is. I have also tried to explore the values that religious have always sought through the practice of evangelical poverty and to suggest how these values might be pursued in the vastly changed circumstances of our own times. Let me conclude with a simple, tentative definition of religious poverty. Religious poverty is an evangelically inspired and structured relationship to material creation which involves owning well, using well, and suffering well for the purpose of transforming human existence, our own included. Its goal is a community in which all have the material supports necessary for truly human living whose fullest realization is that total openness to God which makes salvation possible and real.

Part Three

REFLECTING ON SOME CONTEMPORARY CHALLENGES

Chapter Ten
PERMANENT COMMITMENT
IN A DANGEROUS WORLD

The material for this chapter was originally developed for presentation to a group of lay and religious men and women, married and celibate, who participated in a workshop held at El Pomar Renewal Center in Colorado Springs, Colorado in the spring of 1982. It was refined and revised, in the light of discussion at that workshop and subsequent reading and discussion with religious of my own and other congregations, for presentation to a similar mixed group at a workshop given at Oblate School of Theology in San Antonio, Texas in May 1984.

I. THE CONTEMPORARY SITUATION

If statistics were an adequate description of reality we would have no choice but to conclude that permanent or lifelong commitment is, if not impossible, so difficult as to be an impractical ideal for most people. Nearly half of the marriages in this country, including those between Catholics, end in divorce. And in the past twenty years tens of thousands of priests and religious have resigned from ordained ministry or left religious life. In contrast to the attitudes which prevailed a couple of decades ago few people today, including those who have remained faithful to marital or religious commitments, are inclined to judge harshly those who have left. The reason for this more lenient attitude is not only that we have taken more seriously the Gospel which is much less tolerant of self-righteous condemnation of others than it is of human weakness or failure; it is also that we are aware of factors in contemporary society which militate against permanent commitment in a way that was scarcely imaginable in times past and that we are also aware of the fact that none of us is immune to these influences. I would like to preface my reflections on the meaning and possibility of permanent commitment with a brief look at some of the cultural and historical obstacles to such commitment. This catalogue is in no sense complete, and every reader will be able to suggest additions to it. But the point I want to make is that these factors are qualitatively different in some respects from those of other times and places and that this difference must have a real effect on the way we think about commitments, on the way we prepare people to undertake such commitments, and on our attitudes toward those who, for one reason or another, set aside such commitments once they are made.

A. Cultural Factors

A first cultural factor influencing both those considering undertaking a permanent commitment and younger people who have already made such commitments is the fact that many young people today reach maturity without having had any realistic experience of commitment among the adults to whom they look for example and guidance. Fifty years ago the child of "a broken home" was rare and pitied. Today we do not even use the expression. Increasing numbers of children are growing up in single parent homes, in joint custody arrangements, with a step-parent or even a series of step-parents. Grandparents, who should function as a kind of symbolic assurance of the continuity of generations founded on marital fidelity, often come and go in children's lives like the tumbling patterns of a kaleidoscope. Little children are assigned public roles in the second and third weddings of their parents and given little or no chance to mourn the loss of a departed parent or to adjust to new relationships which would tax the emotional resources of well-adjusted adults. Even children of seemingly stable marriages know how frequent divorce and separation are and cannot be unaware of the vulnerability of their own families to the disaster that strikes around them in school and at play.

The same instability characterizes the once secure religious context of Catholic children growing up today in the Church. In years past virtually no young Catholic knew a priest or sister who had left the ministry or religious life. Today most know at least some. The kind of rock-like solidity of parish life assured by the commitment of religious personnel, even if the individual

ministers changed from year to year, is not part of the experience of young people growing up in today's Church. The persons they call "Father" or "Sister" today and know are
committed to lifelong celibacy may be married next year.

Even for the child who is sheltered in a two-parent family
and blessed with a religious environment in which commitments
have endured, the media make it impossible to believe that this
situation is normal or widespread. Even infidelities which were
never mentioned in a child's presence a few decades ago are part
of the common vicarious, if not real, experience of even pre-
schoolers today.

In short, the experience of most young people growing up
in this country is that permanent commitments, although fac-
ilely made, are not always or even usually kept. Nor are the social or religious sanctions such as to suggest that anyone really
expects that they will be. In such a situation it is more than a little
difficult for a young person to form an ideal of commitment, to
image commitment in a way that is compelling as she or he enters adult life.

A second cultural factor militating against the making and
honoring of permanent commitments is that we live in a con-
sumerist society which powerfully inculcates an ethic of personal fulfillment that is essentially hedonistic and self-centered.
Every television advertisement advises us that if something is
not "paying off" in terms of personal satisfaction the only sensible thing to do is to get rid of it and try something else. One
not only gets rid of the toothpaste when it does not work for us;
one also gets rid of the person who uses the inferior product.
The ideals of a fulfillment which might come through suffering,
of fidelity over the long haul when it does not seem to be paying
off, of not taking the available escape route when one is hurting,
seem masochistic to someone raised in a throwaway culture. The
business of life, so our culture says, is to find personal satisfaction and meaning during the short and only time allotted to us
on this planet. To remain trapped in a situation which is hurtful,
or even unpleasant, is to waste one's life; there are options and
a sensible person will take them. If there were not a grain of
truth in this cultural wisdom it would be easier to argue with it.
But even then the argument would have to appeal to an expe-

rience of the real rewards of fidelity in the face of suffering and apparent non-satisfaction, and that experience is not readily available in our world or Church.

The situation is further complicated by the fact that many commitments, both marital and religious, of recent years were badly made, and bringing them to a close really does seem to be, and probably is, the best solution. The number of young people who have married much too young has swelled the ranks of the divorced. The reasons for these youthful marriages include the bizarre socializing patterns of our culture, rampant eroticism of the most superficial kind, and the understandable desire of many young people to escape intolerable home situations. And we have to admit that there is little reason for young people to pay much attention to adults whose own marriages have failed, sometimes repeatedly, or to celibate ministers who seem not to know what love is all about, when these adults try to warn them against early marriages. Not all young people enter early marriages, and not all such marriages fail. But in a society in which nearly half of all marriages fail, the chance for the failure of a youthful marriage is compounded and the statistics corroborate this conclusion.

The situation is not a great deal better among religious and priests. Until quite recently seminaries and novitiates took candidates at such an early age that often no realistic decision about their lives was possible. Furthermore, religious and priestly life, like marriage, could easily appear to a confused young person as the solution to terrifying life problems. Religious life, with its vows of poverty, celibacy, and obedience, has appeared to many young people as an ideal shelter from the seemingly insurmountable challenges of becoming an adult in a socially, economically, and politically chaotic world. The celibate lifestyle seems to offer the possibility of avoiding questions of sexual identity, the challenge of intimacy, and the burdens of parenthood. And there is little secrecy today about the fact that an all-male, celibate ordained ministry is the last (or first!) resort of many homosexual men who find in it a "virtuous" and socially acceptable way to escape the pressures of a homophobic society. And finally, mandatory celibacy for the ordained has led many men, truly called to both ministry and marriage, to undertake a burden which they cannot (and should not) carry for an entire lifetime.

Needless to say, this dismal description is not the whole picture. Many people marry well; and many priests and religious, both homosexual and heterosexual, undertake their commitments for the right reasons. But the fact that the cultural situation in both the society at large and in the Church in many ways encourages bad vocational choices means that the dissolution of marriages, resignation from ordained ministry, and dispensation from religious vows cannot be unreservedly condemned. In many cases it is the only reasonable, even virtuous, thing to do. And if in some, even many, cases the breaking of commitments is justified, who is to say in which cases it is not? An ethos in which permanent commitment is culturally and religiously sustainable is one in which most commitments are made and honored for the right reasons. In such a situation the breaking of commitments can be realistically regarded as aberrant, and even the failures will sustain the ideal. But we do not participate in such an ethos. This does not mean that permanent commitment is impossible in our situation but it does mean that our approach to it must take into account a very different set of cultural factors than were operative thirty or fifty years ago.

B. *Historical Factors*

Aside from these cultural factors there is a second set of factors that arise from modernity itself, from the place in history where we find ourselves, and which tend to undermine the possibility of permanent commitment. The first is the fact of greatly increased longevity among a population that is occupationally and geographically extremely mobile and psychologically more self-aware than any generation we know anything about. Because life expectancy is much longer today the average adult commitment, if it lasts a lifetime, will last fifty to eighty years and during that time the average adult can expect to change careers at least three times and geographical location half a dozen times. This same person will traverse a number of "stages" of adult development involving various crises and sometimes major personality changes and developments. Spouses must adjust not only to their own but to each other's changing locations, careers, and selves. Priests and religious face the same problems of personal, geographical, and career changes often compounded by the frustrations caused by institutional rigidity and non-responsiveness to their personal development on the part of ecclesiastical officials who see them more as cogs in an endangered power structure than as persons with human needs and desires.

Another historical factor that affects the possibility of life commitment is the higher expectations that most first world people have as a result of exposure to the available goods of our society. People in our society, no matter what their occupation or status, expect much more of life in terms of education, satisfaction in personal relationships, travel, recreation, and opportunity for growth and development than did their nineteenth century counterparts. For all but the desperately poor in this country survival is not the all-consuming concern. Quality of life is the primary objective. Commitments can really or apparently stand in the way of satisfying expectations which seem in no way exorbitant even though such expectations would have seemed utopian a few decades ago.

A final historical factor that must be recognized is that the rate, direction, and content of change in our society is such that even the relatively immediate future is literally unimaginable. A middle-aged person today has only to mentally catalogue the world modifying developments that have occurred in his or her own lifetime to realize the possibility that two or three years could so modify life on this planet that practically nothing we now engage in, value, hope for, or fear would have the slightest relevance. It has always been true that a person making a life commitment was, in a certain sense, signing a blank check. We have all heard stories of the young couple involved in an accident on their wedding night leaving one of them widowed or the lifetime partner of a helpless cripple. Projects have collapsed, homes been destroyed, and loving companions lost to drink or crime or violence. But the disasters or changes were imaginable. Today no one can have any realistic idea what even the short-term future holds. The changes are not variations on the themes of death, sickness, poverty, failure. They are cosmic modifications that raise a very serious and very real question about whether it is possible to honestly make a commitment intended to embrace the next fifty, sixty, seventy years during which life on this planet will certainly change so radically that we have no idea what it will look like. How can one speak for that which one cannot even imagine?

All of these cultural and historical factors, as well as many others we have not discussed, are important ingredients in any consideration of permanent commitment today. As will soon be clear, I do not want to argue that they make such commitment inconceivable, unwise, or impossible. But I do want to say that permanent commitment today is a qualitatively different project than it was at other, even relatively recent, times and that any realistic image of such commitment must take account of this difference. It is insufficient to maintain that commitment has always been difficult and that young people today (or adults for that matter) are just less generous or responsible than were their counterparts of previous generations. The problematic of permanent commitment needs to be re-examined today in light of the historical-cultural situation in which we live. And young people contemplating such commitments must be prepared differently than we were prepared twenty or thirty years ago. Such a re-examination is the burden of this essay, and therefore the reflections and conclusions in it are tentative and meant to be suggestive. My intention is not to solve the problem or answer the question (since I am not competent to do either) but to reflect on it and invite others to do the same.

II. THE MEANING OF PERMANENT COMMITMENT

The topic we are discussing could probably be more accurately designated *life* commitment because it concerns not so much chronological time as such but the totality of a human life. However, there is a profound reason why we speak of life commitment as permanent commitment, namely, the temporal or historical character of human existence. Our concern is not primarily chronological time, but existential time. As modern philosophers like Martin Heidegger have made us aware, human beings are the only truly historical beings. Temporality is a fundamental characteristic of our human mode of being. Clocks

can create the impression that time is an objective quantity outside ourselves but, in fact, it is not. Anyone who has ever experienced the dragging of a day spent in a hospital bed, the
interminable wait for a loved one, or the seemingly instanta-
neous disappearance of the allotted time in a prison visit or during an exam knows how subjective time is. Time is relative to our
desires, projects, relationships, hopes, fears. As far as we know
only human beings experience time as time. Only we experience
ourselves as the child of our own past and the parent of our own
future.

Temporality, or historicity, comes from our realization of
the fact that we are going to die. Only human beings, as far as
we know, can envision the future and know that inevitably they
will die. And thus we alone speak of that span of time between
our birth which we can look back toward and our death which
we can look ahead to as "my life." We do not know how long it
will be, but we do know that it is radically and inalienably
"mine." Each person's life, no matter how many other people
live at the same time and in the same place, is unique, not only
because each one's life belongs to him or her alone but also because it is the only life each person has. This fact of having a life
to live, rather than simply being the subject or object of what is
going on in the world, creates the uniquely human challenge to
"make something of oneself," to "do something with one's life."
Human beings experience their life as a project.

As the medieval philosophers tell us, any project begins
with the end, and this is part of what makes a project different
from just "going with the flow" or tumbling along through a series of disconnected episodes. Whether the project is to build a
house, have a child, get an education, make money, or save the
world, it must begin with an image, however vague, of the final
product. Everything that will be done to bring the project to
completion will be chosen in view of the imagined end. It is entirely possible that many changes will be made in the plan before
a major project is completed, but they will be changes in a plan,
not random action. The great project of every human being is
his or her own life. There are undoubtedly people who never
undertake the project, who drift aimlessly through life doing
whatever their mood suggests and becoming whatever the

forces around them make them to be. But we do not regard such people as truly significant human beings. They are walking tragedies whether they see themselves that way or not, for tragedy is the failure of one who is called to greatness, and every human being is called to greatness. Not all are called to public prominence, but each is called to make of his or her life a work of art.

The way in which human beings undertake the project of their lives is by the promise. A promise is what linguistic philosophers call performative language. By what we say (to ourselves or to others) we actually embrace and shape our own future. The promise is truly "sacramental" in that it brings about what it signifies. To say "I take John for my lawful wedded husband" actually causes a permanent and public relationship to exist between the speaker and John. It is a relationship which has social, economic, and legal consequences recognized by everyone in the society. By means of a promise we project ourselves into the future and commit ourselves to be or become or do something. This commitment is an espousal of the end and involves the enlistment of our energies and resources in the bringing about of that end. Furthermore, it shapes the expectations of others. Others have a right to expect that we will be faithful to what we have called into being by our promise. By the breaking or keeping of our promises we support or shatter the faith of others. By keeping promises human beings weave among themselves a fabric of trust which is the only viable context for truly meaningful life among free people.

When we apply what can be said of any promise to the promise we call life commitment we see immediately the importance and power of this radical act. Life commitment, properly speaking, can only be validly made to a person or persons. People who have given their lives to money, to projects, to institutions, are deformed by that commitment because it is not worthy of total human self-gift. The true life commitment is the ultimate realization of faith, hope, and love in their interrelationship. We *believe* that this person is worth the *love* we promise and so we *trust* that this self-gift will bring about the true fulfillment of our deepest longings in this one and only life we have to live. This promise is the embracing of the end, not primarily in the sense of chronological time, but in the sense of existential time, of human temporality. We choose the song we will sing with our life, the role we will play in the cosmic drama of human history. This choice involves our whole life because it is precisely what makes of our life a whole. But its primary objective is not time. Rather time is the "stuff" that will allow us to become what we have set out to be. The commitment, one way or another, will take all the time we have. Thus, we frame the commitment in terms of time, of life itself. The project we have undertaken is our own life; the promise that expresses it can only be framed in terms of permanence, lifelong fidelity to what we have undertaken, to the love which alone makes a life human.

However, a profound irony abides in the heart of the situation of life commitment because life commitment must usually be made before we have the experience which can adequately inform and ground such a choice. Adults are infamous for their warnings to idealistic young people about the unknowns that a life commitment involves. But such warnings are relatively useless. Furthermore, one cannot experiment with the risks of the commitment because, prior to the commitment, whatever risks one encounters are precisely *not* those of the commitment. There is really no such thing as a "trial marriage" because prior to marriage the commitment is not a marital commitment. The simple fact of the matter is one cannot wait until the middle of the project to make one's commitment, for without a beginning there is no middle. The piece must be played from the beginning. This is precisely what makes every individual's greatest act of love essentially new, pristine, original, unfounded on any real proof. Commitment is the great adventure, and it is an adventure no matter how many persons have made it before us because *we* have never made this trip before. Others can warn us of dangers, but they are not the dangers we will face; they can assure us of joys, but they are not the joys we will savor. Every life commitment is as unique as the life to which it gives definitive shape.

In the Christian context life commitment takes on sacramental significance. Every Christian's fundamental commitment is to God, in Christ, through the power of the Spirit received in baptism. Our commitment is a response to God's self-gift to us, the shaping of the life God has given us according to our perception of God's dream for us. Thus, when the Christian experiences the attraction to marriage or to consecrated celibacy the attraction is experienced as a vocation, as a call from God to actualize the basic Christian commitment through the mediation of this person or through a union with Christ in consecrated celibacy which foregoes exclusive human mediation. The faith, hope, and love that must come to expression in any truly human life commitment have for the Christian a theological quality, for it is God who addresses to me this invitation and to whom I respond. Thus, in different ways both Christian marriage and consecrated celibacy are witnesses to the fidelity of God to us, human images of that wholeness and fullness which characterizes God's self-gift in Christ to the Church community and which informs our total self-gift to God in response.

Although life commitment is made not to things but to a person or persons, Christian life commitment is realized in an institutional context. Both marriage and consecrated celibacy are institutionalized and the institution is intimately bound up with the reality, the self-gift, which constitutes the commitment. In chapter four we examined in some detail the light that the Gospel of St. John throws upon the relationship, intimate but not absolute, between commitment and its institutional embodiment. What that examination suggested was that the institutional context of any commitment, even that of divinely established Judaism, must not be absolutely equated with the commitment itself. Institutions, even those we recognize as divine in origin, remain human in realization and therefore relative, no matter how closely associated with the will of God for individuals or groups. While we must be extremely reserved about deciding that what God has instituted is no longer valid for us, and must never conclude that it is invalid in itself, nevertheless it is possible that historical developments beyond our control might make it necessary for us to move beyond the legitimate institutional framework of our commitment. My reason for stressing this point is that there was a tendency in the past, still operative today, which creates very serious difficulties for many young people, namely, the tendency to absolutize the institutional context of life commitment in such a way as to suggest that the object of the commitment is marriage or religious life or ordained ministry rather than the person or persons to whom one is giving one's life. This can easily make the context appear as a kind of "trap," a *cul de sac,* rather than as the social and religious framework which facilitates fidelity. While stressing the intimate, and ordinarily unbreakable, connection between the commitment and its institutional context, we need also to acknowledge that there can be situations in which the commitment must seek another institutional expression. These situations cannot be generalized. But they must be recognized if the emphasis is to be kept where it belongs, on the relationships established and the life project thereby undertaken rather than on juridical procedures and arrangements.

III. PERMANENT COMMITMENT TODAY

Having considered life commitment as an ideal as well as the historical and cultural obstacles to such a commitment today, we are in a position to reflect on the reality of permanent commitment in our own times. If an achieved permanent commitment is the ultimate realization of the self, then the shaping of the life project, no matter how difficult, must be both possible and fulfilling for us as it has been for people of previous generations. No doubt the emphasis will be different. It will fall less on chronological time and more on existential totality. The important thing is not *that* one spends a whole life doing something but *what* one does with one's whole life and *how* one does it. The important thing is not that one does not change state of life but that one does change, unceasingly, so as to be able to grow into the fullness of life that was dimly outlined by the initial promise. It is this fundamental commitment to change and growth that allows us to see life commitment not as entrapment in static structures but as ongoing dynamic involvement with the whole of life, whatever the circumstances may be.

This emphasis placed on existential totality must be accompanied by a much sharper sense of the distinction (not separation) between the commitment which is always to person(s) and the institutional context of the commitment than might have been the case in times past. Fidelity is an attitude and disposition toward persons, a commitment to continue to love and to grow in love, no matter how things and circumstances change. Fidelity in a Christian life commitment is three-dimensional: fidelity to God, fidelity to self, and fidelity to the other person or people involved. Fidelity to God will involve ongoing discernment of the Spirit's action in one's life, a delicate and prayerful sensitivity to the dynamics of the call. Fidelity to the self involves a commitment to continue to grow, that is, to learn, to risk, to face criticism and challenge, to engage in ongoing conversion. And fidelity to the others involved engages us in an ongoing and ever-renewed devotion to them and to their real good, a continuing resolve to take them into account in all our decisions.

The real danger to commitment is not that circumstances will change or situations be modified; the real danger is stagnation, tepidity, the inauguration of a kind of cold war from which true love is excluded, or the giving up on self, others, and life itself which turns commitment into an endurance contest or a trial by ordeal rather than the dangerous but ultimately worthwhile adventure of the human spirit in quest of authentic self-realization.

The genuine value of the permanence of life commitment lies not in its chronological duration but in the existential possibilities that only permanence can offer. Personal growth and relationships take time, and unless the commitment to take that time precedes the difficulties one will inevitably encounter, the latter will precipitate a pulling out before growth can take place. The assurance of time is the best framework for working out long-lasting solutions to serious problems, and the working out of real life challenges is finally the only path to maturity. We are more likely to work at relationships that we are committed to sustaining, and others are more likely to work things out with us if they can count on our commitment and we on theirs. The tendency, much encouraged by our society and culture, to "drop out" of problem situations, to walk away when the going gets tough, is a tendency to remain a child forever. Not all problems are worth our time and energy, but some are. And commitment is the context within which, finally, the worthwhile problems of life must be solved because good solutions are precisely those which promote our life project, which help us to be and to become what we have chosen to be in the one and only life we have to live.

Our culture, with its hedonistic ethos, tends to disguise from us the human and spiritual meaningfulness of "bad times." When a marriage hits rough water, or when religious life begins to look dull and meaningless, the first temptation is to conclude that the original choice was a mistake or that whatever made us choose this life was illusion. The sooner we can get out of the situation and start over, the better. As we have already acknowledged, there are indeed mistaken choices and commitments that should never have been made. But a well-made choice is no guarantee against bad times. It is perhaps only in such times that we hear the invitation to enter into the emptiness which God alone can fill. It is only in such times that we can plumb the mystery of fidelity unto death, the fidelity by which the Son of God became Savior of the world. It is only in such times, when we experience our lostness and emptiness and sinfulness, that we can give God the chance to truly save us because, like Peter sinking in the sea, we cannot save ourselves. It is in the bad times that we discover our deepest resources, energies of love and power of enduring that we did not know we possessed. We have all met older married people or religious who have passed through all the turmoil and suffering that a true life commitment can offer and who now radiate the peace, serenity, and wisdom of people who have indeed "made something of their lives." It may well be true that life commitment, never easy, is even more difficult in our times. But it remains the great glory of human life and it is possible because of the one who "having loved his own who were in the world . . . loved them unto the end" (Jn 13:1).

Chapter Eleven
FRIENDSHIP IN THE LIFE
OF CONSECRATED CELIBATES

> The material in this chapter was originally prepared for a group of priests, religious men and women, and lay people as part of a series of lectures on issues in contemporary spirituality given at Oblate School of Theology in San Antonio, Texas, May 31 to June 1, 1984. It was revised for presentation to a group of women religious attending a conference sponsored by New Ways Ministry entitled "Exploring Our Sexual Orientation" which took place in Burlingame, California, November 30 to December 2, 1984. Between the two presentations the manuscript was read and critiqued from various points of view by religious brothers and sisters, a few priests and bishops, and several lay persons.

I. FRAMEWORK FOR UNDERSTANDING CONSECRATED CELIBACY

Before addressing the main topic of this paper, namely, the possibility, necessity, and appropriate forms of friendship in the life of the consecrated celibate, it is necessary to clarify certain terms and notions about which there is both confusion and disagreement today. I certainly do not wish to claim that my understanding of these matters is the only or the best way to understand them. I only hope to give cogent reasons for the positions I take so that the reader can decide for himself or herself whether they make sense and are helpful in this very important area of religious life.

A. *Distinction between Celibacy and Consecrated Celibacy*

First, although it might not always have been necessary to do so, I think it is important in our times to distinguish clearly between celibacy and the consecrated celibacy which is vowed by religious. Celibacy is simply the state of being, for whatever reason, unmarried.[1] The celibate person, by definition, is free to

207

marry if and when she or he chooses to do so. In the Christian context celibacy ideally involves, as its appropriate form of chastity, abstention from sexual relations, that is, from fornication or adultery. It is important for religious to realize that in our culture simply being celibate, that is, unmarried, is not in and of itself religiously significant to our contemporaries. Furthermore, few people today assume that because a person is celibate he or she is not sexually active. People choose not to marry for many reasons, ranging from the transcendently selfless to the totally ego-centered including such reasons as political statement, social protest, and sheer apathy. What this means for religious is that if the celibacy of our lifestyle is to witness to anything in particular it must involve more than celibacy as such.

It is difficult to find an appropriate term for religious celibacy. Chastity is certainly inadequate because all Christians are called to chastity and religious chastity is no more chaste than married or single chastity. Referring to the religious lifestyle as chaste in a pre-eminent way contributes to the reprehensible elitism that has long characterized religious life in the Church and which religious have been striving, since Vatican II, to eliminate from their attitudes and rhetoric as well as from their behavior. For purposes of clarity I will refer to religious celibacy as consecrated celibacy and trust that my reasons for the choice will be at least clear, if not convincing, from what follows.

Consecrated celibacy involves, first of all, a free choice to remain unmarried for the whole of one's life, that is, to make non-marriage a state of life. One cannot meaningfully embrace consecrated celibacy out of necessity, misfortune, coercion, or inertia. Nor can one embrace consecrated celibacy for a time, for example, until one meets an appropriate partner. Consecrated celibacy is the defining characteristic of religious life as a public lifestyle in the Church, and it has the same intrinsic exigency of permanence that matrimony, the other consecrated lifestyle in the Church, does. This is not meant as any kind of judgment on people who have left religious life or sacramental marriage. It is a statement about the consecrated states of life as such. Whatever the vicissitudes of real life make necessary in individual cases (and judgment in such cases is God's affair, not ours) permanence remains an essential characteristic of the life commitments of matrimony and religious profession. In both these respects, as a free choice of non-marriage and as an intentionally permanent commitment, consecrated celibacy differs from other instances of celibacy.

Sexual abstinence, that is, abstinence from genital relationships, is the appropriate form of chastity for the consecrated celibate as it is for any Christian celibate. The reasons for this have to be taken up in more detail later, but for the moment I am merely stating it for purposes of completeness in our preliminary description of consecrated celibacy.

So far I have been describing consecrated celibacy materially, that is, trying to spell out its distinguishing visible characteristics. But far more important for an understanding of consecrated celibacy is a consideration of its inner meaning for the person who undertakes it and its significance for the ecclesial community within which it is undertaken. It seems to me that there are at least five dimensions to the interiority of consecrated celibacy that can contribute to our consideration of celibacy and friendship.

First, consecrated celibacy is *religiously motivated and personally meaningful* to the person. I am convinced, both from my study of the history of religious life and from my experience of listening to the life stories, struggles, and joys of many religious, that there are several valid types of motivation for the choice of consecrated celibacy. They seem to fall into two groups, those which are primarily rooted in ministerial concerns and those which reflect primarily a concern with the particular relationship to Christ that celibacy embodies and expresses.[2] But in all cases, genuine consecrated celibacy is freely chosen as religiously meaningful for the person who chooses it. I am sure there are people who would want to argue that celibacy could be validly accepted as a condition for access to some religiously meaningful life or activity, for example, ordained ministry, rather than as religiously meaningful in itself for the person involved. I do not think that this is true, and my conviction on this subject affects a great deal of what I will have to say about the sexual implications of consecrated celibacy. My assumption throughout is that genuine consecrated celibacy must be freely chosen as personally meaningful and for religious motives.

A second interior characteristic of consecrated celibacy is that it is chosen as the *best path to affective growth and development* for the person who chooses it. Celibacy is a way of determining how we will live our sexuality. Our masculinity or femininity, that is, our sexuality, shapes our relational capacity, our potential for self-transcendence in love for others, whether those of our own sex or of the other sex. Happiness, health, and holiness depend in a crucial way on our finding a way to live our sexuality, that is, our relational capacity, which is both personally fulfilling and life-giving for others. For most people the best path to full sexual fulfillment is a lifelong commitment to one other person in a relationship which allows for growth in identity and intimacy and which finds its fullest expression in the sharing and fostering of human life. The person who chooses consecrated celibacy embarks on the road less traveled. The person is convinced, for reasons of the heart that may never be clear to others or even fully clear to oneself, that celibacy is the best way to affective maturity for him or her. Repression, confusion about sexual identity or orientation, fear of full sexual living, a need for security, or a preference for a same-sex community context is totally inadequate as the basis for a valid choice of consecrated celibacy. This is not to say that such factors do not play some role in most adolescent choices of religious life. But if they are not resolved, if the person does not eventually discover in himself or herself a genuine and uncoerced conviction that celibacy is the most authentic path to affective wholeness and maturity for himself or herself (in more traditional terms, that one is truly called by one's Creator to this form of life), celibacy can perhaps be borne as a burden but it cannot become the source of affective energy for a fully human life.

Third, consecrated celibacy is not solely an intrapersonal reality. Religious profession is essentially both a personal commitment to Christ and an *ecclesial commitment to public ministry*. The ministry of religious, like that of all Christians, is rooted in baptism. But it receives its specific form from the vows of profession. By the profession of consecrated celibacy religious commit themselves in a particular way to the healing and transformation in Christ of the social order in its interpersonal dimensions.[3] This ministry differs from age to age because the disorders and the potentialities of interpersonal life vary according to historical and cultural setting. In our own time and place we can surely recognize the excesses and violences of our culture, hedonism, unbridled eroticism, pornography, and sexual violence as particular areas of concern. What is perhaps the most important social movement in world history, the liberation of women and men from the perversion of patriarchy and sexism, creates a special sphere of ministerial concern for the twentieth century consecrated celibate. The effort to achieve an appropriate integration of heterosexual and homosexual persons into one Christian community free of violence and intolerance and marked by charity and mutual acceptance has taken on a particularly public and urgent character in our own day. Reconciliation and community building in all their forms are ministry to the social order that have become crucial in a nuclear age. This is not an exhaustive list but merely an indication of the ministerial implications of the choice of consecrated celibacy in the twentieth century Church.

A fourth dimension of consecrated celibacy is the *public witness* the celibate gives in the Church, not to the totality of the Christian mystery, but to certain important aspects of it. Both married and celibate persons must live the whole of the Christian mystery, but we each give striking public witness to part of it and our complementary witness proclaims the good news. Some aspects of the Christian mystery to which consecrated celibates give particular witness (although they must never claim to "own" these as their private experience!) are the inviolability of the personal inner sanctum, the wholeness of the person before God, the absolute priority and real all-sufficiency of God in the Christian life, the totality of the demand of the reign of God, and the reality of the resurrection life both in this world and after death. This is the experience of every mature Christian, but it stands out with particular clarity in the single lifestyle of the consecrated celibate whose celibacy is not a burden accepted but a path freely chosen in response to a genuine personal vocation.

Finally, and very closely related to the foregoing, consecrated celibacy is a *sacramental or effectively significant living out* of one important aspect of the human and Christian condition in all its mysterious paschal density. Part of the experience of being human is the *ultimate aloneness and loneliness* of each of us. Whether celibate or married, none of us can escape the realization of the limits of human intimacy, the final and ultimate aloneness that even the most intense experience of physical and psychological union cannot obscure or alleviate for more than a fleeting moment. For all of us loneliness must become fruitful solitude or it will become deadly and sterile isolation. Marriage is no guarantee that human loneliness will mature into true solitude; neither is celibacy. But consecrated celibacy is a choice to live that loneliness in a particularly stark and vibrant way, to drink to the dregs, as it were, the mystery of human aloneness, in the confident hope that the other side of loneliness is union with God. A fulfilled celibate life is a sacrament of human solitude transubstantiated by the love of God into the life-giving bread of human solidarity. It is a rare enough achievement, perhaps even more rare than the truly sacramental marriage, but both are a splendid gift not only to the Church but to the world.

B. Celibacy, Sexuality, and Genitality

A second basic notion, following upon the distinction between celibacy and consecrated celibacy, has to do with how we understand the genital expression of sexuality. I want, at this point, to distance myself from the attitude that is so prevalent in our culture that sex is an absolute need for all normal persons. On the contrary, it *is* possible to abstain from sex, for a time, or even for a lifetime, without damage to oneself if it is done freely for the right reasons. Sex is a very strong drive, but it is not, as some people would have us believe, an appetite like that for food and drink. If the sexual drive is not satisfied one does not die. As a pure biological need, sex is an animal instinct designed for the preservation not of the self but of the species. In other words, sex and sexuality are not the same thing. As human beings we are not the subjects of a purely biological sex drive. We have a choice about how we will integrate our sexuality into our total life experience of aloneness and relationship. That choice may involve sex, that is, the genital expression of our sexuality, or it may not. The all-important issue is not whether we have genital relations but why or why not and how and with what result for ourselves and others.

When tempted to romanticize the urgency of sexual desire it is useful to remember that all healthy and chaste people, whether married, single, or celibate, must learn non-repressive ways to control their sexual desires because no one can responsibly satisfy them at will. Even the most happily married person with the most sexually responsive spouse must learn to be considerate of the dispositions of the partner. Illness, absence, or even physical accommodations can make short-term or even long-term abstinence necessary. Admittedly, celibates face a much greater challenge in committing themselves to a life of sexual abstinence. But it is wholesome to remember that everyone must learn to deal with some degree of frustration of normal sexual desires.

However, if religious are to become sexually integrated individuals who are relatively proficient in this matter of sexual self-control, or chastity, it is clear that they need much more realistic preparation for a life of celibacy than has been characteristic of formation programs in the past—and is still characteristic of some. Knowing the definition of chastity, which is about all that formation for this virtue involved in times past, does not make a person forthwith proficient in its practice. The implied expectation that one called to celibacy never experiences serious or prolonged temptations in this area, and certainly never fails, has led to dishonesty, guilt, and protracted immaturity which add up to prolonged anguish and vicious cycles of self-hatred and perfectionism. Chastity, like any other virtue, is learned slowly by trial and error, and the learning could be facilitated by the honest acceptance of the difficulty involved and by an early-acquired knowledge that everyone struggles with the same problems. If we are not ashamed to admit to young religious that we all get angry, are all lazy at times, all fail occasionally to practice appropriate moderation in food and drink, all get discouraged and are tempted to abandon our commitments, all at some time or another deliberately hurt others, all fail to accept

our responsibilities—why do we create the impression that no
good religious has ever sinned against chastity? If a person is
convinced, consciously or otherwise, that a good religious never
fails in the area of chastity, this unrealistic self-image makes the
creative use of failure nearly impossible. Since incessant success
in the spiritual life is not possible, only the person who learns to
use failure wisely will grow and develop. A perfectionistic self-
image, especially in the area of chastity, leads only to deceit, self-
hatred, and neurotic guilt.

A second factor in helping religious develop the virtue of
chastity is helping them attend to and thus learn something
about their own sexual responses. If every sexual movement
comes as a shock and is met with denial, instinctive repression,
and guilt, the young person will never learn appropriate and
healthy ways to handle his or her sexuality. General rules in this
area are not much help, especially when their sole content is
"Whatever you're thinking about, don't do it." Each of us has to
learn how our own sexuality functions if we are to integrate it
into our own personality in healthy ways.

A third factor in formation for chaste celibacy is more important in our times than it was in the past. Religious today must
learn to live and behave in a two-sex universe. A sexually healthy
adult, whether homosexual or heterosexual in orientation, must
be able to relate to, to enjoy the company of, and to work well
with people of both sexes. The challenges are somewhat different for people of heterosexual orientation and those of homosexual orientation. But neither can be excused from developing
the capacity to relate well with members of their own and the
other sex. At times the problem is overcoming fear and/or aver-
sion and at others learning to be with the attractive other without sexually loading the situation. But in any case, the days of
living in a virtually one-sex world are over, and the attitudes of
fear, arrogance, superiority or inferiority, prudery, and cold-
ness which created and sustained such worlds are not only obsolete but counter-productive.

Finally, if religious are to practice a chastity appropriate to
their public profession of consecrated celibacy they must develop adequate reasons for sexual abstinence as well as healthy
alternative routes to human maturity in the relational sphere.

An arbitrary law, anti-sexual and repressive moralism, tradition, social pressure, or fear of the consequences are not adequate reasons for lifelong sexual abstinence no matter how effective they may be in controlling external behavior.

C. The Issue of Sexual Abstinence

This brings us to the third and final area of preliminary considerations, namely, the difficult issue of sexual abstinence. The question which has become especially important and urgent for many religious today is whether it might be permissible under some circumstances for a religious with a public vow of consecrated celibacy to maintain a responsible, private, genitally expressed relationship with someone provided it causes no scandal and does not harm either party or their other relationships and does not interfere with their primary community and ministerial commitments. This arrangement is sometimes referred to as "the third way" because it is proposed as an alternative, on the one hand, to a publicly recognized sexual relationship such as marriage or some other permanent sexual commitment, and, on the other hand, to sexual abstinence within the context of celibate commitment. In my opinion, the third way is not a viable option. I do not intend my remarks as a moral condemnation of celibates who have become sexually involved nor of their relationships (which it is certainly not my business to judge) but as a statement of principle and the articulation of what I consider to be the ideal. I want to offer four considerations that have led me to this position which might well seem unduly restrictive and unrealistically demanding to many but to which I can see no fully authentic alternative.

First, and most importantly, it seems to me that sexual relations between persons who are not committed to each other in a permanent, faithful, and exclusive relationship that is open to and oriented toward shared generativity (whether physical or spiritual) is fundamentally inauthentic no matter how deeply felt or mutually satisfying. Our body is not a possession. It is the symbol, that is, the effective sign of ourself. To give full and unreserved access to our body-person to another and to accept the same gift from that other is to symbolically express total self-commitment. Total personal self-commitment cannot be transitory or shared with several. To become one flesh with another necessarily involves the intention to forge a shared destiny, to undertake a common life-project, to belong exclusively to one another as each belongs to no other. It commits and calls both persons to undertake the sexual journey of learning to speak the language of intimacy by repeatedly coming together in physical, psychological, and spiritual union, and it gives each the right to expect this repeated self-gift of the other, not when it happens to be convenient, but according to a mutual commitment which gives priority to the development of this special form of communication. Sexual intercourse is not just one way of expressing affection, an intensified handshake if you will. It is the expression of total and exclusive self-commitment to another. Such a commitment is not compatible with another total life commitment, especially one from which the beloved is excluded at times.

The second consideration flows directly from the last remark. Sexual relations with someone to whom one is not permanently, faithfully, and exclusively committed can never really be fair to the partner no matter how willing the other is. And mutual unfairness is no more defensible than unilateral exploitation. Sexual relations outside of a permanent life commitment say to the partner something that is not true, something that cannot be true as long as one's real life commitment lies elsewhere. The heartbroken tales of women who have been mistresses of married men or priests bear eloquent testimony to the ultimate futility and despair of such relationships. No matter what protestations of undying love the otherwise committed partner brings to their sexual encounters, the cold fact remains that the kind of love that is being expressed sexually cannot and will not be embodied in the only lifestyle that can adequately express it, namely, a full, public, permanent, faithful, and exclusive relationship. The same is true for the religious whose fundamental life commitment is not to the sexual partner but to the life undertaken by profession and who cannot therefore publicly claim the relationship or acknowledge the role of the other in his or her life.

A third consideration has to do with the very meaning of

consecrated celibacy itself. To secretly fill the loneliness of celibate life, publicly undertaken as a witness to the adequacy of divine love, with the kind of sexual relationship deliberately surrendered by the profession of celibacy radically subverts the celibate witness in the Church. A sexually active consecrated celibacy is a contradiction in terms and in fact. The single lifestyle, undertaken for evangelical reasons, is meaningless if it is not a life of solitude but rather of coupling, differing from marriage or other lifelong sexual commitment only in virtue of being secret, committed to never establishing a family, and unsteady because of basic life-commitments of the partners which do not include the other. One might also reflect that it is somewhat childish, if not radically selfish, to seek the sustaining joys of a publicly committed relationship without undertaking its responsibilities and obligations either to the other person or to society.

Finally, I think we must attend to a consideration that is more important than many would like to think, namely, that religious profession is a public commitment. Public commitments, whether to one's life partner, to the fulfillment of civic responsibility, or to the practice of celibacy for the reign of God, are a fundamental component of that fabric of public trust which alone permits us to live together in society in non-coercive and mutually respectful ways. The publicly committed celibate who engages in an ongoing sexual relationship lives a lie in a sacramental context, and that lie undermines the trust of the entire Church. Just as adultery undermines the reality of matrimony, whether or not the adulterer is caught, so the "third way" undermines consecrated celibacy as a state of life in the Church and weakens the fabric of public trust which clothes all of us against the harshness of a climate of mutual suspicion and perpetual defensiveness.

For all of these reasons I am forced to conclude that however difficult it may be, and however many mistakes and failures each of us may make and suffer along the way, abstinence from genital relationships is integral to consecrated celibacy and must remain the ideal within which and not outside of which we raise the important questions of friendship and its role and appropriate expression in religious life.

II. CELIBACY AND INTIMACY

Important as these considerations are, however, it must be acknowledged that the most demanding challenge of religious celibacy comes not from the sexual abstinence it involves but from the sacrifice of marriage. My primary concern in this chapter is with the profound implications for the person of the choice not to marry for religious reasons.

According to the renowned psychologist Erik Erikson, there are three crucial developmental tasks for the adult: achieving identity or the sense of self; achieving intimacy or the capacity to transcend the self in self-giving love, to be able to cross the boundaries of the self and allow those boundaries to be crossed without losing one's identity but, on the contrary, enhancing it; and the fruition of selfhood and relationship in generativity or the undertaking of caring responsibility for the next generation through physical or spiritual parenting.[4] The normal context within which most adults experience and grow in intimacy which alone can adequately ground authentic and selfless generativity is marriage. This does not mean, of course, that all married people achieve intimacy. If our divorce statistics are any indication it is a rather rare occurrence. Nevertheless, marriage does supply the normal context and framework in which to devote oneself seriously to growth in intimacy. It provides the privacy, the commitment, the exclusivity, the fidelity, the sexual expression, the public support that foster such growth.

Celibacy, especially lifelong religious celibacy, is a dangerous choice because one thereby renounces the normal context for meeting this developmental challenge. To remain celibate involves the very real risk of never developing the capacity for genuine intimacy. I think it is important for us to face this risk before considering the possibilities of surmounting it. It is simply not sufficient to affirm that love of God fulfills all our human hungers and that the religious who are faithful to their obligations will be protected by God from any psychological harm their commitments could entail.

The harsh fact is that many religious do not develop affectively and we have all seen the results. In the human sphere these men and women remain childish all their lives. After Vatican II many women religious became progressively more embarrassed and angry at their depiction in films and cartoons as over-sized little girls giggling their way through the tragedies of life, demurely submitting to "father's" every whim, and considering themselves adequately compensated for the gift of their lives by being occasionally herded to the amusement park where they squealed in delight on the ferris wheel and tangled their veils in the cotton candy. The religious women of the Church today are recognized as leaders in the struggle for justice in Church and society and they are rarely pictured as little girls. But there is no denying the real basis in people's experience of pre-conciliar religious for the perception of them as immature "innocents" ill-equipped to participate in an adult world.

Male religious have not really presented a more mature picture, although their membership in a male dominant society which is more tolerant of affective immaturity in men often obscures their childishness. The "no-girls-allowed" ethos of male celibate groups is more typical of the activities and attitudes of sixth grade boys than of affectively well-developed men. The locker-room camaraderie, little-boy nicknames and horseplay, physical rigidity, projection of fear of the sexual onto women seen as universally seductive, and social awkwardness of many male celibates is a thin disguise for the insecurity of men who have never grown up affectively, who are out of touch with their own sexuality and scared to death of that of others. The occasional exposures in the press of clerical child-molestation, homosexual promiscuity, and less serious manifestations of arrested sexual development have made us aware of problems that were better hidden in earlier times but which are not new.

Besides the immaturity that failure to engage the challenge to intimacy of adulthood involves, it also almost necessarily results in the displacement of intimacy needs in unhealthy ways. Over-dependence on and subservience toward superiors, reliance on authoritarian uses of power in work relationships, hypochondria, over-eating and addiction to drugs and alcohol, compulsive masturbation, drivenness in work, perfectionism, unhealthy forms of ritualistic piety and rigid adherence to rules and rites are just some of the ways unmet intimacy needs surface

in the disguise of narcotization, control and defense mecha-
nisms, and alienation of authority.

To call attention to the immaturity and displacement behaviors of celibates, the outward manifestations of stunted affective growth, is not to claim that only celibates fail to achieve
maturity in this area. But it is intended to undercut the myth,
still propagated and believed by many religious, that somehow
the making of vows absolves one from the major developmental
tasks of adulthood which have to do with the achieving of affective and relational maturity.

Perhaps the most tragic result for religious of the failure to
negotiate the crisis of intimacy occurs in the spiritual realm. The
ability to love God and neighbor wholeheartedly, which is after
all the only fully adequate motivation for the choice of celibacy,
rests on the capacity for human intimacy. It sounds platitudi-
nous to say that one who cannot love human beings cannot love
God, but it is not a platitude. It is a cold, hard fact. The religious
who has never experienced love, who has never loved and been
loved with a real, warm, human, sexually alive and enlivening
human affection by a real, concrete, singular human being, can
talk endlessly about the beauties and joys of divine love but will
not be very convincing to anyone who has known the agonies
and ecstasies of the real thing. One has only to read the great
mystics to know that their imagery is not derived from hearsay
or fantasy. One of the most consistent characteristics of the great
lovers of God and personally effective ministers in Church history is their capacity for deep personal relationships and their
actual friendships.

A second cold, hard fact is that one cannot achieve intimacy
alone. One must have some capacity for solitude and have
achieved some real sense of personal identity if one is to be capable of intimacy, but the achieving of identity is not completed
prior to the development of intimate relationships. Finding out
who one is is not a stage which is completed before one addresses the challenge of relationship. In real life, while intimacy
is based on an initial sense of self, one's identity is achieved and
grasped in new and deeper ways through the experience of intimacy with another. To a large extent we find out who we are
by finding out what we mean to others and especially to partic-

ularly significant others. However, one cannot be intimate with others in general. Nor can one substitute a kind of universal affability or even apostolic generosity for concrete individual relations with real individual persons. And this is precisely what constitutes the challenge for the religious who has vowed consecrated celibacy, who has renounced the normal path to human intimacy which is the lifelong, committed relationship with one other person that comes to full symbolic expression in genital sexual union.

The purpose of the foregoing somewhat stark reflections is to ground our discussion of celibate friendship in an unflinching realism about this subject. If consecrated celibacy is to be lived integrally it involves foregoing the normal path to human affective maturity. But to fail to develop affectively means to fail to become fully human and, more importantly, to subvert the possibility of coming to a full experience of the love of God and a full development of ministerial potential. In other words, the stakes are very high. Unless the religious can find an alternate path to human intimacy, the chances are very good that he or she will sabotage the very project for which consecrated celibacy was undertaken. Bypassing the challenge to intimacy is not a viable alternative. It is a resignation from the human adventure, a self-consignment to perpetual childhood. Consequently, the concern with affectivity in the life of the consecrated celibate must not degenerate into strategies for avoiding sexual relations or rigid catalogues of what is and is not permissible. Our task is not to get through life without having sexual intercourse, or to eke out enough human warmth to survive without incurring paralyzing guilt. It is to find the authentically celibate way to adult intimacy and therefore to affective maturity.

It seems to me that there are two elements, or two dimensions, to the celibate quest for intimacy. The first is not often mentioned in discussions like this one, and there are good reasons why it is not. On the one hand, it can easily play into the unrealistic spiritualism of those who deal with life by denial; on the other hand, it can cause discouragement in those who understand the issue. I am speaking of contemplation, mystical prayer in the strict sense of the word. I am not speaking here of paranormal phenomena such as ecstasy or levitation, but of deeply experienced union with God or, more specifically, union with Christ. Contemplative prayer differs in important ways from the kind of prayer we can engage in by our own efforts of thinking and willing. Contemplation is freely given by God. We cannot bring it about no matter what we do. Precisely for this reason it fills the one receiving it with a profound conviction of the reality and the presence of God. It is an affectively involving, psychologically transforming experience of the presence and activity of God in the very depths of one's being. In its joyful moments it is an experience of being marvelously and intimately touched, loved, cherished—and enabled to respond from depths one does not control, did not even know one possessed. In its moments of suffering it continues to involve the contemplative in an experience of the Other which cannot be escaped or relativized. Even in times of utter aridity the longing for the Beloved is a psychological involvement with God whose reality is not simply accepted in willed faith but experienced even in and through God's felt absence.

By definition, mystical prayer is not something one can achieve by the exercise of one's will. But it is the flowering of a life of enlightened fidelity to prayer. God does not forever hide the divine face from those who seek God in sincerity and truth. It would seem that a religious life which does not involve at least some experiential union with God, however rare or brief such moments might be, and however laced with aridity and suffering it usually is, lacks the most important element in dealing constructively with the absence of a human life-partner. Furthermore, if a person grows into deep and involving human relationships in the course of his or her life, it is difficult to see how these can be integrated into the celibate commitment if an experienced union with the One to whom his or her life is given does not provide the context for such integration.

What this means in the concrete is that formation for a life of prayer, solid grounding in such a life, and a firm commitment to its development no matter what the obstacles is absolutely necessary for a meaningful religious life. Religious who, at the age of forty or fifty, come to the realization that their prayer life has been a vaguely boring, uneventful, even if fairly steady performance of duties that has never been psychologically involving or meaningful, much less satisfying and fulfilling, often also discover that loneliness has so endlessly filled their lives that they are now chronically depressed, without energy or motivation for anything further, or else that their sexual urges seem completely out of control. If anything, they should thank God that the symptoms have become painful enough that the problem must be dealt with. Intimacy with God, not dutiful performance of routines but experienced union with One whom we know (not think or believe, but *know*) loves us individually, tenderly, and in psychologically fulfilling ways that defy communication to others but which deeply nourish our heart, is essential to the life of consecrated celibacy. This is not a suggestion that we should turn our prayer into a quest for unusual experiences. It is a suggestion that we should become people of profound prayer, knowing that God who is faithful beyond our power to imagine will fulfill our deepest human desires in ways we could not think to suggest and could never describe. Intimacy with God is not one way to live religious life meaningfully. It is the only way. It is as crucial for the religious as intimacy with one's spouse is for the married person, and for the same reasons.

The second element or dimension of the celibate quest for intimacy is human friendship. Friendship is necessary for all people. For those involved in a lifelong committed relationship the first friend, of course, is the life companion. Other friendships, though enriching and important, are of secondary importance. But for religious whose life commitment is to the invisible God, friends who are not life-partners are of supreme importance. One might say that friendship is the characteristic road to human intimacy for the celibate, a kind of "sacrament" of celibate love.

Friendship has been discussed by philosophers, theologians, students of human nature, and friends themselves from time immemorial. All agree on certain points. Friendship is a relationship between equals, those who are equal to start with or those whose love of each other renders irrelevant whatever discrepancies in wealth, status, power, social position, education, or talents exist between them. Thus friendship is a relationship of mutuality to which domination, debts, and protocol are as foreign as respect, service, and endless delight in each other's company are natural. True friendship is the climate for that total sharing of gifts human and divine that is possible only occasionally in any life but which, when it is realized, involves an experience of intimacy that surpasses even that which can be achieved in and through sexual union. Spouses who have grown to maturity together testify to the superiority, finally, of the intimacy of friendship over any and all other experiences of union.

Needless to say there are degrees in friendship, but all true friendship tends to grow toward a capacity and desire for mutual self-revelation in the fullest sense of the word. On the way, there is room for many degrees of relationship. Among our relationships are some which, while not involving the intimacy of fully developed and irrevocable friendship, are, nevertheless, characterized by equality, mutuality, free and generous sharing, ease of communication, support and affirmation, joy in each other's company, and the general enhancement of energy that comes from being with and doing things with people whose presence we truly relish. It is of these friendships that I wish to speak first of all.

All of us, whether celibate or permanently committed to a life partner, need in our lives a variety of close friends of both sexes. For the religious this means friends within and outside of one's own community. Some people have numerous friends; others a chosen few. But the important thing is that true friends call us out of the isolation that celibacy can easily engender. Friends are people with whom we can be ourselves, people for whom we do not have to perform, to whom we do not relate out of role or according to prescribed expectations. Among friends we can, indeed must, shed the *persona* which so many religious wear so constantly that they eventually cannot distinguish it from their real selves. Friends are people with whom we share not just ideas, projects, or things but ourselves. With friends we can talk about ourselves, our feelings, our fears and hopes. We do not need an "opening" or an "excuse" to come out from behind the protections we necessarily construct in order to carry on our business in the everyday world of relative strangers. With friends we are always vulnerable but never in danger.

One of the great sufferings of isolated persons, especially

as they grow older, is the deep and aching realization that no one really cares for or about them. People may express interest, keep up perfunctory or even genial contact. But the isolated celibate knows, deep down, that there is no one who is really "there" for him or her. They look enviously at married acquaintances who seem to have that immensely life-giving assurance that they are "number one" in someone else's life.

For the celibate who has real friends the situation is otherwise. Friends are people who care. They do not care because they have to or are expected to but because they cannot help it. When we hurt, they hurt; when we are happy, they are too. A celibate's friends may not always be able to be at his or her side in times of crisis or rejoicing. Part of the celibate situation is that other responsibilities which belong to the primary life commitment, distance, and other factors may make physical nearness impossible at times, even in times of real need. But we know that wherever the friend is, he or she is with us. We are not humanly alone. This does not abolish the realization, integral to the celibate experience, that we are not "number one," not the primary or exclusive love of any other human being. But it does help us gradually to integrate that realization into our own primary love, the love for Christ, so that the loneliness of celibate life does not become bitter isolation but a mature solitude sweetened and deepened by genuine human love that is neither possessed nor possessive but nonetheless real and intense.

Friendships do not just fall into anyone's life, although the development of a real friendship always has a certain "miraculous" quality to it and leaves us feeling graced. Friendships are developed deliberately by people who have achieved sufficient human maturity to be capable of intimacy. If a fraction of the effort that was once devoted to keeping young religious from making friends were devoted to encouraging genuine friendship and helping young religious live through and work out the complexities of relationships with their peers in and outside the community, we would probably have fewer isolated and bitter old religious and priests living out lives of quiet desperation. One of the most important tasks of young adulthood is to develop friendships, to learn to live the challenges and joys of intimacy, of being ourselves with another in vulnerability and mutuality. But unfortunately there are still some young religious, especially young men in religious communities and seminaries, who are being formed to a suspicion and fear of intimacy, to viewing all relationships in terms of power over or subservience to, to being always the "givers" of ministerial gifts incapable of even admitting need much less accepting help. The smooth plastic finish of such priests and religious is completely scratch-proof by the time they exit from formation. They seem to be composed of a material which gets neither hot nor cold, never gets dirty, can be endlessly battered without denting, but which is universally recognized as a cheap substitute for that rich natural substance that characterizes living beings. If religious could be formed to prayer and to friendship, whatever else was left undone, they would probably be capable of rich, full, and happy lives, and have at least a realistic chance of entering into the depths of the mystery of divine love.

III. THE SPECIAL FRIENDSHIP
IN THE CELIBATE LIFE

The growing recognition in the last couple of decades of the importance of friendship in the celibate life as well as the long-overdue breakdown of the barriers between religious and other people has given rise to a problem which was practically non-existent in more cloistered days, namely, that of what we might call the "special friendship." I am speaking here of a friendship which carries an erotic tone not present in most of one's relationships. All relationships, positive or negative, are "sexual" in the sense that our masculinity or femininity shapes all of our relational experience in profound ways. But most of our friendships are sexual in this sense without being erotic. That is, the urgent impulse toward genital expression of our love is not a major part of the experience. However, for the unmarried person who has multiple relationships with people of both sexes it is almost to be expected that, depending on one's sexual orientation, some erotically attractive person of the same or the other sex will eventually come into one's life. This, of course, also happens to married people, but celibates lack the inhibiting factor constituted by the daily physical presence of and psychological interaction with the life partner.

In some cases, especially among younger religious who do not as yet have much experience either of their own sexuality or of erotically freighted relationships with others, the first encounter with an erotically attractive other can precipitate a full-blown case of infatuation with all its genital urgency, its agonizing desires, and its intoxicating joys. It may well be that such an experience is practically a necessity if a person is to grow up sexually. A person has to have lived through such an experience to fully empathize with the truly infatuated person. And it seems to me that part of the task of older and more experienced religious is to help their younger companions survive and grow through the experience of infatuation toward mature celibate friendship.

In the case of more mature and experienced religious the arrival of such a friend in one's life may not be the tumultuous experience of "falling in love," of infatuation with all its distortion, emotional upheaval, and self-centeredness. It is more likely to be the case that two people who have worked together, who have come to know each other through shared ministry and relaxation, who have discovered common interests in and outside of work, who have imperceptibly grown closer to each other in many ways and at many levels, become aware that a relationship has developed between them that neither really has with anyone else. The level of comfort in being together, the freedom of communication, the depth of sharing, the range of common interests, the confidence and trust in the other's loyalty and love, have gradually become part of a friendship which is altogether special. The free, deep, frequent, mutual self-revelation, in other words, the intimacy that such a friendship involves, can and often does give birth to a deep desire for total expression of that intimate love in physical union.

Whether one "falls in love" or grows into love, whether the friendship is between persons of the same sex or opposite sexes, whether the two share the same state of life or not, the problem presented by the development of such a relationship is the same. How can the claims of such an intimate relationship be honored within the context of an integral celibate commitment? What I would like to do in the final paragraphs of this essay is to suggest a few thoughts that might be helpful in handling one of the most difficult challenges a religious has to meet. It would be utterly presumptuous to think that any set of suggestions will solve this problem or make living it to a successful resolution easier for anyone. But perhaps such suggestions, based on much shared experience with religious and priests who have faced this challenge and have emerged well or badly from it, can help somewhat in reflection upon the issue.

First, such a relationship, in my opinion, is not to be avoided or run from in fear. If it can be successfully integrated into the celibate commitment, it enriches the life of the religious with a joy, courage, and fulfillment that nothing else can supply. While it would be foolish (and probably futile) to set out to establish such a friendship, it is usually self-destructive to run from it. It is a gift and a challenge, a gift of immeasurable worth but a challenge with very high stakes.

Second, before such a relationship develops in a person's life there can be some preparation for it. For one thing, young religious can learn what it means to *be* celibate in a conscious and communicative way. There is a way of dressing, walking, talking, relaxing, in general a way of communicating, that, while being genuine and warm, is, at the same time, non-seductive. It communicates that one is personally but not sexually available, that one is interested in the other and open to friendship but not seeking a sexual relationship. This is something young people have to learn. Much in our culture, sometimes even parental modeling and social pressure when children are very young, inculcates a kind of perpetual seductiveness in girls and perpetual prowling in boys. Young religious are often genuinely surprised and shocked when someone "makes a pass" at them, unaware that they are sending very sexually freighted messages in all kinds of ways. The art of being personally open but sexually self-contained, of being both warm and reserved, which any faithful married person certainly has to learn, also has to be learned by religious. To expect that simply because one has made a vow of celibacy one is protected by an invisible shield from the normal interactions of our highly eroticized culture is unrealistic in the extreme. Others respond to the interpersonal signals a religious sends just as they do to the signals anyone else sends. And sending the right signals is learned behavior.

Another part of the preparation for a mature handling of deep friendships is attitudinal. The religious who wants to remain celibate does not drift through life "being open to whatever happens" in the affective sphere. She or he has to realize and interiorize the fact that religious are not single—they are celibate. Their approach is not "I don't intend to have any non-celibate relationships develop in my life but you never know what might happen and I'll handle it when it does." It is rather "I intend not to have any such relationship develop in my life." The first attitude is somewhat like that of the single person who takes contraceptive precautions before going out on a date. The second is more like the person who does not take such precautions because he or she knows they are not going to be necessary. He or she has taken other precautions, at the level of personal decision, which make them not open to a sexual encounter and that is what they communicate indirectly, or, if they have to, directly. This is in no way a counsel to rigidity, prudery, or suspicion but to the internalization of one's life choice that makes one communicate, from the inside out as it were, that one's commitments are not open to negotiation, not because of fear or personal uncertainty but because one is happy in them and wants to share their meaningfulness with others in integrity.

The fruit of an awareness that in a mobile, relatively free, two-sex universe one's commitment to celibacy cannot be naive or childish, that one must, without becoming defensive, nevertheless stay in command of one's turf, is that one is less vulnerable to the experience of "love at first sight," of sudden and utterly overpowering infatuation. A relationship which begins with one or both partners swept off their feet into total mutual self-absorption is necessarily much more difficult to integrate, is much more likely to move swiftly and prematurely toward physical and psychological intimacies which compound the problem, than a relationship which develops within a context of respectful mutual reserve in which boundaries are explored and evaluated before they are crossed rather than being toppled by impetuous assault from both sides.

In what follows I am assuming that we are talking about a

mature celibate who has neither initiated nor fostered the development of an irresponsible erotic relationship but who has developed a special and intimate friendship with someone who is worthy of that friendship and now, together, they face the very real challenge of integrating that friendship into their primary life commitments. Is there anything that can be said that might be helpful in such a situation?

First, I think there is great value in "starting at the end" rather than at the beginning. By this I mean that if both friends are perfectly clear about where the relationship is not going to go, namely, into a genitally expressed sexual relationship, they have a basis for some of the decisions they must make individually and together. The decision that the relationship is not going to develop in certain ways is actually a commitment to not saying what we do not mean so that we can learn to say what we do mean. This presumes, of course, all that was said above about the symbolic significance of full sexual union. The committed celibate who intends to remain such is not open to that full self-gift and merging of personal destinies in lifelong partnership and common generativity that genital sexual union signifies. The decision to preclude from the friendship the expression of what is not meant is a mutual choice of authenticity, of taking sexual language utterly seriously and agreeing not to make a toy, an instrument of passing pleasure, of that which is our most adequate way of expressing ourselves in relationship. It is also an agreement that the two people will not use each other to satisfy, without assuming responsibility for public life commitment, the longings and desires that celibacy necessarily leaves unfulfilled.

The decision not to become genitally involved does not solve the problem. But it gives direction to the effort to find mutually satisfying and acceptable ways to integrate this friendship into both lives. If genital involvement is renounced in a definitive way and the friendship is to develop and deepen, the friends are going to have to find ways to express their love for each other that do not set in motion a psycho-physical process which can only be arrested at the price of violent frustration. In other words, the friends are going to have to find out how they can express affection without sexually arousing each other to an intolerable pitch. As we will mention later, this is going to lead to a developed preference for less physical kinds of expression. But it does not seem to me that any real human relationship of friendship can or should progress in the total absence of any kind of physical expression. The Gospels give us the very clear suggestion that Jesus was at home with physical expressions of affection from both his male and female friends and that he did not condone the prudery of the self-righteous on this score. And modern psychological research suggests that human beings, of all ages, need to be touched at times, to be held by other human beings and to experience physically the support and strength that we can offer each other by bodily as well as by spiritual communication.

Part of learning how to relate to a friend with whom we experience deep personal intimacy and who is, at the same time, erotically attractive to us is learning how to express affection in ways that are not deeply sexually arousing to one or both of the friends. Individuals are very different in their sexual responses. Even more to the point, men and women are very different in their sexual responses. What may be for a man an intense but episodic experience is often, for a woman, less intense but more pervasive and enduring. The friends will almost necessarily have to have some frank conversations on this subject. Most sensitive people will shrink from this for many very good reasons. For one thing, mature people know that talking about sex with someone one loves is itself sexually exciting. Also, people who love each other a great deal and whose love was born and has grown in the context of each other's religious commitment are very hesitant to take a chance on suggesting to the other that he or she is causing a problem in one's spiritual life and even more hesitant to arouse guilt or remorse in the friend. And, finally, neither person wants to inhibit or seem to set bounds on what is acceptable from the other because the real experience is that, in fact, everything the other wants to express is welcomed and cherished. It may be that the mutual admission of these very real hesitations will have to precede any conversation about the erotic dimensions of the relationship itself. But the alternative to some kind of mutual clarity about what each other is feeling is a kind of blind experimentation that runs very real risks of ending up where neither wants it to go.

Against this background let me make a few final observations on practical points which may or may not be helpful but which have a certain amount of shared experience behind them. First, in actual practice many people involved in a deep friendship have found that there is great strength in the deliberate effort of both to regard the other's primary commitment as primary to both. To talk together about the importance of one's own commitment and the friend's commitment is mutually confirming and helps to keep active and productive in the friendship the real identity of both people. The love they share cannot progress by diminishing in one another what is most important to each.

Second, the erotic dimension of any relationship is intensified by secrecy and exclusiveness. Many people who have succeeded over many years in this kind of friendship testify to the importance of each friend having someone with whom he or she can freely and openly discuss the relationship. Such a person might be a spiritual director or another close friend who is not a close friend of the other party to the relationship. Being able to talk about the relationship openly in a context of complete confidentiality relieves the erotic pressure that can build up, gives distance and thus a certain perspective on the experience that reduces the confusion of over-involvement, and gives a very important affirmation to the commitment to maintaining the friendship in its proper relationship to other commitments.

Third, it is very helpful if the friends can share their relationship with other friends, in other words, if the friendship can be inserted into the social context of each other's lives. Many religious communities today, and even some rectory communities, are beginning to be open to the presence and importance of the friends of their members. To be able to invite a close friend home without excuses or subterfuges and to have the friendship accepted without suspicion is a very affirming and supportive experience. It clarifies the fact that the friendship is an integral part of one's life commitment, neither a dark marginal note nor the real secret center of life but an important and enriching dimension of what one is really about. To be able to tell one's companions that one is going out to dinner or is spending a day off with the friend and to expect that to be accepted as normal and healthy and in no way suspicious or dangerous helps to make one experience the friendship that way.

Fourth, the willing acceptance, indeed embracing, of the very real renunciations that such a friendship involves constitutes an authentic and strengthening asceticism. The discretion called for in public, especially ministerial situations, can often be painful. But it is necessary if both friends are to be fully available to others and to enable their friendship to be accepted by others as non-threatening and non-exclusive. Celibate friends are not a couple, and they must avoid setting in motion in regard to themselves the social dynamics appropriate to couples. Every occasion which brings this fact home to the friends is bound to be a painful reminder of the real renunciations that a celibate commitment involves; but every generous acceptance of these renunciations strengthens them in and for a friendship that is filled with challenge. It is well to be aware, however, that very few people can practice asceticism in one area, especially the sexual one, if they do not lead a generally disciplined and even ascetical life from day to day. The person who is not disciplined in regard to food and drink, sleep, work, physical self-care, ministerial responsibilities, and community obligations is not likely to unearth some superhuman strength of character in regard to his or her relationships. Perhaps one of the best motivations for helping young religious develop a positive and healthy asceticism of daily living is that self-discipline is necessary if one is to maximize the most precious opportunities of life such as intimate friendship.

Fifth, both friends can be vigilant regarding signs of exclusiveness or possessiveness in the relationship. Jealousy, suspicion, prying, checking on one another, losing interest in projects that do not involve the other, are feelings and behaviors that are clear danger signals. Celibate friends are not life-partners nor lovers, and while privacy and intensity are characteristic of intimate friendship, exclusiveness and possessiveness are not, or should not be, characteristic of celibate friendship. Again, great maturity is necessary to exercise such vigilance and to surrender freely those very natural and spontaneous feelings which can gradually transform a celibate friendship into an erotic involvement.

Sixth, the friends must consciously develop and deliberately give preference to non-physical ways of being intimate. Conversation, writing, sharing of aesthetic and intellectual interests about which one or both are truly passionate, the sharing of important ministerial involvements (not just tasks), can become ways of being together, of sharing intimately, that reach the depths of one another. Many life partners for whom sexual expression has been temporarily or permanently inhibited have had to find other than physical paths to intimacy. It is not impossible, but it is not easy. In one sense, the easiest and quickest way to intimacy is sexual expression, and for this very reason it is also the way that can be most deceptive and superficial and finally alienating. Learning to communicate is the essence of the development of an intimate friendship and the deliberate foregoing of much of the physical expression of that intimacy can, paradoxically, foster the communication in which the friends relate to the whole of each other rather than taking easy flight into sexual expression. It is well known that not only adolescents but adults as well are often tempted to substitute sex for communication. Celibates are no exceptions to this temptation but they have special motivation for not succumbing to it.

Finally, friends who enjoy a deep, mature, and intimate relationship and who are sincerely committed to maintaining that relationship as an integral part of an uncompromised celibate commitment will learn, probably by trial and some errors, in what ways some physical expression of affection in private can both express and deepen their love for each other while reducing or alleviating sexual tension before it becomes explosive. If mistakes are made in this learning process they need to be admitted, to oneself and to the other, and appropriate measures taken to avoid repeating them. Perhaps one of the most important factors in the development of authentic humility, that liberating self-knowledge upon which all spiritual progress depends, is experience with one's own very real bodily humanity which cannot be intellectualized or spiritualized in a genuine human relationship but which must be transformed, slowly and painfully, in the image of Jesus who was fully human.

If the Son of God learned obedience through the things that he suffered, we can be sure that he learned intimacy from the people whom he loved. The Gospel assures us that Jesus had intimate friends, Mary Magdalene, Peter, Martha and Mary of Bethany, the Beloved Disciple, and others. He loved and was loved. He touched and was touched. He had relationships which were not entirely public, and he did not escape the malicious suspicious of jealous observers. He experienced betrayal as well as support, and he was not able to resolve all the conflicts in all of his relationships. One of his friends committed suicide because of the unresolved complexities of their relationship, and others of his friends finally gave their lives because of their relationship with him. Jesus does not set us the example of a frigid and rigid celibacy. He did not protect himself by dress, titles, lifestyle, behavior, or attitudes from intimate relationships with both men and women. Jesus' life does not call us to the safety of perpetual affective childhood. He challenges us to love deeply, and to answer such a challenge is to risk mistakes, suffering, disappointment with ourselves and others, even real tragedy. Not to answer it is to choose not to live. But an unlived life issues no Gospel invitation to anyone. Both our capacity for intimacy with the God to whom we have given our lives and our capacity to offer Gospel life and love to others depends upon the development of our own affective potential. Jesus' last address to his disciples included his incomparable self-gift, "I no longer call you servants: but I have called you friends" (Jn 15:15) as well as his final and ultimately only command, to love others as he has loved us.

Chapter Twelve
THE CHANGING SHAPE AND FUNCTION OF COMMUNITY LIFE

> The material in this chapter was originally presented in oral form to a mixed group of men and women, religious and lay, at a workshop held at Oblate School of Theology, San Antonio, Texas, in May–June, 1984. It has been significantly revised in light of subsequent discussion with women and men religious.

I. THEOLOGICAL AND ECCLESIAL CONTEXT OF CONTEMPORARY REFLECTIONS ON RELIGIOUS COMMUNITY LIFE

One of the most noticeable changes in religious life since Vatican II is the evolution of community life. This may well be partly due to the extreme rigidity and uniformity of religious community life in the post-Tridentine period in contrast to which any flexibility or diversity was bound to appear at least striking if not radical. But it is also due to the suddenness and speed of the change, after centuries of sameness, and to the variety of developments which have occurred not so much because of conscious decisions about community but as accompaniments of other changes in religious life such as the diversification of ministry, a sharp decline in numbers, and the breaking down of barriers between religious congregations. In any case, there is developing a felt need among many religious to reflect seriously on the community dimension of religious life and to make deliberate choices in this regard for the future. The reflections that follow are intended as a contribution to that reflection.

As a background for the more experimental suggestions of the second part of this essay it would seem useful to insist at the outset on two points which are not under question, either theoretically or practically, in these reflections. The first is that the equation of community with "common life" as it was eventually defined in the 1917 code of canon law is an historical development which is not necessary to religious life as such. In the course of the history, community has been lived among religious in a variety of forms ranging from eremetical life with a minimal participation in the most essential dimensions of ecclesial community through the most developed forms of monasticism to the kind of common life characteristic of apostolic communities of simple vows in the nineteenth and early twentieth centuries.

The common life into which most religious over forty were socialized involved all members of the religious congregation living in houses composed exclusively of the members of their own congregation, under a single superior, and sharing a life that was virtually uniform in regard to clothing, food, recreation, travel, education, ministerial activity, horarium, and so on. This pattern became so entrenched over a long period of time, especially for women and non-clerical male religious, that it had come to seem the only imaginable form that community life could take. Any other arrangement seemed to be either an abandonment of community life altogether or a temporary dispensation from it. It seems to me that there is little historical and no theological basis for this conclusion. This does not solve the problem of what community can and should look like today, but it should liberate us to examine our current experience as a new, but not necessarily aberrant, development in the long and diverse history of religious community life.[1]

The second point that is not under discussion is the essentially communitarian nature of religious life which derives from its intimate participation in the life of the Church. Christianity is communitarian by nature. The God of Christian revelation is a Trinity of equal persons whose very identity as substantial relations establishes the nature of divine life as love. It is into this love-life that Christians are initiated by baptism and which the life of the Church community is called to incarnate in this world. Our ancestors in the faith, the Israelites of old, were called as a people to covenant union with God and, even as God radically personalized and individualized that vocation, Jesus intensified its communitarian nature by calling his followers to share his own filiation as children of the one God and as a community of friends who would be recognized as his disciples precisely because of the love that bound them to one another.[2]

As a deeply ecclesial reality religious life is, of its very nature, community life. But it is not simply a variation of the "1960's commune" or even of the utopian communities of nineteenth century America. Like the Church itself the religious community is bound together by the indwelling Spirit of love communicated to the Church and to each of the baptized by the glorified Jesus. Christians in every walk of life today are coming to a renewed (or new) realization of the essentially communitarian nature of Christianity and seeking ways to make this important dimension of their Christian vocation concrete for themselves. The experiments have ranged from full-scale covenant communities sharing residence and economic resources to subgroups in parishes or on university campuses meeting periodically for a sharing of faith, prayer, and mutual support. But in any case, neither religious nor lay people any longer regard the community character of religious life as something which radically distinguishes religious life from other forms of Christian commitment. The question we are raising has to do with the forms of community life which are life-giving for religious in the twentieth century. In other words, community as a Christian and religious value is not under question; it is community as a lifestyle that raises questions for us at the present time.

II. SITUATING RELIGIOUS COMMUNITY WITHIN THE INSTITUTIONAL EMBODIMENT OF ECCLESIAL COMMUNITY

At least in the Roman Catholic embodiment of Christianity there has always been a solid conviction that the communion in the Spirit which is at the heart of the mystery of the Church implies existential sociality. It is perhaps less than satisfactory to put the emphasis on "visibility" because there is certainly more to community than what can be seen, and what can be seen is especially open to corruption. But community is not a purely spiritual reality that can be realized in truth without leaving any trace in the experiential realm. Community among humans, to be real, must involve some kind of experienced being and living together, physical, psychological, and spiritual. And once we start talking about more than a very small group of people this being together will require some kind of institutionalization.

It would seem that there are at least three levels of such institutionalized sociality in the Church and that the three are quite different. It might be helpful to examine these three levels and try to situate religious community in relationship to them. First, there is the macro-level, that of the Church universal or the Church as a whole. At this level there is maximum institutionalization and visibility and minimal community in the experiential sense of the word. At the present time, unfortunately, institutionalization at this level makes the Church look very much like a divine right monarchy being run like a multi-national corporation. One of its most noticeable features is its hierarchical and bureaucratic organization and its lack of effective communication with much of the membership. This state of affairs is not intrinsic to the Church at the macro-level. Many people in the Church sincerely hope and energetically work to bring about real changes in Church organization at this level. But, phenomenologically, that is the situation at the moment.

The intermediate level of the Church is harder to describe. It includes all the institutional arrangements which mediate between the macro-level and the micro-level or the face-to-face contexts within which Christians actually experience and live out their faith. For one thing, the intermediate level comprises a much more diverse kind of institutionalization, especially since Vatican II. At this level we find dioceses and large parishes and various kinds of national and international groupings of both clergy and laity organized to promote concerns of the Church. There is considerable variation from culture to culture and within cultures. At this level we are not talking about the virtually inaccessible structures of power of the Vatican and its representatives in various countries nor about universal laws, practices, and customs nor about shared membership in an organization of people who have never met each other or shared any kind of faith experience and who probably never will. Nor, on the other hand, are we talking about the real relations between people whose histories, lives, and hopes intersect with some frequency on a regular basis and who affect one another in an ongoing way. The intermediate level embraces all those institutional components of Church life which have some real impact on the life of believers who, in turn, have some access to the structures, personnel, and procedures that operate on that level.

The micro-level of institutionalization is the point of insertion of the individual Christian into the faith life of the Church. At this level we usually have minimal institutionalization and maximum community experience. Here we are talking about primary communities: the family, the small parish or parish group, the prayer group or ministerial team. Many people participate in more than one such community of faith, the emphasis in each being on a different aspect of the person's life. Thus, one might share primarily ministerial concerns with the faculty of the school in which one teaches, intellectual/spiritual concerns with the Bible study group in which one participates, total life concerns with the family, and one's own most intimate spiritual concerns with one's spiritual director, while participating actively in one's parish.

As is readily apparent, any such analysis of levels of community in the Church reveals the somewhat "messy" overlapping of levels and of organization within levels. It may be that in a certain diocese various diocesan organizations actually provide primary group experience for some people while certain covenant communities have become bureaucratic institutions run by secretive power elites. But my point in trying to distinguish three levels of institutionalization is not to prescribe how the Church as community ought to be organized but to describe at least three very different meanings of the word "community." The reality denoted by the one word is quite different when we speak of the community of the Church universal, the community of the local Church of the United States or of Chicago, the community of St. Anne's parish, and the community of people who meet at the Smiths' every other week for Scripture sharing and prayer.

Until a few years ago religious communities were very monolithically organized and it was easy to delineate levels of institutionalization and to specify the kind of community appropriate for each level. Effectively, the institute or congregation as a whole was an intermediate level institution. It was neither the immediate point of insertion of the individual member nor was it an anonymous and inaccessible power structure. The individual member was directly affected by decisions made at that level and had, in various ways, some access to the personnel and some influence on the procedures that took place at that level. However, the primary experience of community of the individual member took place at the level of the so-called local community. The local community, housed together in the convent to which the members were assigned for some specified length of time, presided over by an appointed superior, engaged together in the same ministry, and living a virtually uniform lifestyle, was the immediate context for the realization of the individual's religious life. The ideal of community at this level was one of charitable, but never intimate, equal relationships among the members under the delegated authority of the local superior who was accountable to the congregational superiors but not to the members of the local community. Mutual support, understanding, forbearance, and tolerance were expected of the members. But at the same time, one was expected to avoid all emotional involvement or attachment to either the group or an individual member of the group. Daily formal prayer together was virtually the only form of faith sharing.

No one would claim that the ideal proposed was realized in all or even most local religious houses. On the one hand the expectation of compatibility among people assembled at the beginning of the year by executive fiat without much attention to the desires of any of them, living under a superior who was often appointed because of administrative qualities that had little or nothing to do with human relations skills, and living a lifestyle to which they had made no contribution, was exorbitant to say the least. And on the other hand, despite the best efforts of superiors to enforce the most restrictive rules, friendships were formed, deep affections were shared, and hearts were torn by separation. Perhaps the most amazing thing about pre-Vatican II religious community life was the fact that it was as successful as it was in providing a reasonably meaningful human environment and faith context for most of its members.

What has given way under the impact of massive changes in religious life and ministry since Vatican II is the unambiguous clarity of this system. The intermediate level has become much less remote because individual religious have assumed more immediate responsibility for what is going on in their congregations and religious in leadership positions have taken more seriously than have most ecclesiastical authorities the call to collegiality, subsidiarity, and co-responsibility. On the one hand, as local communities have been completely transformed by the abandonment of most of the uniformity that served as social glue in pre-Vatican II convents, the congregation itself has become a more immediate point of insertion into religious life for many religious. And on the other hand, local communities, whether composed of the members of one congregation or of several different congregations or consisting of some mixture of religious and lay people in a ministerial setting, have become more real as communities while becoming less recognizable as strictly "religious communities" in the classical institutional sense of the term.

The "confusion" in terms of institutionalization has led to a renewed examination of the very meaning of religious community, an examination which is, in fact, long overdue but which was unlikely to arise as long as the pre-Vatican II system was firmly in place. I would suggest that what is happening in religious life in regard to community is analogous to what Dolores Curran in her recent book, *Traits of the Healthy Family*,[3] says is happening to the American family. Curran says that the functions of the family have changed drastically since the turn of the century and therefore the structures of family life and the expectations people have of it have also changed. I suspect that the functions of religious community have also changed and that this is what accounts for the changes in institutional forms. If this is true, a re-examination of religious community life should start not with an ideal institutional formula, whether derived from canon law or from sociological theory, but with a frank assessment of the functions of community within the context of religious commitment. Once the major functions have been delineated, questions can be raised about how to organize religious community for the accomplishment of those functions.

III. RELIGIOUS COMMUNITY AT THE INTERMEDIATE LEVEL

Since our primary concern in this essay is with community life at the micro-level, the level of immediate day to day living of the individual religious, we will cast only a brief glance at the intermediate level of community, that is, the congregation. The reason for looking at this level at all is that it has certain functions which, if they are not accomplished at the congregational level, will create problems at the local level.

I would suggest that there are at least five functions which pertain particularly to the intermediate or congregational level of community life. First, the congregation as a whole holds and administers the collective assets of the group including property, financial resources, influence and leverage, and so on. Therefore, it is at the congregational level that institutional provision must be made for equality of access by the members to community resources, for participation in the decisions about the use of community goods and leverage, and for the selection of community leaders and the determination of their roles. While congregational officials have always been responsible for the handling of community goods and the public representation of the institute these functions have changed dramatically. Congregational officials are no longer unaccountable administrators of community goods but stewards who are expected to be continuously and openly accountable to the membership for their exercise of this ministry. Furthermore, they are expected to represent the membership to the larger Church community, not to decide for or to take the place of the membership. They are not independent agents making unilateral decisions about the education, ministerial involvements, and lifestyles of the members but partners in such decisions whose task is to represent the concerns of the congregation as a whole in dialogue with the concerns of local communities and individuals. In other words, one function of the congregation through its leaders is the administration of the larger body in such a way that it is representative of the membership, supportive of them, and responsible to them.

Second, it is at the congregational level that provision must be made for an equitable sharing of responsibilities for the ongoing life of the group as a whole. Such tasks as the formation of the younger members, the care of the aged, and the ongoing care of personnel through counseling, life-planning, education, and spiritual enrichment must be organized and staffed. Again, this is not a new function since congregational authorities have always had responsibilities in these areas. But the way this function is realized today has changed immensely as anyone involved in any of these congregational responsibilities will readily testify. Among the major changes is the insistence of the membership on input into both the choice of personnel for these responsibilities and how these responsibilities will be fulfilled.

Third, and perhaps most radically new, is the function of organizing the ongoing general participation of the membership in the self-determination of the congregation as a whole. In pre-Vatican II days the members of a congregation had very little to do with the decision-making processes of the congregation except for voting for delegates to the general chapter once every several years. All major (and even very minor) decisions were made either by the chapter or by the major superiors and administered by local superiors. Today participative government has become the common form in most renewed religious communities. The congregational leaders must not only facilitate that participation but implement its decisions and keep the membership abreast of that implementation.

Fourth, a function of the congregation as a whole which is slowly evolving but has not been well realized in most communities is that of facilitating accountability. Structures and procedures for due process are in rudimentary stages of development but, as participative and non-coercive forms of government gradually replace hierarchical and autocratic forms, the necessity for mutually recognized instruments for the assurance of responsible interdependence is going to become more and more necessary. If unity is to be preserved while lifestyles become more diverse, the membership more far-flung, theologies more pluralistic, and ministries more varied, it is imperative that forums be established in which differences can be adjudicated according to mutually recognized norms and by just procedures.

Finally, the congregation as a whole must somehow carry the collective history of the group and transmit it to succeeding generations. Many congregations have discovered the importance of occasional "events" which bring members together for multi-leveled sharing which keeps alive the spirit, the *esprit de corps,* of the group as a whole. The keeping of records, the organizing of archives, and all the other tasks that facilitate corporateness not only among present members but between generations is a function of the congregation at the intermediate level.

This list is probably not complete but it should suffice to make the point that there are functions, some actually new and some different versions of long-standing functions, which can only be carried out at the intermediate level. They concern the community as congregation in relation to the macro-level of the Church universal and to other Church institutions at the intermediate level (such as the diocese, parishes, etc.), as well as in relation to secular society and its institutions. These functions facilitate the lives of individual members by keeping the congregation itself alive and operative. But the congregation as a whole, the intermediate level institutionalization of community life, is not the day to day life context of the individual member however intensively she may participate in its operations.

IV. RELIGIOUS COMMUNITY AT THE MICRO-LEVEL

Terminology is a major problem when we turn our attention to the immediate context of community life for the individual religious. To speak of the "local community" is as ambiguous as to speak of the "local Church." For one thing, most Christians, including religious, participate in several "local communities" and it is not always easy to designate one of them as primary because, from different points of view, different groupings are primary. But, more importantly for many religious today, the immediate context of day to day faith experience may not be that of a collectivity of his or her own brothers or sisters. The religious may be living alone, with members of one or several different congregations, or in a mixed community made up of religious, ordained, and lay people. In other words, religious may not belong to a "local community" of their own congregation in the traditional sense of the word.

I am of the opinion that little is to be gained by pretending that this situation is an anomaly, an aberration, or an exception, and continuing to discuss "community life" as if almost all religious are or will soon be living in convents with members of their own congregations. Declining numbers, ministerial diversification, and financial necessity combine to point to a future in which such group living by members of a single congregation is going to be the exception rather than the rule. Congregations will own fewer large institutions staffed by their own members; members will undertake ministries where they open up, whether or not other members of their own congregation are located nearby; and in any case there will be far fewer religious in the foreseeable future and they will necessarily be spread more thinly geographically than they are even now. Consequently, realistic re-examination of religious community life at the micro-level, it seems to me, will have to involve discussion of two kinds of experiences: small group living (whatever the composition of the group), and the community experience of those who live alone. Discussion of these two forms of religious living from the point of view of function giving rise to structures and procedures rather than the other way around might yield more usable results.

A. Small Group Living

Most of what follows concerning small group living will be applicable also to solitary living since the religious living alone today is not a hermit deliberately avoiding contact with other people but simply a person whose contacts with others, including the members of her congregation, take place outside her home.[4] Those contacts will function in her life in much the same way the members of a living group function in the life of a religious living with others. And she will have the same problems with and joys from those contacts. Most people living in small groups do not spend most of their time at home any more than does the person living alone. Living in a group offers certain advantages and involves certain limitations as does living alone. But both lifestyles involve a person in the satisfaction of certain basic life needs through interaction with other people.

The model of group living that defined the community experience of pre-Vatican II religious was that of the primary family. The primary family is the family into which one was born, in contra-distinction to the secondary family which is the family one founds. In the first one is a child in relation to parents and siblings. In the second one is a spouse and parent in relation to spouse and offspring. "Subjects" in religious communities experienced the community as a primary family in which they were children in relation to the superior who functioned parentally. "Superiors" experienced community more as a secondary family in which they functioned as parents in relation to children. For many years now most post-conciliar religious have been aware of the inadequacy of this familial model for religious community, but it is well to briefly recall some of the reasons why this model must be definitively set aside.

The primary family model requires that most of the members function as children most of the time that they are at home. Since all the members of a religious community are at least chronologically adults and ideally psychological and spiritual adults as well, it is counter-productive if not destructive for them to play the role of children at home while trying to function as adults in all other arenas of their lives. This play-acting leads to infantilism, psychological regression, alienation of responsibility, guilt, and malformation of conscience among other things. The appropriate relationship between members of a community, whatever their role in the group, is that of adult to adult. Whatever else it might be, the religious community is not a two-generation family and the primary family model is radically inadequate.

Having laid aside the primary family as a model for religious community living we face the problem of finding another model which is more adequate. My suggestion is that the appropriate model is that of a community of friends who are co-disciples in ministry. Later I will suggest that such a community might look a good deal like a family of grown siblings after the parents are deceased. But first, let me describe the functions of this community of friends and then we will turn to a description of its possible forms and structures.

A community of adult friends in ministry will be, of course, a voluntary society, a group of people who are together not because they were born to the same parents or because of economic or political necessity. Their voluntary association, like any such grouping, will involve each member in the acceptance of certain characteristics of some members and certain features of group life for which she might not care. Nevertheless, each member has freely joined the group; it has not been imposed upon her. She has joined it because the group provides for the satisfaction of certain needs and embodies certain values that are important to all the members.

In a community of religious, among these values will probably be a shared concern for ministry, a shared vocational context of celibacy, and in some sense a shared history, if not as members of the same congregation at least as women religious who have lived through the conciliar evolution of religious life. Some of the needs which the community will meet will be that for worship, prayer, and faith sharing in the spiritual sphere; the supplying of mutual assistance, support, affirmation, the space to be oneself and to grow, reasonable and caring confrontation when necessary, and a sense of belonging, interdependence, and friendship in the psychological sphere; and the sharing of resources and opportunities for growth and development in the professional and ministerial spheres. Obviously, communities will vary greatly in their capacity to meet the needs of their members in these various spheres, but the point here is that these are real and legitimate needs of religious which a community can be legitimately expected to fulfill in some measure, and it is realistic to evaluate a community in terms of its capacity and willingness to function in these ways.

At the same time there are functions which a community of adult friends in ministry should not be expected to exercise. The members of such a community should not expect to be parented. There are obvious and not so obvious ways to seek parenting. We have all known religious whose hypochondria, or cultivated ineptitude, or inability to be alone, or refusal to master the ordinary skills of adult living such as cooking or balancing a checkbook, or moodiness and emotional instability is a manipulative demand for endless parenting. Such behaviors were not only tolerated but even sometimes encouraged in preconciliar communities organized according to the primary family model, but they are inappropriate in an adult community.

Second, members of an adult community should not expect to parent. The sacrifice of parenthood is integral to the celibate commitment, but not all religious come to terms in explicit and definitive ways with this sacrifice. The need to run the lives of other people, the conviction that we know what is good for them, the need to fuss over others, intrusion into the private affairs of others, the imposition of "rules of order for the house," and similar patterns of behavior often betray the secret "parent" who is not happy unless taking care of someone. In a community, of equal adults there are no parents. The only appropriate way to deal with fellow community members is as one autonomous adult with another.

Third, members of a voluntary community brought together not by marriage and mutual life commitment but by a common commitment to Jesus and to ministry to his people cannot realistically expect to experience the intimacy and total mutuality characteristic of marriage partners. If friendship in the most intense sense of the word develops between community members they share a rich and gratuitous blessing. But it is unrealistic to expect that one's intimacy needs will be automatically met by membership in a religious community. Even if the members of the community came together partly because they liked each other (and this is not always possible), their primary reason for being together is not each other; the primary affective commitment in the life of celibates is to Christ and the primary overflow of that affective commitment is ministry, including that within and to the community. The expectation that community life will be an experience of totally fulfilling intimacy grounds one of the most frequent and bitter disappointments of some young religious today. Without being cynical or encouraging low ideals we could probably do them a service by helping them to recognize and come to terms with their real intimacy needs and locate appropriate channels for fulfilling them before they unleash exorbitant demands on a community which cannot be expected to function in this way.

Finally, the community is not an extension of the workplace and community members are not fellow workers at home, even if the members participate in the same ministry. Today it is often the case that the members of a community each work in a different ministry or location. But even when several members of a community share the same ministry, the need of professionals to "go home from work," physically and psychologically, is real. This is just as true for people whose professions are ministerial as for others. The community member who cannot or will not relate to others except in terms of or about work, who maintains the same social stratification in the home as at work, deprives her community of that relaxed fellowship among equals which everyone needs if she is to function altruistically and professionally in the ministerial setting.

So far I have tried to describe the small group community in terms of its functions. These functions, as can be seen, are primarily relational rather than occupational or disciplinary as might have been the case in times past. However, the relationships are not those of the primary family nor that between spouses. They are relationships among equals, structured by common allegiance to certain values, and profoundly shaped by the shared spiritual life and ministerial commitment which is the primary concern of each member. The most adequate designation and the ideal of these relationships is Gospel friendship, that love of one another as Jesus has loved us that is the sign of discipleship.

Let me now undertake a kind of phenomenology of the small group community "from the outside." What might such a community look like today? As mentioned above, it might well resemble a family of grown siblings. First, each of the members will have her own work, friends of both sexes outside the community who may or may not be friends of other members of the community, professional interests and associations, educational and developmental projects, interests and causes, and family connections which are not of primary significance to other members of the community. In other words, each member will have a personal life whose wealth enriches her and overflows into the community's shared life but which is not shared in detail with the other members of the community.

Second, living together will more than likely not mean virtual constant companionship but regular coming together for spiritual enrichment, companionship, and the handling of community concerns. Unlike the pre-conciliar convent community, our small group might not be together more than a couple times a week, and that will probably have to be planned just as grown families must plan to get together if they want it to happen.

Third, there will probably be considerable in-depth sharing on a one-to-one basis as well as strong affective bonds. Concern with one another's well-being and projects, mutual support, pride in each other's achievements, affirmation, and encouragement will be important ingredients in relationships which are sustained more by their affective quality than by physical proximity.

Fourth, organizational patterns, including leadership, will tend to be collegial and cooperative rather than hierarchical or coercive. One of the purposes, whether acknowledged or not, of the kind of community life away from which women religious are moving was control. Never being out from under the eye of the superior, having to be present at such frequent intervals that nothing of significance or at any distance could possibly take place between appearances, having no private space or time in which to relate to anyone outside the community had disciplinary potential the loss of which is precisely what is disturbing to certain authorities. But this form of control is inappropriate for adults and, in any case, will probably not be accepted by the religious of the future who know that it contributes nothing to the development of a mature religious life.

This brief glance at the "appearance" of a modern religious community opens up the possibility that such a community might be realized even by people who do not live under the same roof. The religious of a particular congregation in an area might well form a community that has all of the characteristics mentioned above and exercises all of the relational functions discussed previously but whose members live in different locations because of the demands of their ministries, educational pursuits, or other duties. This is, in fact, the case with many religious today. It is a way for religious of the same congregation who live within manageable distance from one another to maintain and strengthen congregational identity and participate actively in congregational affairs even when living with members of one's own congregation is not possible. In such cases phone calls, letters, individual visits, shared vacations, holiday gatherings, and the like take on particular importance as they do among relatives for whom the family is important. And it has been the experience of many religious that under such circumstances being together is more enjoyable, more productive, and more important than pre-conciliar community life was.

B. *Living Alone*

In the context of what has just been said we can raise the issue of sisters "living alone" which has become an increasingly frequent occurrence. Of all the variations on community life that have emerged in the last two decades, this one seems to many to be least compatible with the very notion of community. I suspect that the reason it is so problematic in theory for most religious, including those who are doing it, is that our understanding of community has been so profoundly shaped by the primary family model understood in terms of "common life" that it is difficult to conceive of someone participating actively in community who is not in the physical company of the other community members on a daily basis. However, I also suspect that the reason why it is so problematic in practice for certain members of the hierarchy is because it raises such a challenge not only to the exercise of control but even to the principle. The person living alone is not under the constant supervision of a superior and is not subject to a pattern of life determined by those in authority. To the extent that such authoritarian concerns are at the basis of expressed apprehension about religious living alone, the apprehensions need not concern us. Religious life is not a form of fascism and religious are not minors. Control is certainly not what religious life is all about, however deeply imbued with such concerns some people might be.

Our concern is with the actual experience of religious who "live alone." The expression itself is misleading because such religious spend most of their time with other people. Let us begin, then, with specifying what is meant by "living alone." Such religious are not hermits, that is, they have not chosen a solitary form of life. They are not deliberately avoiding the company of other humans for ascetical or contemplative, much less misanthropist, reasons. They are active ministers who are also members, presumably active and in good standing, of congregations for whom community life is an important value. They live alone only in the sense that there is no one else inhabiting the same domicile.

We are not, of course, concerned here with religious who have "moved out" of community psychologically as well as physically, who are isolating themselves from others in their communities, who are blocking out community leadership, who are running from social involvement, or are running to inappropriate social involvement or sexual liaisons. These religious have problems which must be solved, and their living arrangement is the least of these.

The reasons why religious might choose, or find themselves, living alone are numerous and varied. The most common is that the ministry someone has undertaken is in a place where there is no suitable religious community which can incorporate the newcomer. The religious, for ministerial reasons, finds herself "alone" physically and takes up solitary residence because that is the best or the only option.

Sometimes there are several members of one congregation living in the same area, but for reasons of cramped housing and lack of natural compatibility it seems preferable for all concerned not to attempt living in close physical quarters where natural antipathies are going to be exacerbated on a daily basis. This is not necessarily a surrender to unmortified living; it may well be a reasonable choice about where and how energies are to be expended. If the primary charism and ministry of a congregation is community life it might make sense to put prime energy into the developing of viable community despite the lack of natural compatibility. If the primary ministries of the individuals are in other areas the deliberate creation of a living situation which will be highly conflictual is self-defeating behavior. The possibility that real and life-giving community of the kind we described in the last section can be developed among these religious is actually enhanced by their not living together in the same house.

For some religious, especially introverts whose ministerial involvments are especially intensive and usually in the public arena, living alone might provide a very necessary solitude that allows them to nurture the kind of interiority that alone enables them to remain spiritually and psychologically healthy in the midst of a hectic lifestyle. For the genuine introvert, solitude provides what good company offers to the extravert, namely, an energizing resource. Of course, introverts need company just as extraverts need solitude. What differs is the proportionate role company and solitude play in the life of each. Especially today, when the houses of religious are no longer cavernous enclaves but small residences in busy neighborhoods, and when religious life is no longer lived according to a schedule that provides for silence during most of the day, intentional solitude and silence can become real necessities for some people. Living alone can provide at least a few hours, morning or evening, of guaranteed solitude and silence for such people.

For certain life activities, for example, prolonged study, writing, or spiritual renewal, living alone might be much more conducive to the immediate goals than living with a group. I have known a number of religious, engaged in an intensive renewal program of which community social and liturgical life was an important part, who chose to live alone during that year precisely in order to ensure the complementary solitude required to integrate the experiences of the program. Such people were actively and appropriately involved in all the activities of the renewal community, including liturgy, socializing, workshops, peer group reflection, and so on. But living alone provided a healthy experience of "apartness" for which there was a felt need.

The point of the foregoing reflections is that living alone, in and of itself, is "community-neutral." The question is whether the reason for living alone is valid and whether the person participates actively and fruitfully in community even while dwelling in a separate domicile. Leaders in various religious congregations have testified that some of their best community members live alone. These are people whose interest in, involvement with, and contribution to the ongoing life of the congregation can be counted on, who have in no sense psychologically distanced themselves from the community, who are open to and with community leaders, who are hospitable, frugal, and responsible in lifestyle and who readily cooperate with community policies and procedures. Needless to say, living alone is a lifestyle not particularly suitable for the newest members of a community. Socialization to religious life requires lived experience with mature religious. But once the religious has assumed adult status in the community and demonstrated a consistent capacity to organize and direct her own life in accord with community ideals and standards and to handle the everyday problems of life in the real world, the question of where she will live becomes relative to other much more important factors than physical togetherness.

V. COMMUNITY LIVING AND BASIC LIFE NEEDS

One of the reasons for community life (whether of the enclosed "common life" variety or the more open type we have been describing in the previous two sections) is the satisfaction of certain basic needs that all persons, including religious, have. As Genesis 2:18 reminds us, "It is not good for the human being to be alone." (Note, it does not say to "live alone," but to "be alone.") We are social beings and some of our most fundamental needs arise from this existential condition. Let us look at four of these needs, identity, intimacy, generativity, and achievement, in relation to community life. To what extent and in what way can we look to community for the satisfaction of these needs and to what extent is it inappropriate to ask this satisfaction of community?

Identity: To some extent a person should have resolved the basic issues of identity before entering a religious community. But all of us have the need for a permanent context for commitment, a "place" where we belong in a stable way, people with whom we are interdependent on a lifelong basis. Those who lack such permanent contexts of relationships within which they have a sense of who they are in relation to significant others are those we call "loners" or "drifters." The religious congregation and, more immediately, the community provide that context for religious as the secondary family does for married people. In this context one can legitimately expect to experience mutuality, support, participation, belonging, personal affirmation and appreciation, opportunities for self-development, and gradually increasing responsibility for the shared enterprise. One cannot realistically expect to experience all of these values in an intense way at all times. But a healthy community should provide enough of a life context to nurture the maturing sense of personal identity of its members. Religious are not loners; they belong. It should mean something to them and to others when they identify themselves as religious of such and such a congregation.

Intimacy: The need for close personal relationships is one whose satisfaction was ill provided for in pre-conciliar religious communities. The assumption that celibacy involved a renunciation of intimacy justified practices that made the formation of close friendships, inside or outside the community, virtually impossible and always suspect. As we now know from sad experience, the life deprived of intimacy is a life half lived. People whose lives are devoid of intimacy remain immature, shallow, and usually unhappy. Although it is possible that intimacy with God can develop in a life empty of human intimacy (all things are possible to God!) it does not seem to be the usual case. Human intimacy is ordinarily essential to full adult living and therefore to deep spirituality as the lives of the saints richly demonstrate. Religious have renounced marriage, the normal route to intimacy. But they have not renounced, because as human beings they cannot, the need for close personal relationships in their lives. As we have tried to show in chapter eight, friendship, in the strictest and most intimate sense of the term, with persons of one's own or the other sex (and ideally with both) is the characteristic path to human intimacy for consecrated celibates.

Although I am sure there would be religious who would strongly disagree with me on this point, I am convinced that the satisfaction of intimacy needs cannot be realistically demanded of one's immediate community. Intimacy cannot be called into play on demand. Friendship is a mystery which arises (we know not how) when and where it arises. The kind of compatibility on which it is based is not something that can be achieved by the assiduous practice of virtue by one or both parties. Although it is certainly the case that many religious find their closest friends in their own congregations, it is not always the case (although it is more common today than in times past) that one's ministry allows one to live close to one's community friends and/or in the same immediate community with them. The immediate community, whether those with whom one lives or the more extended community we have described under the heading of living alone, may be composed of people one likes and admires but may not include anyone with whom one experiences that intimacy which characterizes friendship in the strict sense of the term. It is both a gift and challenge when close friendship develops between two members of the same immediate community. Although there are not the same suspicions and strictures which militated against friendship in pre-conciliar religious life it can still be difficult to avoid inappropriate exclusivity and to invest oneself enthusiastically in the life of the group if one's own needs are being more than adequately met in a single relationship. But whether or not friends find themselves in the same immediate community it seems to remain true that the community as such cannot be asked to fulfill the intimacy needs of its members. Community life meets, or should meet, many of our affective needs, such as those mentioned in the previous section, but all of us, finally, have to make our own friends.

However, the corollary of the exemption of the community from the obligation of meeting the intimacy needs of its members is the requirement that the community be capable of accepting the friendships of its members with people outside the immediate community, whether members of the congregation or others. People need time and space to spend with friends. They need to be trusted and supported in such relationships. They need to feel that the community, if it lives together in a single house, is reasonably open to the reception of members' friends and their appropriate inclusion in the life of the community. Such an atmosphere of openness and inclusiveness, of trust and support, as well as corresponding tact and sensitivity on the part of the individual religious who have obligations to their community as well as to their friends, is not a spontaneous achievement and may well be one of the most taxing challenges of modern community living. It is greatly reduced in situations in which religious are living alone and have the possibility of entertaining without involving the rest of the community as well as the possibility of being fully present and attentive to community life and activities when these are the agenda. But conflicts are not eliminated, even in this case, and one of the skills modern religious will undoubtedly have to develop is the capacity to integrate their personal and community affective life in minimally stressful ways. Pre-conciliar "common life" solved this problem by largely suppressing personal life and replacing it with fairly monolithic collective living. We can see, in hindsight, the impoverishment of personhood that this often caused. But as we seek alternative lifestyles that take the human and spiritual need for intimacy more seriously we will also have to face the stresses that complication inevitably introduces into life.

Generativity: The work of developmental psychologists has made us explicitly aware of the need of healthy adults to be generative, to nurture the next generation and thus cooperate in assuring the future of the race. Parents, of course, experience generativity as the main preoccupation of a good part of their lives (although it is painfully obvious that many are not equal to its demands). But those who do not marry, if they become fully mature adults, also experience a deeply felt need to foster the growth and well-being of other human beings. This need can, of course, develop neurotically, as in the case of parents whose generativity needs become a compulsive need to be needed. And it can easily go berserk in religious as well. But we are speaking here of a healthy need to love, to give, to nurture which is the overflow of a fullness of life and which is well balanced with the need for self-development and for peer exchange.

It would seem that the most appropriate sphere for the expression of generative love is that of ministry *as* ministry. I am not suggesting that religious ministers should infantilize those to whom they minister and make surrogate children out of their adult clients. But most ministry does consist in meeting the

needs of others, of children or adults for education, of the sick
for health care, of the indigent for social and legal services, of
the political system for insight and challenge. Ministry, if it is
real, is addressed to real needs and in this sense calls for a generosity, an un-self-centered attention to the needs of others, that
does not seek reward or demand reciprocity.

Again, this suggestion is certainly open to challenge, but I
am of the opinion that, at least ordinarily, the generativity needs
of religious should find their primary satisfaction in ministry as
such and not within the community. A community should be a
unit composed of equal adults whose relationships are primarily
characterized by a love of mutuality tending toward friendship
(with all the reservations noted several times above). Such mutuality will involve all the members in service of one another and
sometimes in a one-way service that, for the moment at least, is
not reciprocated. But when some members of a community become exclusively "givers" or "servers" and others exclusively
"receivers" or "takers" we see the development of a highly manipulative situation which serves no one's real needs but feeds
compulsions on the one side and immaturities on the other. If
the religious community, as we have suggested, is a community
of equal disciples in ministry it will be most appropriately characterized by relationships of mutuality, cooperation, free sharing of gifts, full participation according to personal
endowments, and shared responsibility. Such a situation might
well be characterized as one of mutual ministry, of reciprocal
care, but it would not have the same characteristics that ministry
itself does. A fulfilling community life supplies some of the
strength needed for ministry just as a strong marital relationship fosters the ability to parent generously and wisely. We can
be truly selfless in some situations, without manipulating or
dominating those we serve, if we are not trying to be or expected
to be selfless in all situations. One of the problems with the ideal
of unremitting selflessness that was sometimes proposed to religious in times past was that it encouraged compulsive "giving"
that dominated the receivers and impoverished the givers. The
over-emphasis on self-development that is still with us is not
hard to understand as a reaction against a univocal definition of
religious adulthood in terms of generativity. Adults have many

needs, one of which is to nurture the life in others. When those needs are kept in balance and are met with some degree of adequacy they are healthy impulsions toward full living. When they are not, they become tyrannical drives that infect ministry and community life alike and do little to promote the growth and holiness of the individual religious.

Achievement: Even to acknowledge the need of religious for achievement will activate instinctive resistance in some people. The intense indoctrination against pride and ambition to which most religious were exposed is not easily overcome. Again, I am expressing an opinion with which some might disagree, but I am convinced that religious have the same basic needs in this sphere that other people do. Psychologists often refer to the need for recognition. However we name it, I think it is based in the need we all feel to do things well, to become better people, to grow and produce. Recognition, not necessarily public acclaim or notoriety but the simple affirmation we receive from some others in our life which corroborates our own sense of making a difference in our world, is a real need. Like any need it can, of course, develop neurotically. There are people who need such constant positive feedback that it taxes the energy and good will of everyone around them. They manipulate others to obtain this feedback by constant self-deprecation which they expect to have contradicted, or by incessant if subtle boasting, or by just getting sick if they do not receive regular "fixes" of praise and appreciation. We are not talking about such neurotic needs but about the ordinary need of healthy, productive people to be appreciated for their contribution and to experience some recognition by which to measure their actual growth.

I have long suspected that one of the underlying causes of morale problems among both the ordained and religious is that the work structures in which they are involved have very few built-in provisions for regular and appropriate recognition and ordained men and religious were taught that desiring even these was inappropriate or wrong. Religious in a teaching order, for example, both coveted and denied desiring to move to a higher grade because, on the one hand, it was almost the only affirmation that one was a successful teacher but, on the other hand, desiring it was considered to be "ambition" or a sign of pride. This double bind led to subconscious dishonesty as well as to sometimes very inappropriate uses of personnel.

Transferring achievement needs, the need for recognition and reasonable positive feedback honestly earned, to the community undermines the basic equality underlying the truly Christian character of religious community. It is certainly to be hoped that members of a community will be the first to rejoice in a member's success and achievements. But if the only success or achievement members experience must be achieved within the community (as was often the case in times past) the community will have to be structured hierarchically and members will have to compete for status and positions of power. The most distressing example of this situation is certainly the clerical system. The stratification of what should be a collegial system is so rigid and finally meaningless that it has created a power structure capable of destroying men and communities.

What I am suggesting is that the appropriate sphere for the satisfaction of the need to achieve and be recognized is ministry *as* profession, or as one's "work." Now that many religious are ministering in institutions and settings not owned and operated by their own congregations they are experiencing, almost as a salutary reality therapy in some cases, ordinary human reward systems. Getting and keeping a position, getting paid a real salary for work done, and receiving promotions and public recognition for signal achievement, as well as losing ground for ineptitude, laziness, or uncooperativeness, are realities of ministerial life today. I suspect that this is a very healthy development. Religious who are achieving in their work do not need to demand, often in subversive and neurotic ways, the satisfaction of their needs for recognition within and by the community. The jealousies, competition, and unadmitted coveting of the few positions of power available in the small social system of the community are no longer necessary. People come home from diverse work situations able to share their successes and failures, their real frustrations and cherished hopes with people who have no secret vested interests in the situation and who can, therefore, be honestly interested in the person who is sharing.

Needless to say, the satisfaction of achievement needs in the sphere of life work can lead to serious conflicts. The work of religious is, from one point of view, a profession, but from another it is ministry. The call to generativity in ministry can come into conflict with the need for achievement in work. And even if religious in a community are not all involved in the same professional situation there will always be a diversity in levels of success and recognition among the members. The insensitive achiever can become an oppressive presence for less high-powered companions, just as the underachiever can be a burden for more highly-motivated and self-starting companions. The need for recognition, long repressed and denied especially among women religious, can reassert itself in exaggerated forms turning previously meek religious into ambitious climbers. There are no limits to the perversions we humans can devise, but it seems to me that the present situation in which achievement needs, as well as their possible deviations, are frankly recognized and in which the professional character of ministry is accepted and allowed to function as an appropriate source of realistic experiences of success and failure is potentially healthier than its predecessor.

In summary, then, my thesis is that religious have a variety of human, psychological needs which must be met if religious are to become and function as mature adults and that holiness normally finds its substrate in such human maturity. The immediate community, whether it is the small group living in the same residence or the more diffuse group in which some or all members do not live in the same house but come together in various ways to corporately participate in congregational affairs and to support and sustain one another in religious commitment, cannot and should not be expected to meet all of these needs. Specifically, it is the corporate identity need, the requirement for ongoing and meaningful belonging to a social unit larger than oneself with whose ideals, purposes, and members one can affectively identify and within which one can be oneself without pretense, that is primarily met by community membership. The need for intimacy is primarily met through personal friendships within and outside of the congregation and immediate community; the need for generativity is primarily met though one's ministry as ministry; and the need for achievement and recognition is primarily met in the sphere of ministry as work or profession. This theory departs significantly from the understanding of the community as the total and exclusive context of the religious' life as well as from a totalitarian conception of the institute or congregation. The immediate community is seen as a coming together of congregational members, each of whom brings the riches of an adult personal life, and the placing in common of those riches which together form the primary, ongoing context of the life of the members.

VI. THE THEOLOGICAL SIGNIFICANCE OF RELIGIOUS COMMUNITY

So far we have been looking at religious community from the standpoint of its relationship to the psychological/spiritual well-being of the members. In this final section I want to take up the question of the meaning of religious community from the theological/spiritual point of view. We began these reflections by affirming that Christianity is essentially a communitarian phenomenon which is called upon to incarnate in this world the Trinitarian life of God in the community of the children of God which Jesus founded. Isolation is not an option for Christians. Our primary ministry is always to participate in the great mystery of reconciliation and union which Jesus initiated by his death on the cross and his glorious resurrection.

Different states of life in the Church make differing contributions to this realization of and witness to community. The Christian family, rooted in its sacrament of matrimony, bears primary and striking witness to intimate life-giving love. Religious life, with its celibate commitment, offers primary witness to the character of Christianity as "eschatological community." By eschatological I do not mean that which lies in the future so much as that which focuses hope. The community of reconciliation which the Church is called to be and to foster is a community of friends, of equal persons loved for themselves, who freely give and receive as they participate in the ministry of transforming this world into the place and material of the reign of God. The eschatological community is not composed of selected companions and is not held together by need or force. It is an inclusive community bonded by shared love of Christ and devotion to God's reign. The religious community, ideally, is a realization, however limited, of this community. Its members come together, not because they are compatible or because of needs or under duress. They are not held together by ties of blood, power, or wealth. They are together because they choose to love inclusively and to commit all the resources of their lives to extending that community of reconciliation to the ends of the earth.

To be community in this evangelical sense of the word is one of the tasks which contemporary religious must undertake in a very changed religious and ecclesial setting. To make the reality of what they are visible so that it can function as witness in Church and world is a further task. The kind of automatic visibility which the "common life" community had in times past is no longer available to many religious. But, on the other hand, it is much more possible today to allow people to witness religious community life from the inside than it was when religious life was an entirely exclusive phenomenon viewed only from the outside and deliberately presented as a monolithic and perfect collectivity rather than as a struggling human reality. Few people, I suspect, had any desire to model their ecclesial experience on what they thought life in a pre-conciliar convent was like; many people today want to find ways both to participate in the life, ministry, and spirituality of religious communities and to found voluntary lay communities modeled on those religious communities they know.

Religious community has evolved so rapidly in the last two decades that the question of evaluation is premature. I think, however, that certain conclusions can safely be drawn. First, the functions of religious community have changed drastically and so the form must change accordingly. Religious life is no longer a quasi-primary patriarchal family organized according to the pattern of a divine right monarchy and functioning as a kind of branch office of centralized Church authority; it is a voluntary and self-determining community of equals sharing discipleship and ministry. Therefore, its forms will be less and less totalitarian, hierarchical, and control-motivated and ever more egalitarian, participative, and responsibly free.

Second, the equation of community with "common life" has

been historically undermined. The forms community takes will vary greatly under the influence of decreasing numbers, diversification of ministries, and alterations in resource-disbursement patterns. While most religious will probably continue to choose living together in small groups, there will be increasing numbers of religious living alone or in intercongregational or mixed communities. Therefore, community at the intermediate or congregational level will be proportionately more important and community at the immediate level will be more diversified in form and probably more intentional in function.

Third, community life will increasingly be evaluated in terms of both its capacity to foster the psychological well-being of its members and therefore their spiritual maturity and its capacity to incarnate and witness to the reality of eschatological community. This will be in sharp contrast to the evaluation of community in terms of regularity, order, discipline, and control.

The task of contemporary religious is not to find the definitive form of community and set it in concrete for the next several hundred years, but to cherish the value of Christian community and seek with ongoing flexibility to find appropriate ways to realize it in ever-changing situations. The value in question is that which Jesus described when he prayed to God his Father that we might all be one even as he and the Father are one so that the world might know that God had sent him and loves us even as God loves him (cf. Jn 17:20–23).

Chapter Thirteen
PROPHETIC CONSCIOUSNESS: OBEDIENCE AND DISSENT IN THE RELIGIOUS LIFE

Much of the material in the following essay was originally developed for the members of the National Religious Formation Conference, delivered at their bi-annual meeting in Philadelphia in November of 1981, and published in their 1981 *Proceedings: Formation in the American Church*. It was later reworked at the invitation of the Leadership Conference of Women Religious and the Conference of Major Superiors of Men, delivered at their joint annual meeting in San Francisco in August of 1982, and published in their 1982 *Proceedings: To Build a Bridge*. It has since been used by a number of congregations in their respective renewal processes, in preparations for chapters, and as input for committees working on revisions of constitutions.

Discipleship, as we all know, is a vocation to which one can never respond in a final and definitive way. It is a call to ongoing conversion, to an ever deeper appreciation of the mystery of Christ. To be a disciple is to incarnate the identity and mission of Jesus in our own personal, historical, and cultural context. For us, then, discipleship means living ever more deeply and effectively the mystery of Christ in the American Church of the late twentieth century.

There is a characteristic of our recent American Catholic experience that is at once glaringly evident and profoundly confusing, particularly because it is so discontinuous with the experience which formed most of us as American Catholic children. I am speaking of the deep ambivalence toward the authoritative institutions of both our country and our Church that many of us contend with on a daily basis. Nothing was more integral, even central, to the formation of young Catholics in the American parochial school system of the 1940's and 1950's than

266

the positive evaluation of lawfully constituted institutions summed up in the oft-cited, though decontextualized quotation from Romans: "All authority comes from God."[1]

Obedience to parents, to Church law and personnel, and to civil officials was all of a piece expressing filial submission to the ultimate authority, God "himself," variously imagined as a stern father, a heavenly pope, or the policeman in the sky. Adult Catholics who were sophisticated and discriminating professionals in their secular lives lived unquestioningly with the virtual equation, on the moral level, of eating meat on Friday, murder, contraception, and missing Mass on Sunday. All were mortal sins that would send the unshriven perpetrator to hell. This was the authoritative teaching of the authoritative institution, and obedience to lawfully constituted authority was strictly identical with obedience to God (unless, of course, the action commanded was sinful).

Much the same attitude characterized the American Catholic in respect to the civil institution. Catholics were, of course, taught that in a conflict between Church and state it was not only legitimate but obligatory for the Christian, in imitation of all the martyrs down through the centuries, to obey God rather than human authority (God = Church; human authority = state). However, two factors conspired to keep this teaching largely theoretical for most American Catholics. First was the position in moral theology resulting from the affirmation that just civil law, although human, was sanctioned by divine authority. Therefore, Catholic moralists were never really comfortable with the theory of the purely penal law, that is, a law whose infraction, though entailing a just penalty, was not immoral. To deliberately break any just law, however morally neutral its content, was a rebellion against lawful authority and therefore against God in whom all authority originated. The second factor was the American political system itself. The separation of Church and state enshrined in the First Amendment guarantee of religious liberty made the likelihood of a real conflict between the civil government and the Church remote and assured legal redress of grievances if it should ever occur. America was the promised land, born in the passionate quest for religious liberty, and committed to assuring the freedom and well-being of its own citizens and of all the world's huddled masses yearning to breathe free. The civil government of the United States was, American Catholic children learned, a just government of, by, and for the people, and therefore legitimately enjoyed divinely sanctioned authority. Respect for and obedience to civil authority was just as much an obligation as obedience to religious authority.

This attitude toward authority which characterized most Catholics in their relations with both ecclesiastical and civil institutions was not mindless subservience. It was the expression of a profound conviction that both Church and state were, despite human weaknesses, divinely instituted social orders, perfect societies, designed to foster the common good on earth and lead eventually to eternal life in heaven.[2] What I want to explore in this chapter is the radical change which has taken place in the American Catholic consciousness in the last twenty years in regard to institutional authority, both ecclesiastical and civil. The basic trust in the overall soundness of these institutions and therefore in the legitimacy of their authority which grounded the presumption in favor of obedience even in conflictual situations has been seriously eroded by events of the last two decades. The result is a profound ambivalence of many Catholics, including many religious, toward both Church and civil government and a resulting need to rethink the entire problematic of authority and obedience as it concerns institutions.

For some combination of historical reasons, the exploration of which is beyond the scope of this chapter, human consciousness has undergone some kind of quantum leap during our lifetime. Humanity has always, up to our own time, accepted as inevitable and therefore legitimate the determination of some people's lives by other people's decisions. Masters have controlled slaves, the rich have controlled the poor, whites have controlled people of color, men have controlled women, clerics have controlled the laity, superiors have controlled subjects, and so on. Hierarchy was considered the natural, universal, God-ordained principle of all sound social organization. For the first time in world history, in our generation, this arrangement has been repudiated on a worldwide scale. Group after group, in nation after nation, has claimed the right of self-determination.

Every liberation movement of our time is the expression of the claim to self-determination by some previously subordinate group. Whatever the cause of this phenomenon, it is indeed a fact, and the massive failure of both Church and state to come to grips with it is in my opinion a, if not the, major factor in the undermining of institutional authority. Conflict after conflict in both institutions has taken the same shape, namely, the resistance of a sizable group of members to the institution's attempt to limit their self-determination. American blacks rose up against their imprisonment in a second-class citizenship. For the first time in our history young men in America during the Vietnam War decided that they would not kill or be killed because the government said they should. Catholic spouses responded to *Humanae Vitae* with a resounding refusal to have the role of sexual love and procreation in their marriages determined in an absolute and unilateral way by ecclesiastical authorities. Women in both Church and state have decided that men must no longer sit in all-male council determining the nature and function of women in secular or ecclesial society. Examples abound, but the point is that neither Church nor state has been able to come to terms with the claims of its members to equality and self-determination and the result has been a rapidly increasing series of situations in which large numbers of American Catholics are resisting the institutional authority they once accepted as the evident manifestation of God's will in their lives.

The situation is complicated by the fact that these resisters do not dispute the legitimacy of the institutions as such nor the existence of genuine authority. They are not planning to overthrow the American government or the Vatican. Nor do most of them intend to renounce their American citizenship or their membership in the Catholic Church. They intend both to remain and to resist. It is this phenomenon of dissenting membership that is the focus of these reflections. How are we to make sense of this experience, in which many of us are involved, of ongoing radical criticism and behavioral non-conformity within the institutions that most profoundly structure our lives and identities? As a journalist once asked me, "Are we not talking about Catholicism (or citizenship) a la carte?" In other words, does it make any sense to talk about accepting authority if one reserves to oneself the right to decide when and if one will obey? Can we realistically talk about an ecclesial or civil community if each member takes to himself or herself the right to determine his or her own position on matters of vital common concern and the right to act on that position even when it contradicts the directives of institutional authorities? In short, is radical dissent compatible with loyal membership and, if it is, how are we to understand that compatibility?

I suspect that neither I nor anyone else has a fully satisfactory theoretical solution to this problem which is, after all, quite new. But what I would like to do is suggest a way of thinking about this experience of dissenting membership which might at least allow us to situate ourselves within the question with a little more clarity and conviction.

In what follows I am immensely indebted to a wonderful little book by the Old Testament scholar Walter Brueggemann entitled *The Prophetic Imagination.*[3] In the book Brueggemann explores the ongoing tension between the monarchy and prophecy in ancient Israel. I am going to use Brueggemann's analysis to explore the meaning and relationship between the prophetic and royal dimensions of Christian identity and mission. My thesis is that there is a dialectic, a tension which can be either creative or destructive, between these two dimensions of Christian discipleship and that it is precisely this dialectic which is at work in the phenomenon of dissenting membership. If prophecy and royalty can come to function in our lives as they did in the life of Jesus, they will energize our commitment to bringing about the reign of God in this world by the effective preaching of God's Word. If, on the other hand, our royal identity degenerates into a participation in what Brueggemann calls the "royal consciousness" our prophetic mission will be domesticated and denatured; and if prophecy loses touch with the reign of God that it must serve, we will become rebels without a cause, blind leaders of the blind.

Let us begin our analysis by briefly recalling certain features of the history of Israel's experience of prophecy and monarchy. Israel was constituted a people by her rescue from Egypt and her entrance into the covenant with Yahweh at Sinai. From that time on Israel was a holy nation, the people of God (cf. Ex

35). Yahweh alone was King and Lord, and so, while Israel had judges and elders, military leaders and priests to facilitate the ongoing religious and political life of the people, Israel had no human king, no monarch who stood above the community as a superior source of law and order. All the members of the community, whatever their functions, were subject to the same Law, namely Torah, which did not originate with any earthly ruler but had been given to the community by God.

When, in the eleventh century B.C., for political and military reasons that are quite understandable, the people asked the prophet Samuel to give them a king so that they could be like other nations, the prophet protested that setting up a king in Israel would be idolatrous (cf. 1 Sam 8:4–21). God is presented as interpreting the people's request as a rejection of Yahweh's reign in favor of a human monarch (1 Sam 8:7). Nevertheless, God acceded to the people's demand and Samuel was sent to anoint Saul, thus inaugurating the Israelite monarchy. It was understood from the beginning that the king was chosen by God, was anointed by God's servant, and was subject as were all the people to Torah, God's Law for the covenant community. The king was Yahweh's visible representative among the people but in no sense a vicar, one who took the place of God. God was always present and active among the people. The king was a concession to the community's need for security, in other words, to its lack of faith. Consequently, the monarchy was always an ambiguous reality from a theological point of view.[4]

In very short order the monarchy became concretely problematic in the disobedience and superstition of Saul, whom God finally rejected (1 Sam 15:22–29). David, Saul's successor, came closer than any of Israel's kings to realizing the truly religious role of the monarch as God intended. David, despite his sins, never forgot who was really king of Israel. But after David's death, his son Solomon progressively appropriated to himself the divine royalty, and so, after him, the monarchy was divided and slipped deeper and deeper into infidelity until both the northern kingdom of Israel and the southern kingdom of Judah came to ruin[5] and kingship in Israel became a glorious memory founding a messianic hope for the renewal of the Davidic dynasty (2 Sam 7:8–16).

Throughout the period of the monarchy the prophets constituted a kind of loyal opposition. They were so consistently opposed to the policies and procedures of the kings that opposition
to the monarch came to be almost a sign of a true prophet,
whereas telling the king what he wanted to hear raised a strong
suspicion of false prophecy (cf. Jer 23:16ff). The prophets did
not oppose the institution of kingship as such. They opposed the
way it operated. And the kings never disputed prophecy in principle; they exiled the prophets for their opposition to the royal
regime. Although prophecy and monarchy were both accepted
as divinely established institutions in Israel, they were almost always in tension with one another.

What Brueggemann does is to abstract from the concrete
experience of Israel the inner structure and reality of the conflict. He discusses not the historical struggle between King Ze-
dekiah and the prophet Jeremiah, between King Ahaz and the
prophet Isaiah, but the tension between what he calls the "royal
consciousness" and the "prophetic imagination." It is this par-
adigm whose potentialities I want to exploit in relation to the
dilemma in discipleship of the American Catholic which I have
called dissenting membership in Church and state.

First, let us try to understand what Brueggemann calls the
royal consciousness. What primarily characterizes the royal consciousness is its identification with the present, with the current
regime, with the political and social status quo. Obviously, it is
only within the present structure that the king *is* king. If the
monarchy falls the king's reign comes to an end.

Now there are various possible grounds for asserting that
the present system should remain in force. One is that it is really
serving the true interests of the people. But this is, in one sense,
a very precarious basis on which to found one's royal claims because, if it should happen (as it well might) that many people
become unhappy or discontented, the legitimacy of the monarchy, or at least of the incumbent's exercise of it, becomes open
to question. The king whose reign is justified by its efficacy, its
capacity to meet the real needs of the people, is really in a position of dependence on the people rather than vice versa. Such
a monarchy is not an absolute one at all. It might be a monar-
chically structured regime, but in substance it is a genuinely

communitarian arrangement because the community's needs have a real priority. This, of course, was the kind of monarchy God intended for Israel, one in which the king pursued God's own concerns for well-being and justice among God's people.[6]

There is, however, another way to legitimate a regime, one that can claim that the present system is permanently and irreversibly legitimate regardless of its efficacy in meeting community needs, namely, to claim that the regime was instituted by God and therefore enjoys perpetual legitimacy which is not subject to review nor accountable for performance. This is the claim of Israel's unworthy kings, of Egypt's pharaohs, of Rome's emperors, of divine right monarchs down through history and, frequently enough, of ecclesiastical hierarchy. We notice in each of these regimes the tendency of the monarch to self-identification with the divinity which is characteristic of hierarchical social structure when it wishes to lift itself above the vicissitudes of human change and possible revision. The pharaohs and the Roman emperors deified themselves; Louis XIV called himself the "Sun-King"; the Church talks of its officials as "other Christs" and of the Pope as the "Vicar of Christ"; religious superiors have often claimed that their will expressed the will of God for their subjects. The royal consciousness legitimates its identification with the status quo by claiming that the present regime is of divine institution and the presently reigning personnel are God's vicars.

Once it is established that the monarchy is not the product of human initiative but of the divine will, the monarch ceases to be truly answerable to the people. He is accountable only to God. The people, on the other hand, are accountable to the king who controls access to God as well as to all material benefits. This double control of both divine and earthly goods gives the monarch immense power which he can then exercise with sovereign liberty because to call his arrangements into question is to oppose God's will. As the monarch accumulates power and wealth the people become progressively more dependent, and only those who are in favor with the monarch have assured access to well-being. We see this dynamic at work in our own day in Latin American dictatorships, in some American dioceses, and occasionally in the houses or provinces of religious orders.

This is, of course, exactly what happened in Israel. Solomon represents the ultimate realization of the royal consciousness. As he became immensely powerful and wealthy the people became progressively poorer and more powerless (cf. 1 Kgs 5:13ff). Solomon so appropriated to himself his divine identification that he eventually took it upon himself even to mitigate the demands of monotheism. When it served his political purposes he allowed the cults of other gods to flourish in Israel (cf. 1 Kgs 11:1–13). Solomon considered himself, and the people considered him, immune from opposition, for he was, after all, God's anointed, not the representative of the people.

The only voice that could be raised against the divine right monarch was the voice of the prophet who spoke for God. The prophet was a member of the community, subject like other community members to the royal authority. But the prophet had an independent, charismatic access to God, an access which the king did not control, and on the basis of which he could call the king to account in God's name. The prophet spoke for the community not as its elected representative but as God's representative. In the prophet, championing the rights of the people, we hear the voice of God reclaiming the covenant people from the unfaithful shepherd who has failed in his trust, who has not pastored and protected God's people, but has victimized them for the sake of his own regime (cf. e.g. Jer 23:1–8). The prophet challenges the king's claim to divine immunity from accountability and reminds him that he was to represent, not replace God; that he, too, is subject to Torah, not above the Law (see also Is 3:14–15; 10:1–4 and elsewhere).

Let us look, then, at the *prophetic imagination*. The prophet is one who can imagine, against the royal contention that the present regime is an eternally valid and inviolable arrangement, an alternative reality. The prophet refuses the royal injunction to worship the status quo as the inevitable and divinely sanctioned dispensation. The prophet looks back to the past, to the promises made to the ancestors and the covenant which enshrined those promises, to the people's free commerce with the living God when they cried out from their needs (Jer 2:1–3). And the prophet laments the incongruity between what was promised and what now exists (Jer 2:4–37). Because the prophet sees the inadequacy of the present against the fecundity of the promises, he can imagine and announce a different future (Jer 3:11–4:4). This is the danger of the prophet to the king. The prophet, by his evocation of the past and his imagining of the future, undermines the present order of things and threatens to bring the king's reign down around his ears (Jer 26:1–11). And the prophet does all this in the name of the very God to whom the king appeals for the legitimacy of his regime.

To sum up briefly, then, the royal consciousness is structured by its identification with the status quo. It tries to present itself as the eternal now, the unchangeable order. It is an order in which power and wealth inevitably accumulate at the top of the hierarchical system and which is immune, as divine institution, from accountability to those at the bottom. It is a system which even God cannot change because, to do so, God would have to act against God's own dispensation.

The prophetic imagination, by contrast, nourished by a living rememberance of the past, threatens the present status quo by its capacity to imagine and announce an alternative future. For the prophet, God is not irrevocably implicated in any earthly dispensation, no matter how it originated nor how sacred it is. God remains sovereignly free to act again in favor of God's people if only they will recognize Yahweh as the one on whom their true good depends (Jer 3:12–18; Hos 14:1–9). The prophet sees clearly what neither king nor people see, namely, the difference between the God whose representative the king is called to be and the self-divinized monarch who has surreptitiously taken God's place in the lives of the people (e.g. Jer 22:1–5). The prophet announces that God is still on the side of the dispossessed, the lowly, the poor, the powerless as God was on the side of the Hebrews against Pharaoh (Jer 22:13–23). The prophet recalls both king and people to the covenant, to trust in God rather than in human strength, to true worship which repudiates any and every claim of king or foreigner to take the place of God among the people.

Now, it is crucial to our purposes to realize that the royal consciousness and the prophetic imagination are not limited to realization in historical monarchs and ancient prophets. The royal consciousness asserts itself in any situation in which the of-

ficials of an institution so identify with and invest themselves in
the institution that preservation of the status quo begins to take
precedence over the real good of the people the institution was
created to serve. This perversion does not have to be the expression of deliberate malice. Usually this self-investment in the institution results from and is expressed as a conviction that the
preservation of the status quo is identical with, or at least necessary for, the good of the community.

By the same token, the prophetic imagination emerges
whenever fidelity to a community's founding inspiration is effectively evoked to energize movement toward an alternative future which stands more in continuity with that past and thus
stands a better chance of improving the condition of those victimized by the present regime.

Basic to the situation with which we are concerned in this
chapter, namely, that which involves many American Catholics,
and especially religious, in the experience of dissenting membership, is the fact that there is an inveterate tendency of institutional responsibility to give rise to the royal consciousness in
even the most well-motivated officials. People are elected or appointed to office in institutions because the institutions are necessary instruments of the common good and these institutions
cannot perdure or function without the responsible dedication
of those who administer and lead them. Officials are chosen precisely because they see the importance for the community of the
institution. It is this insight that frequently leads the office
holder to opt for the institution over the members. The classic
principle of institutional expediency, "It is better that one person die rather than that the whole nation perish" (cf. Jn 11:49–
50), contains a built-in escalation factor. During the Vietnam era
it was invoked to justify the sacrifice of a whole generation to a
misguided notion of national honor. There is a grim possibility
that it will be the epitaph of the earth incinerated for the same
empty cause. It has been invoked in religious congregations to
justify the repression or expulsion of truly prophetic members
in order to ward off the descent of ecclesiastical wrath on the
whole order. The royal consciousness is seldom the result of
freely chosen malice or naked hunger for power. It is the creep-
ing disease that is the occupational hazard of office.

On the other hand, the prophetic imagination, precisely because it is a charismatic quality deriving from personal experience of God and the resulting commitment to God's people, especially to the most oppressed, is notoriously difficult to discern. Jim Jones offered an alternative future to some of the people most victimized by the American system. Only the spectacle of nine hundred people dead at their own hands around a cauldron of cyanide revealed the horrible character and tragic dimensions of his ego-blinded vision of salvation. Hitler offered an alternative future to a humiliated Germany and eloquently persuaded a whole nation to look the other way while he exterminated six million Jews to bring it about. There is nothing simple about the struggle between the royal consciousness and the prophetic imagination.

My suggestion is that it is only by contemplating, and making our own in disciplined practice, Jesus' living of the tension between the royal and the prophetic dimensions of his vocation that we can begin to mediate between our own legitimate institutional commitments and our prophetic vocation to combat the royal consciousness which corrupts those very institutions into shrines of the status quo rather than servants of the community and its purposes.

The early Church recognized in Jesus the fulfillment of all Israel's messianic expectations. He was the long-awaited Davidic king; he was the transcendent realization of the prophetic vocation of Moses, Elijah, and Jeremiah. But we have become so used to speaking of Jesus as prophet and king that we often fail to attend to the fact that he related very differently to each of these two dimensions of his messianic identity and mission.

During his public life Jesus resisted any application of royal titles to himself and fled from the people who wanted to make him king (e.g. Jn 6:15). It is important to note that he not only refused to allow himself to be made a political king in opposition to the Roman imperial rule; he also avoided participation in the religious power structures of his own people. Jesus was not a Pharisee, a lawyer, a scribe, a member of the Sanhedrin, or a priest. He was a simple layman who held no official position in either the ecclesiastical or the civil sphere. Consequently, while he manifested an appropriate respect for both institutional regimes he was not personally identified with either (cf. Mt 5:17; 22:15–46; 23:1–31 and elsewhere). By his own choice, there was no soil in the human experience of Jesus in which the royal consciousness, in either its religious or its civil form, could flourish. Jesus did not assume his royal identity until he entered Jerusalem to be handed over for execution by the institutional authorities (cf. Jn 12:13). It is interesting that tradition has never been able to establish conclusively whether Jesus' execution should be attributed finally to the animosity of the Jews or of the Romans. It is perhaps more to the point to realize that at the deepest level, the level of their opposition to Jesus, the two institutions were identical. Jesus the prophet was put to death by the institution in the grip of the royal consciousness. The fear of the Jewish authorities that the continuance of Jesus would lead to the Romans "taking away our place and our nation" (cf. Jn 11:48) and the Roman fear that this man would overthrow the representative of Caesar (cf. Jn 18:33–38; 19:12–13) are the same fear. Jesus' message was as dangerous for the synagogue as it was for the palace because what he was announcing was that both regimes, even though legitimate, were provisional, relative human institutions. God was alive, well, and present in Israel and God had not transferred the divine preference from its age-old object, namely, the poor and the oppressed, to the prestigious and powerful who held office in Church and state. Jesus announced the end of both regimes by calling into question their identical false claim, to be eternally valid, divinely sanctioned, absolute dispensations. For Jesus the only absolute regime which made the only truly royal claim was what the evangelists call the *basileia tou theou,* the reign of God. No civil or ecclesiastical regime was identical with or the exhaustive incarnation of that reign. All human institutions, religious and civil, exist to help realize that reign among God's people, not to take its place.

The true royalty of Jesus, which had nothing to do with the royal consciousness, but was rooted in his divine filiation, was expressed in his identification with the reign of God. Consequently, it was not something he could claim during his public life because he knew well that the royal consciousness was as much at work in the hearts of the victims of the oppressive regimes as it was in the officials. The people wanted to make Jesus king, not because he inaugurated among them the reign of God by preaching the good news to the poor, but because he seemed to be a better version of their earthly rulers. They wanted to replace their current institutional idols with a new idol. As Jesus says to the crowd, "You seek me, not because you saw signs [that is, not as a locus of divine revelation], but because you ate your fill of the loaves [that is, because you think I could fulfill your immediate material needs better than the current regime]" (Jn 6:26).

Jesus refused a royalty already corrupted by the royal consciousness and functioned openly only as a prophet. As prophet he evoked the past, the covenant God made with the people in their poverty and powerlessness, and he energized them to hope for an alternative future. He announced that the reign of God would belong to the poor, the meek, the hungry, the dispossessed, the powerless (cf. Mt 5:3–12; Lk 6:20–23). It is a reign in which mutual love among equals (cf. Jn 13:34–35 and elsewhere)[7] will replace all the hierarchical relationships built on inequality, the relationships of power and domination which structured the society of the pagans and oppressed the people of God (cf. Mt 23:8–12; Mk 10:42–45).

But Jesus did not just promise a future reign; he acted to inaugurate it in the present. He broke the grip of the ecclesiastical establishment by declaring all religious laws except that of love relative to human good (e.g. Mk 2:23–28) and by giving free access to divine forgiveness to those who did not qualify for it by meeting institutional requirements (e.g. Lk 7:36–50). He broke the grip of the political establishment by declaring the equality of people as children of God called to mutual love and thus announcing the relativity of Rome's dominion in the present and the inevitability of its demise when the reign of God would come in all its fullness. He broke down the barriers of stratified society so necessary for hierarchy to function by eating with sinners (Mt 9:10–13), consorting with Samaritans (Jn 4:4–27) and pagans (Jn 4:46–54), and calling women to be disciples and apostles along with men (Lk 8:1–3; Jn 20:17–18).[8] Jesus the prophet reminded the people that God's covenant was still effective, announced the reign which was coming, and inaugurated it among them. But he avoided identifying himself publicly as a king until the moment when he was beyond the corrupting reach of the royal consciousness in the people, as the victim of the royal consciousness in the institution. Only when he was definitively involved in the ultimate reversal that characterizes the divine reign, in the poverty and powerlessness of death from which only God could rescue him, did he claim his royal identity. From the cross he reigned as king (Jn 19:19–22).

Our faith teaches us that all of us participate in the royal and prophetic dimensions of Jesus' identity and mission. But from the Council of Trent until quite recently it has been customary in Roman Catholic circles to speak of the hierarchy alone as participating actively while the laity participated passively in Christ's mission. The prophetic dimension of the active Church was usually equated with teaching established doctrine and the royal dimension with hierarchical government. In fact, the teaching function came to be exercised as an aspect of government, resulting in the notion of an absolute authoritative magisterium characterized by the same authoritarian triumphalism that marked the Church's government by a clericalized hierarchy. The laity, whose participation in the identity and mission of Christ had been characterized as passive, were thought to take part in his prophetic identity primarily by being docilely taught and in his royal identity by being meekly ruled. Little attention was focused on the way Jesus had related to his royal and prophetic vocation.

Obviously, Vatican II has legitimated a massive revision of this Counter-Reformation approach to discipleship. But it has not provided much clear guidance for the ordinary Christian disciple in understanding what it might mean for us to participate actively in the prophecy and royalty of Jesus. What I have been trying to suggest in this essay is that participation in the royalty of Jesus has nothing to do with identification, active or passive, with ruling institutions, ecclesiastical or civil. It has to do with identification with the reign of God, an identification in hope that anticipates its final realization, but also an identification in action in helping to realize it here and now by an active and effective commitment to peace and justice for all God's people.

One of the most important insights of post-conciliar ecclesiology is that the Catholic Church is not identical with the reign of God but exists to serve that reign.[9] To absolutize the institution of the Church (and *a fortiori* the nation) is not a recognition of, nor a participation in, the royalty of Jesus. It is an exercise of the royal consciousness against which, as prophets, we must cry out, for it is an idolatry that blinds people to the coming of the reign. To participate in the royalty of Jesus ·˃ to so identify with the reign of God that we see clearly the rel ıvity of all human regimes, that of the ecclesiastical institution as much as that of the civil institution. To participate in the prophetic identity of Jesus means, at least in part, to combat the royal consciousness in ourselves first of all, but also in the Church and state, especially when they sacrifice persons to systems. As humans and as Christians we participate in institutions; but as disciples of Jesus we recognize only one regime as absolute, the reign of God.

I suspect that many committed American Catholics are acting out of an experiential but unthematized realization of the relativity of institutions to the absolute claim of the reign of God when they dissent from oppressive institutional policies and practices of both Church and state while remaining respectful members of both. What they are refusing to do is to concede to the royal consciousness, no matter where it emerges, its claim to absolute validity. They are not refusing to admit the real but provisional legitimacy of human institutions.

It may well be that the ecclesiastical institution presents a more painful challenge to conversion for the contemporary Catholic, especially the person actively involved in ministry, than does the civil institution. It is easier for most of us to exercise our prophetic discipleship against the government because the blasphemy of a claim to absolute validity and authority is more blatant when it is made by a non-religious institution. It is much more difficult for Catholics, especially those of us who were brought up in the most absolutist period of Church history, the Counter-Reformation, to relativize the institution of the Church. The great temptation is to connive with the royal consciousness when it emerges in ecclesiastical officials, even if we ourselves are the victims. We have been so educated to respect the religious claim to obedience which the institutional Church makes that we are ill-prepared to accept ourselves as dissidents, even when our most fundamental individual and collective rights are at stake or the good of the people we serve is being subverted.

There are times, of course, when we can legitimately suffer persecution for justice's sake as Jesus did. But we pervert the Gospel ideal of meekness when we make it an excuse for allowing ourselves to be dominated rather than face the struggle to achieve maturity in our relationship with institutional authority. Not to resist the royal consciousness is to support and encourage it. What victimizes us today will claim a sister or brother tomorrow.

Even more problematic is the temptation to stand by silently while others in the local or wider Church are victimized by the abuse of power. It matters little whether those in power are being deliberately and maliciously oppressive or whether, like the religious officials Jesus warned of, they think that by destroying their ecclesiastical enemies they are giving glory to God (cf. Jn 16:1–2). Our commitment to the reign of God is a vocation to prophesy, in season and out of season, against the royal consciousness whenever it prefers the good of institutions to the good of human beings.

One of the most difficult aspects of the responsible assumption of our vocation to prophecy is accepting the necessity that falls eventually on most of us to resist or to criticize those institutions in which we are most intimately and immediately involved, for example, the local Church or our own religious congregation. Jesus warned us both that our enemies would be those of our household (Mt 10:34–36) and that the prophet would be least acceptable in his or her own country (Mt 12:57; Mk 6:4; Jn 4:44). It is difficult enough to denounce injustice and oppression in distant lands and in remote institutions—this must, of course, be done—but it is more psychologically painful and dangerous to denounce them from within the institutions in which we live and minister. It is easier to challenge our government's participation in Latin American oppression than Vatican persecution of theologians. We are more comfortable denouncing civil discrimination against women than crying out against the oppression of women in and by the Church. We will more willingly align ourselves with the struggle for self-determination of South African blacks than with the struggle for self-determination of our own religious congregation. Examples could be multiplied but the point is painfully obvious. We must bring our prophetic ministry to bear within the community of the Church. As the Synod of Bishops declared in its 1971 document, *Justice in the World,* "The Church . . . recognizes that anyone who ventures to speak to people about justice must first be just in their eyes."[10] And the same Synod went on to honestly indicate that there are numerous aspects of Church life in which contemporary people cannot readily recognize the justice which the Gospel demands and the Church proclaims. It is upon these issues that the prophetic dissent, criticism, and even resistance of loyal Catholic individuals and groups, including religious congregations, is increasingly and rightly coming to bear.

In taking our bearings from the Scriptures, especially the Gospels, we must remind ourselves that the prophets of old, including Jesus, were people called to rise up in the midst of their own religious community. They were sent, not primarily to foreigners, but to the house of Israel. The primary objects of their critique and resistance were the religious authorities to whom the community, including themselves, owed obedience, the religious establishment to which they belonged and which they never ceased to love, the Church for whose salvation they were willing even to be persecuted, banished, and executed by those who sat in the chair of Moses. This is the root explanation of that painful paradox of the prophetic experience, the marriage in the heart and activity of the prophet of compassion for and condemnation of the religious institution to which they belonged and even of its highest representatives. Jesus both wept over Jerusalem and predicted its well-earned destruction (cf. Mt 23:37–39), and in this he only followed in the great tradition of Hosea, Jeremiah, and the other prophets of the Old Testament.

We are doubtless correct to question seriously our own credentials for this lonely and agonizing vocation. Indeed, anyone who aspires to be a prophet is either completely uninformed or clinically insane! Probably one of the surest signs of the call to prophecy in the Church today is the experience of that same terror in the face of such a task that made Moses stutter, Jeremiah rebel, and Jesus sweat blood. The more afraid we are of the consequences, the more unworthy we feel in the face of our own sins to call anyone to repentance, the more deeply we love the Church and reverence its ministry of leadership, the more resolutely must we face the implications of the vocation to prophecy in the contemporary Church. This will only be possible if our wholehearted commitment to Jesus gives rise in us to a passionate and ultimately fearless identification with the reign of God, that regime of reversals whose great sign is the resurrection of an executed Prophet.

NOTES

INTRODUCTION

1. Perhaps the best available contemporary theology of religious life is John M. Lozano, *Discipleship: Towards an Understanding of Religious Life,* tr. B. Wilczynski (Chicago/Los Angeles/Manila: Claret Center for Resources in Spirituality, 1980). See also Alejandro Cussianovich, *Religious Life and the Poor: Liberation Theology Perspectives,* tr. Y. Drury (Maryknoll, NY: Orbis, 1979); Francis J. Moloney, *Disciples and Prophets: A Biblical Model for the Religious Life* (New York: Crossroad, 1981); Leonardo Boff, *God's Witnesses in the Heart of the World,* tr. R. Fath (Chicago/Los Angeles/Manila: Claret Center for Resources in Spirituality, 1981).

2. The assigning of priority to experience is one of the salient characteristics of feminist theology. While feminist theology is undoubtedly not the original source of renewal in feminine religious life it has become a very congenial resource for the evolving theology. The most comprehensive feminist theology available is Rosemary R. Ruether, *Sexism and God-Talk: Toward a Feminist Theology* (Boston: Beacon, 1983).

3. See, for example, the SCRIS document, "Essential Elements in the Church's Teaching on Religious Life as Applied to Institutes Dedicated to Works of the Apostolate," May 31, 1983.

4. An excellent example of such a process of study and publication was the Contemporary Theology of Religious Life study commissioned by the Leadership Conference of Women Religious in 1976 which culminated in the publication of *Starting Points: Six Essays Based on the Experience of U.S. Women Religious,* ed. L.A. Quiñonez (Washington, D.C.: Leadership Conference of Women Religious of the U.S.A., 1980). The process of this study is described in detail in Appendix I of this volume, "The Contemporary Theology Project Process" by Diane Fassel (pp. 125–132).

2. TOWARD A THEOLOGICAL THEORY OF RELIGIOUS LIFE

1. Interestingly enough, the new Code of Canon Law, promulgated in 1983, in Part II devoted to religious life, includes both "Religious Institutes" and "Secular Institutes" under the title "Institutes of Consecrated Life" and distinguishes from the latter "Societies of Apostolic Life." This change from the earlier code witnesses to the difficulty of making juridical distinctions among charismatic phenomena which are theologically closely related or identical. An English translation of the code is available as *Code of Canon Law: Latin-English Edition,* tr. Canon Law Society of America (Washington, D.C.: Canon Law Society of America, 1983).

2. Members of Secular Institutes and of Societies of Apostolic Life are not, juridically, religious according to the new code of canon law.

3. It is interesting to compare, for example, the controversial theology of religious life developed by Alejandro Cussianovich (see *Religious Life and the Poor: Liberation Theology Perspectives,* tr. Y. Drury [Maryknoll: Orbis, 1979]), in the cultural context of Latin America and within the theological matrix of liberation theology with that of John Lozano (see *Discipleship: Towards an Understanding of Religious Life,* tr. B. Wilczynski [Chicago/Los Angeles/Manila: Claret Center for Resources in Spirituality, 1980]), developed within the framework of classical European theology. Likewise, it would be instructive to compare the essay on religious life of a non-religious priest, Johannes B. Metz, reflecting on this life within the context of the German Synod's document "Our Hope: A Confession of Faith for Our Time" (see *Followers of Christ: The Religious Life and the Church,* tr. T. Linton [Ramsey: Paulist, 1978]) with that of an American Jesuit, L. Patrick Carroll (see *To Love, To Share, To Serve: Challenges to a Religious* [Collegeville: Liturgical Press, 1979]).

4. Even theologians, e.g., Karl Rahner, who have effectively dealt with almost every conceivable aspect of the Christian mystery within the framework of a single philosophical schema, know that their syntheses are limited and conditioned.

5. See *Documents of Vatican II,* new revised edition, ed. A.P. Flannery (Grand Rapids: Eerdmans, 1984).

6. Both *Evangelica Testificatio* and *Venite Seorsum* are available in English in *Documents of Vatican II,* pp. 680–706 and 656–675 respectively.

7. The Canadian conference of major superiors and American conference of major superiors of women collaborated in publishing a predominantly critical collection of essays on *Evangelica Testificatio* entitled *Widening the Dialogue: Reflections on "Evangelica Testificatio"* (Ottawa/Washington, D.C.: Canadian Religious Conference/Leadership Conference of Women Religious, 1974).

8. One of the most objectionable aspects of recent papal and Vatican documents on religious life has been its tendency to revitalize the elitist understanding of religious life. See, for example, John Paul II's exhortation "Redemptionis Donum" (1984) and "Essential Elements in the Church's Teaching on Religious Life as Applied to Institutes Dedicated to Works of the Apostolate" (1983).

9. Although the 1983 Code acknowledges a distinction between solemn and simple vows (canon 1192.2) the distinction has no juridical effect on religious as such.

10. Secular Institutes, which were originally sharply distinguished from Religious Institutes, are now included in the section of canon law devoted to Institutes of Consecrated Life which is divided into two parts: Religious Institutes and Secular Institutes. In other words Secular Institutes are seen to have more in common with religious institutes than with any other group in the Church.

11. Thomas Merton is the Catholic religious who has best demonstrated this co-comprehension of religious across traditional lines, but Bede Griffith, David Steindl-Rast and others have also engaged in this dialogue.

12. We have recently seen chilling examples of the use of official ecclesiastical power to exacerbate such tensions and to forcibly destroy religious membership against the wishes of both the congregations and the religious, e.g., the case of Sister Agnes Mary Mansour, R.S.M. and Fernando Cardenal, S.J.

3. TOWARD A CONTEMPORARY THEOLOGY OF RELIGIOUS PROFESSION

1. It is useful to note that even today there are groups in the Church which, though not canonically religious, are so theologically and which accept the formal engagement of their members without vows. Among these groups, called Societies of Apostolic Life in canon law, are the men of Maryknoll and the Columbans.

2. Cf. Canon 654; *Perfectae Caritatis* 1; *Lumen Gentium* VI, 43–44.

3. It should be noted, however, that the new code of canon law includes among religious those who make continually renewed temporary profession (Can. 607, 2). In effect, members of such groups regard their vows as annual in form but expressive of the intention of remaining religious.

4. Cf. *Summa Theologiae* II–II, 186, 2–7.

5. For a detailed treatment of the development of religious life in the first three centuries see my article, "Non-Marriage for the Sake of the Kingdom," *Widening the Dialogue: Reflections on "Evangelica Testificatio"* (Ottawa/Washington, D.C.: Canadian Religious Conference/Leadership Conference of Women Religious, 1974) 125–197.

6. The Augsburg Confession, 27. English edition available as *The Augsburg Confession: A Confession of Faith Presented in Augsburg by Certain Princes and Cities to His Imperial Majesty Charles V in the Year 1530,* tr. from the German (Philadelphia: Fortress, 1980). Section on "Monastic Vows," pp. 40–47.

7. The Council of Trent (Denz. 1810) declared that it was better and holier to remain in the state of virginity or celibacy for the sake of the kingdom than to marry. It is instructive that the Vatican Council, in *Perfectae Caritatis* 12, says only that such chastity "deserves to be esteemed as a surpassing gift of grace" but refrains from repeating the claim to superiority or even from citing the Tridentine decree in the notes.

8. John Lozano, *Discipleship: Towards an Understanding of Religious Life,* tr. B. Wilczynski (Chicago/Los Angeles/Manila: Claret Center for Resources in Spirituality, 1980).

9. On the hierarchy of the vows, see Thaddée Matura,

Celibacy and Community: The Gospel Foundations for Religious Life,
tr. P.J. Oligny (Chicago: Franciscan Herald, 1968).
　　10. See note 7 above.

4. COMMITMENT: LIGHT FROM THE FOURTH GOSPEL

　　1. R. Schnackenburg, *The Gospel According to St. John,* vol.
I, tr. K. Smyth (London: Burns and Oates, 1968), p. 12.
　　2. Cf. J.L. Martyn, *History and Theology in the Fourth Gospel,*
revised and enlarged (Nashville: Abingdon, 1979), pp. 37–62,
156–157.
　　3. Hans Küng, *On Being a Christian* (New York: Doubleday, 1976), pp. 295–300.
　　4. R. Kysar, *The Fourth Evangelist and His Gospel* (Minneapolis: Augsburg, 1975), pp. 227–233.
　　5. A. Vanhoye, "Notre foi, oeuvre divine d'après le qua-
trième évangile," *Nouvelle Revue Theologique* 86 (1964) 337–354.

6. TOWARD A CONTEMPORARY THEOLOGY OF THE VOWS

　　1. The first unambiguous reference to a public promise
of celibacy occurs in Clement of Alexandria (c. 150-c. 215), *Stro-
matum III*. However, the reference in the First Apology of Justin
Martyr (c. 150 A.D.) to "men and women, disciples of Christ
since their childhood, [who] have remained virgins to the age of
sixty or seventy" (chs. 15 and 29) suggests that some public
profession of celibacy was made even in the first century. For
full references and more complete analyses of these and other
early texts on religious profession see my article, "Non-marriage
for the Sake of the Kingdom," *Widening the Dialogue: Reflection
on "Evangelica Testificatio"* (Ottawa/Washington, D.C.: Canadian
Religious Conference/Leadership Conference of Women Religious, 1974) pp. 125–197.
　　2. The Rule of St. Benedict, for example, specifies that
the monk is to make vows of stability, conversion of manners,
and obedience. Most religious congregations today profess poverty, chastity, and obedience and some have a fourth vow.

3. It suffices to compare Benedict's notion of obedience essentially qualified by stability with Ignatius' notion of obedience as readiness to be sent anywhere on mission to see how differently the same vow could be understood.

4. It is important to realize, however, that the earliest consecrated virgins and celibates did not separate themselves from the community by any of the means later adopted by desert monasticism. And, despite fairly consistent official opposition, religious life has been steadily moving, since the 1500's, back from the desert to the city.

5. The frequently reiterated position of the Sacred Congregation for Religious and Secular Institutes, e.g., in "Essential Elements," as well as most papal statements, e.g., *Redemptionis Donum,* on religious life since the Council, bears witness to the fact that the official theory of religious life is far behind both the Council's ecclesiology and the practical *aggiornomento* that has taken place in religious life.

6. See *Lumen Gentium* IV, 31.

7. The theological question of whether the Church really is hierarchical by divine institution or in what sense this might be so needs to be seriously addressed. Simply repeating the proposition does not illuminate the present situation very much, especially when the people repeating it think of hierarchy as meaning substantially the kind of monarchical organization which now obtains in the Church.

8. A chilling analysis of the potentiality for evil in groups in which individuals project all authority upon the leader is to be found in M. Scott Peck, *People of the Lie: The Hope for Healing Human Evil* (New York: Simon and Schuster, 1983), pp. 212–253.

9. See "Justice in the World" 3, *Synod of Bishops: The Ministerial Priesthood; Justice in the World* (Washington, D.C.: National Conference of Catholic Bishops, 1971), p. 44.

10. "Justice in the World," Introduction, p. 34.

7. CONSECRATED CELIBACY: ICON OF THE REIGN OF GOD

1. Perhaps one of the most spiritually profound treatments of the icon is Paul Evdokimov, *L'Art de l'Icone: Théologie de la Beauté* (Bruges: Desclée de Brouwer, 1970). He deals with the Roublev "Trinity" on pp. 205–216.

2. See Francis J. Moloney, *Disciples and Prophets: A Biblical Model for Religious Life* (New York: Crossroad, 1981), p. 111, for a discussion of this point.

3. See, for example, Quentin Quesnell, "Made Themselves Eunuchs for the Kingdom of Heaven," *Catholic Biblical Quarterly* 30 (1968) 335–358, who adopts the position first proposed by J. Dupont, *Mariage et divorce dans l'évangile: Matthieu 19, 3–12 et parallèles* (Bruges: Desclée de Brouwer, 1959).

4. See Moloney, *Disciples and Prophets*, pp. 106–109.

5. This is the position espoused by Jerome Kodell, in "The Celibacy Logion in Matthew 19:12," *Biblical Theology Bulletin* 8 (February 1978), pp. 21–22, following the thesis first proposed by Josef Blinzler, "Eisin eunouchoi: Zur Auslegang von Mt 19:12," *Zeitschrift für die Neutestamentliche Wissenschaft* 48 (1957) 254–270.

6. See Justin Martyr, *The First Apology*, chapters 15 and 29.

7. See note 2 above.

8. For discussion of Jewish attitudes toward celibacy at the time of Jesus, see Kodell, "The Celibacy Logion," pp. 19–20.

9. Cf. Dt 23:1 which excludes the eunuch from the "assembly of the Lord."

10. See Moloney, *Disciples and Prophets*, p. 112, and notes 19 and 20.

11. Kodell, "The Celibacy Logion," pp. 21–22.

12. Cited from an unpublished manuscript, by Ray Hart in *Unfinished Man and the Imagination: Toward an Ontology and a Rhetoric of Revelation* (New York: Seabury, 1979), p. 219, n. 63. Emphasis mine.

8. RELIGIOUS OBEDIENCE: JOURNEY FROM LAW TO LOVE

1. Henceforth I will use the terms "rule" and "constitutions" interchangeably to refer in general to the particular legislation operative in a religious order or congregation.

2. We will take up the problem of corporate obedience in greater detail in chapter thirteen.

3. Cf. *Perfectae Caritatis*, #14.

4. Obedience, in the sense in which it is traditionally understood, i.e., as obliging the religious to follow the will of the superior according to a rule, is a relatively late development in the history of religious life. It attained its strictly monarchical form and definitive practical priority over virginity or celibacy and poverty only in the sixteenth century with the foundation of the Society of Jesus. However, the view that obedience in some form is somehow integral to religious life pre-dates both the development of the cenobitic form of religious life and the emergence of congregations committed to the apostolate. The original and primary object of religious obedience, in other words, is spiritual rather than functional.

5. See the interesting treatment of the "Scriptural Foundations of Religious Life" in T. Matura, *Celibacy and Community: The Gospel Foundations for Religious Life,* tr. P. Oligny (Chicago: Franciscan Herald Press, 1968), pp. 26–48. Matura concludes that only celibacy can be shown to be a "counsel" in the sense of being a grace and a call not addressed to all Christians.

6. Cf. *Lumen Gentium,* ch. 5, 40: "Thus it is evident to everyone that all the faithful of Christ of whatever rank or status are called to the fullness of the Christian life and to the perfection of charity," and 41: "In the various types and duties of life, one and the same holiness is cultivated by all who are moved by the Spirit of God and who obey the voice of the Father, worshiping God the Father in spirit and in truth."

7. As will be clear in part three, I have no intention of reinforcing the extreme position that family and personal talents or projects become totally unimportant and expendable as mediations of God's will in the life of religious. But they become relative to another set of factors and thus function differently

than they would in the life of an unmarried lay Christian, an ordained minister, or a married person.

8. In what follows I will be discussing the substance of a theory of mediation, not the specific legal forms which have developed in the Church or in religious life to institutionalize that mediation. In other words, I am not concerned with whether the Roman primacy is adequately grounded in Matthew 16:18–19 or whether the contemporary exercise of the papacy is adequately grounded in the theory of Roman primacy. Rather, I am investigating the question of how, given that certain institutionalizations of the mediation of God's will are legitimate, this mediation is to be understood. A second qualification is also important. Although an adequate theology of mediation should apply *mutatis mutandis* to mediation at any ecclesiastical level, there are significant differences between the forms of mediation in the universal Church, the local Church, the family, the state, and the religious community. I am concerned fundamentally only with the last.

9. A very interesting early recognition of this distinction occurs in the Rule of St. Benedict in chapter 2 on "The Abbot." Benedict says that the abbot "holds the place of Christ in the monastery" but immediately adds that in his capacity as abbot he "must not teach or establish or command anything outside the precept of the Lord" (my translation from the Italian of the edition of the monastery of St. Scholastica, Subiaco, 1958). In other words, the abbot must do nothing except preach the Gospel to the monks and, therefore, his words are authoritative and he "holds the place of Christ."

10. Ch. 71 of the Rule of St. Benedict treats of "mutual obedience" among the monks and urges them to obey one another freely. Although he uses the same term "obedience" for this mutual fraternal submission, it is clear that he distinguishes this familial willingness to cede to the will of others from the obedience to the abbot who commands only what the Gospel demands.

11. Actually the traditional theology of religious obedience as reflected in the pre-conciliar constitutions of most congregations does respect this distinction by limiting the legitimate use of the "command in virtue of the vow" to the most serious

matters whose direct connection with the Gospel would, in most cases, be quasi-demonstrable. But the distinction has been almost totally obscured in practice by the unnuanced understanding of the superior as God's representative and all legitimate commands as God's will.

12. *Schema of Canons on Institutes of Life Consecrated by Profession of the Evangelical Counsels* (Draft) (Washington, D.C.: United States Catholic Conference, 1977).

13. *LCWR Recommendations: Schema of Canons on Religious Life* (Washington, D.C.: Leadership Conference of Women Religious, 1977). A very enlightening article on the significance of *The Schema* is R.A. Hill, "Canon Law After Vatican II: Renewal or Retreat?" *America* 137 (Nov. 5, 1977) 298–300.

14. Some interesting recent efforts are the following: The short but excellent analytic description by L.A. Quiñonez, *Patterns in Authority and Obedience: An Overview of Authority/Obedience Developments Among U.S. Women Religious* (Washington, D.C.: Leadership Conference of Women Religious, 1978); A. Cussianovich, *Religious Life and the Poor: Liberation Theology Perspectives*, tr. J. Drury (Maryknoll: Orbis, 1979), which situates obedience (and all of religious life) within the life-experience of Latin American liberation theology; J.B. Metz, *Followers of Christ: The Religious Life and the Church*, tr. T. Lanton (New York: Paulist, 1978), which deals with religious life as a prophetic phenomenon in the institutional Church; T.M.R. Tillard, *There Are Charisms and Charisms: The Religious Life*, tr. O. Prendergast (Brussels: Lumen Vitae, 1977), which explores the charismatic foundations of religious life.

15. The Lukan formulation is "more religious and conventional" as C. Stuhlmueller notes in "The Gospel According to Luke" in *The Jerome Biblical Commentary*, ed. R.E. Brown, *et al.* (Englewood Cliffs: Prentice-Hall, 1968), p. 134, which is a good indication of redactional work. Both Matthew and Mark have the shorter form, another indication of its priority.

11. FRIENDSHIP IN THE LIFE OF CONSECRATED CELIBATES

1. Although the references in this chapter are generally to marriage and other heterosexual relationships, it is my opinion that what is said applies equally to homosexual relationships, whether friendship or permanent, monogamous, sexually expressed unions.

2. This subject has been dealt with at greater length in chapter seven.

3. For a fuller development of this point, see chapter six.

4. The work of feminist developmental psychologists is beginning to challenge the universal validity of developmental theories based entirely on the experience of male subjects. However, I think Erikson's model, at least on this point, is a valid starting point for these reflections on maturity.

12. THE CHANGING SHAPE AND FUNCTION OF COMMUNITY LIFE

1. The 1983 code of canon law says that members of religious institutes "live a life in common as brothers or sisters" (607, 2) and specifies that such a common life requires members to "live in their own religious houses" (665). This legislation was passed when the actual practice of many congregations had been, for many years, quite otherwise. The law permits broad enough exceptions that, one would hope, congregations will not be forced into confrontation with ecclesiastical authorities on this point.

2. Cf. Jn 1:12; 15:15; 13:34–35.

3. Dolores Curran, *Traits of the Healthy Family* (Minneapolis: Winston, 1983).

4. I am using the feminine pronoun in this section because the experience I am describing is much more prevalent among women than among male religious at this time.

13. PROPHETIC CONSCIOUSNESS: OBEDIENCE AND DISSENT IN THE RELIGIOUS LIFE

1. More exactly: "For there is no authority except from God, and those that exist have been instituted by God" (Rom 13:1).

2. See the elaboration of this commonly held thesis in J. Maritain, *Scholasticism and Politics,* tr. and ed. M.J. Adler (Garden City: Doubleday [Image] 1960). Originally published in 1940. See especially chapters 3 and 4: "The Human Person and Society" and "Democracy and Authority" respectively.

3. W. Brueggemann, *The Prophetic Imagination* (Philadelphia: Fortress, 1978). As M. Guinan points out in *Gospel Poverty: Witness to the Risen Christ* (New York/Ramsey: Paulist, 1981), note 1, pp. 87–88, Brueggemann has to be read with some care because he tends to overdraw the conflict between prophecy and royalty in ancient Israel. However, this is more a problem for biblical criticism than a drawback for the present analysis, which is concerned precisely with the struggle between authentic prophecy and the perversion of institutional authority.

4. See Guinan, *Gospel Poverty,* pp. 26–31, for a fuller presentation.

5. Israel was destroyed by Assyria in 722 B.C. and Judah fell to Babylon in 587 B.C.

6. See Guinan, *op cit,* pp. 36–37.

7. See my article, "The Foot Washing (John 13:1–20): An Experiment in Hermeneutics," *The Catholic Biblical Quarterly* 43 (January 1981) 76–92 for a fuller development of this theme.

8. See my article, "Women in the Fourth Gospel and the Role of Women in the Contemporary Church," *Biblical Theology Bulletin* 12 (April 1982) 35–45, for a fuller treatment and justification of this point.

9. See, for example, R.P. McBrien, *Church: The Continuing Quest* (New York/Paramus: Newman, 1970), esp. pp. 67–85.

10. "Justice in the World" 3, *Synod of Bishops: The Ministerial Priesthood; Justice in the World* (Washington, D.C.: National Conference of Catholic Bishops, 1971), p. 44.

INDEX OF BIBLICAL REFERENCES*

*Special thanks to Debbie Blake, S.N.D. and Frances Smith, R.S.C.J. for their help with the indexes.

SUBJECT INDEX

Note: Boldface page numbers signify the major treatment of a subject.